TWO BAD YEARS
AND
UP WE GO!

WADE B. COOK

Lighthouse
Publishing Group Inc.
Seattle, Washington

Distributed by
Midpoint Trade Books, Inc.

Lighthouse Publishing Group, Inc.
Copyright © 2002 Never Ending Wealth, LP

For Library of Congress information, please call the publisher
ISBN 189200872-6

Creative Director: Mark Engelbrecht
Book Design by Jennifer Stolz
Jacket Design by Kerri Ladines

Published by Lighthouse Publishing Group, Inc.
A subsidiary of Wade Cook Financial Corporation
Publicly Traded Company, Ticker Symbol WADE (OTCBB)
14675 Interurban Avenue South
Seattle, Washington 98168-4664
1-800-706-8657 206-901-3027 (fax)

Printed in United States of America
10 9 8 7 6 5 4 3 2 1

Distributed to the trade by Midpoint Trade Books

To Jeff and Debbie Hochstrasser

Explanation of the Dedication

Many who read this book will not know Jeff and Debbie Hochstrasser. First of all, it was Jeff's idea to bring this book out at this time. He saw an incredible need in the marketplace to have this message brought to tens of thousands of people. He has a keen insight on the marketplace, which just did not happen overnight, but has extended back many years. Jeff Hochstrasser is the owner and operator of Highstreet Advertising, whom we have worked with for over two decades. Jeff's agency is on an "M" Street (Meridian) but about as far away from Madison Ave. as can be, in Puyallup, Washington.

At one time in my corporate life, Jeff came onboard and helped me build a company as the general manager. We worked together in that capacity for a few years. We saw our company grow from $6,000 a month to $75,000 a month and upwards from there. When I made the decision to move to Arizona, Jeff decided to move back to Washington, but we continued to work together in a different capacity.

He founded an advertising and marketing company, and we pioneered many new ideas never before found in the marketing and radio industry. We are now approaching one half billion dollars in sales over the last seven or eight years, and I know that Jeff has worked with several other clients and has also had successes with them.

Recently, my wife wrote a book about me entitled, *I Married a Ticker Symbol*. She told part of our history together. The people she mentions in the book, friends from our church, are Jeff and Debbie. Yes, they are indeed the ones who introduced me to my wife and for this, I am eternally grateful.

Jeff and I go back to our teenage years. We were in competing rock'n'roll bands while we were both in high school. We did not go to the same high schools in Tacoma, Washington, but we were in the same church and were able to meet each other quite frequently. It's tough to go from being a competitor to being a business compadre, but our relationship has developed from that point. I know and trust Jeff immeasurably.

Let me give a plug without Jeff's permission. I honestly don't know if he is even taking on any new clients because his business is incredibly busy servicing our company and a few others whom I know he is involved with. However, if you are looking to do nationwide radio, TV or newspaper advertising, you may want to give them a call. Again, no promises that he'll be taking on new clients, but I think you would be in very good hands with somebody who "gets it."

Now to Jeff and Debbie—I want to thank you for all you have done—for your incredible attitudes, your keen insights and your unquenchable spirit of kindness, generosity.

Mit herzlichen Dank. Ohne dich, wäre es nicht möglich gewesen.

Acknowledgement

I've already given thanks to Jeff Hochstrasser, whose idea it was to bring this book out at this time. We felt it very important to bring this book out in a timely manner. Whenever you go on a crash course to get something accomplished, a lot of people have to sacrifice much.

My thanks goes to Jerry Miller at Lighthouse Publishing and their Graphics staff, Mark Engelbrecht and Jennifer Stolz for the typesetting and editing and to Kerri Ladines for the jacket design.

Also, a heartfelt thank you to Cindy Little, Angelina Corona and Angela Laverdure for their "second-mile treatment" of this process.

I'd also like to thank the members of our Research and Training Department. Throughout this whole time they have helped with the research and the actual trades mentioned in this book. They also do the research and training behind the scenes, so that working formulas are brought to the public through the Stock Market Institute of Learning seminar system. These people include David McKinlay, Jay Harris, Paul Lund, Barry Collette and Mark Yohman.

Also, many excerpts in this book were taken from our Wealth Information Network (WIN), and I'd like to thank Todd Doyle and Eric Delahanty.

As always, I would like to thank my assistant Patsy Sanders and the CEO of the Stock Market Institute of Learning, Robin Anderson and her Executive Assistant, Carol Taylor, along with Robert Hondel the Chief Operations Officer of Wade Cook Financial Corporation for their dedication through all of this. Their unfailing loyalty is appreciated from the bottom of my heart.

My family and friends have been very supportive through this process. To my wife Laura, as always, I honor her and give her my deep appreciation.

Contents

Preface

Just before this book went to press, and I mean minutes before it went off to press, the following announcement was made. The Non-Farm Productivity (productivity ratio per man hours of work) was up for the last quarter of 2001. This is October, November and December after the terrorist attack. It speaks well to the fact that Americans are willing to do what it takes to succeed. See further comments at the beginning of Chapter 2.

Imagine a nice summer day and you're out in the back yard with family and friends. Out on the grass is a large trampoline with nine kids jumping up and down. Some are pretty good—they can do flips in the air and other somersault type tricks. Others are not quite so good, but can do a few basic moves. Still others just stand there, or jump up and down and occasionally bounce on their rear-ends. A couple of smaller children are sitting on the side of the trampoline, even though they are not jumping. They are just sitting but feel the shock waves of the bigger kids' bounces. There are a few toddlers playing in the grass around the trampoline, but they're too small to get on the trampoline.

To me the stock market is a lot like this trampoline. The stock market has ups and downs, and unlike the trampoline, it is not stationary. There are high-flying stocks in the stock market with all kinds of bells and whistles. There are stocks that do a few good things infrequently; there are stocks that simply exist, but do not have any upward movements and therefore hardly any downward movements. Then there are the stocks that do basically nothing but feel the effects of other stocks. Just like the trampoline metaphor, there are companies' stocks that have not even climbed into the market yet. I love these small private companies and love to see them become publicly traded. Please refer my comments about Bottom Fishing for these types of companies in Chapter 13, Appendix 2.

Imagine what would happen if everyone on the trampoline decided to bounce simultaneously. Obviously, for the small players on the sidelines, this would not have any impact at all. However, the big players in the middle could really move the stock market down, and then back up.

I have isolated a phenomenon in the stock market which occurs around the quarterly news-go-round. I call this the Red Light- Green Light phenomena. Red Light meaning a period when there is no news, and the Green Light meaning a period when there is either a lot of news, or the anticipation of future news. Red does not mean "bad" and Green does not mean "good." They simply mean "news-period" and "no-news period." I have written extensively on this in an upcoming book called *Red Light, Green Light*. Watch for it in bookstores. However, at the current time I have excerpted some selections from the book and from the *Red Light Green Light Home Study Course*. You will find information about this incredible process in Chapter 6, *Compelling Reasons* and Chapter 11, *Trading on Company News*.

BEAR MARKET RECOVERY TOUR

As many of you know, I am a teacher for a company called The Stock Market Institute of Learning. This company sponsors numerous seminars every week. They have contracted with me to take my seminars to the world. They have done a remarkable job in doing so. Tens of thousands of people have benefited from the information, especially from the incredible Wall Street Workshop, which is an experiential learning formatted seminar.

The market has been so bad for the last two years that many of our students have felt not only bewildered but many of them have seen their trading account valuations decline. It's the same old incredibly flawed, "buy and hold," strategy that has created trouble for myself as well as for a lot of my students. Ironically, many of our cash flow strategies work very well, but when you have a down-trending market and feel like there is nothing you can individually do to counteract it, then for a certain period of time you may become a temporary victim both mentally and physically. See Chapter 9 for my take on why "long-term buy and hold" is a flawed strategy.

For me it seemed like it was time to fight back. I am a classic optimist and I told my staff to get me out on the road again. I left Seattle numerous times and have been to many states and many cities to meet with tens of thousands of my students to encourage them, to pick them back up, to give them fight-back strategies they can use in the current marketplace and, in short, to bring a little light back into their lives.

For some of these students all they needed was to see the light at the end of the tunnel. I hope I brought some of that to them. I also shared with them specific strategies they could do to get going again.

Let me give you an example. In fact, this is the most powerful example I could give, it was the one story I heard from a lady at a Semper Financial Regional Investor's Convention, that was the catalyst for getting me to go on the tour. She was the straw that broke the camel's back.

This woman mentioned that she attended our Wall Street Workshop and started with around $20,000 a year and a half before. She did some pretty aggressive trading and built up her trading account to over $300,000 and felt that was enough. From then on, she switched her plan to more of a monthly income plan; for example, Writing Covered Calls.

When the stock market got hammered, her account went from $300,000 down to $200,000 and she panicked. She was literally paralyzed. She did *nothing* in her account. One of the things we teach is to "paper trade." (Please see the excerpt from David Hebert's book *On Track Investing* in Chapter 10). I asked her at that point if she continued to paper trade, and she said yes, she had.

She told me that when she reached $300,000, she was generating $32,000 to $35,000 *a month* in income. That is very common among those who have learned how to capitalize on their stock holdings with appropriate formulas. Anyone of you can test me on that by calling your stockbroker. Pick any particular stock and then, right around the price of the stock, look for an option strike price—in this case a call option—and instead of buying it, sell the call option into the marketplace and generate cash into your account. You can do this as a paper trade to see how it works. With the cash in your account you can quite often generate between 8-15% per month, sometimes even 20%—of the stock price, especially if the stock was purchased on margin, which means you put up only half of the money. For her to take $300,000 and generate $30,000+ per month is not unheard of, it is very common.

Now that her trading account had backed off to $200,000 in stock valuations, she stopped trading, but continued to do paper trades. I asked her, "How are you doing on your paper trades?" She answered that she was still netting on paper around $20,000 to $25,000 a month. I asked her this question, "How much do you need to live on?" Her answer was that she needed $5,000 to $6,000 a month to pay all of her bills. I said, "Now, on paper, with your $200,000 in stocks, you are making over $20,000 a month and you're telling me you only need $5,000 or $6,000?" She said, "I know, it seems kind of silly, doesn't it, when you think about it?"

I encouraged her and the whole class that day to continue to paper trade but also with certain stocks. Once their confidence had been built up again, to once again start writing covered calls, which generates nice monthly income checks.

Before I go on, I want anyone who comes to my seminars or reads my books to know I am not in this business to make anyone busier. I see people coming to my seminars and getting very excited about the stock market business. They exchange working for another company 50 to 60 hours a week, for working in their personal stock market business 50 to 60 hours a week. Yes, they're then able to operate out of their back bedroom and possibly see their kids a little bit more, but they are still so wrapped up in the business of the stock market that it hardly speaks to living a good quality life. I am into helping people retire. To me, that means helping them learn how to: grow assets that produce income to lower their exposure to risk and liability. To set up pension plans to prepare for a great retirement. To establish Living and Charitable Remainder Trusts and to make sure their church and family receive everything they have worked so hard to build up in their lives. In short, to not only learn how to make money, but to keep that money working for them and their family after they have passed on.

Let me restate the gist; I am not here to get people busier, but to help people build a quality life.

The chapter on trading in and out of this current mini-recession is taken from the Bear Market Recovery Tour. Chapters 4, 5, and 13 are pertinent and timely. They provide many formulas for trading in today's market conditions.

"Our purpose in life, should be to build a life of purpose." Wade Cook

SELLING PUTS

One of my favorite strategies is selling Puts. My favorite strategy used to be Rolling Stocks and as a matter of fact, it was my first love in the stock market. For many years it was the only strategy that generated income, income that would support my family.

My third favorite strategy is writing Covered Calls. My second favorite strategy is Bull Put Spreads. If you would like to learn more about Bull Put Spreads, please see my book *Wall Street Money Machine, Volume 4*— originally titled *Safety First Investing*.

However, the strategy I currently like the most for generating monthly income is Selling Puts. It is so important to me that I have included a chapter on it here. At the beginning of this chapter, I even pulled quotations out of a few news articles that I think will help you see that the big guys do these types of trades. Remember, once again, I'm not into what the retail stock brokers and media writers do, I'm into what the billion dollar traders do. All I've tried to do is learn their information and get good at these types of trades myself. If I feel such trades can be repetitiously duplicated, I try to share them with the students in my seminars as well as anyone who reads my books. I want to provide this knowledge in an easy-to-understand and easy-to-implement way.

The chapter on selling puts is Chapter 12

FINANCIAL EDUCATION COACH

When we were working to get this book out at the beginning of the year, some of my staff came to me and asked if they could put their comments about me in this book. They had originally written an article, which has been excerpted from the *Money Connection Newspaper*, entitled, *Wade Cook: Possibly the Most Controversial Man in America*, and another article which was entitled *Wade Cook = Your Financial Education Coach*. That has been reproduced here and is in Chapter 8.

One of the greatest benefits of being on the lecture circuit is the opportunity to meet incredible students. Some of these students have become Wall Street Workshop instructors. Some have now developed their own books and home study courses. It is such a pleasure to "hang around" like-minded spirits. You will see excerpts in this book from David Hebert, author of *On-Track Investing*, excerpts from Darlene and Miles Nelson's book, *Stock Split Secrets*—which I think is a *must* for anyone who is going to get involved in stock split methods, whether with stocks or options. Also you will find excerpts from Doug Sutton's incredibly valuable book entitled *The Beginning Investors Bible*. You should run, not walk, to your nearest bookstore to get Doug Sutton's book. It is simply that good. I hear that Lighthouse Publishing has many more books coming your way.

The excerpts from these books pick up on the theme of trading in the current marketplace. They are located in Chapter 10.

BACK TO THE TOUR

Being out and about in the country and meeting with my students, flying on airlines and going through airports and visiting hotels, malls and shopping centers all over the country, has given me a keen insight to where the country is right now. Many of the comments you'll read in my three Top Ten lists in this book come from what I have learned and processed as I have visited cities around the country.

I sincerely hope the comments here will not only get you the information you need to trade wisely, but also get you excited about the educational process. I'll encourage you to get educated by people who "walk the walk." I would rather be a great coach than a great player. If you don't use my strategies and the Stock Market Institute of Learning, whom will you use? I remember a commercial for a hospital in Arizona. It said, "If you don't use us for help, get help somewhere!" I agree.

I had Lighthouse Publishing add an appendix of some of my thoughts contained in a marketing piece called *Knowledge is Cash Flow Potential.* It has been included here as Appendix 1. You'll find it at the back of the book. Also you can read highlights of a recent Q&A to shareholders of Wade Cook Financial Corporation in Appendix 2.

Let me conclude with a comment I have made many times since I started teaching seminars over 22 years ago: "If you'll do for two years what most people won't do, you'll be able to do for the rest of your life what most people can't do."

Most people are not willing to pay the price of success. They focus on the prize and not the price. Investing and trading in the stock market has never been easy, but there are learnable skills which can help people provide an income for their families. Stockbrokers will try to sell you a particular investment. Not me. I am here to educate, to edify, to uplift and to hopefully give a bit of inspiration that will help you once again revive your American Dream. This dream for so many has gone blue. Let's turn it into a dream come true.

1

Two Bad Years
and Up We Go

Note: I originally wrote this in August of 2001, before the terrorist attack. I have since updated portions of it, so as to reflect the current marketplace. I also headed out to numerous cities on a Bear Market Recovery Tour. My aim: to show people that we're heading into a new Bull Market, modest though it may be. Well, we had one. A Bull Market is defined as a 20% increase over any period of time—usually one year. In mid-September, the DOW (Dow Jones Industrial average of 30 stocks) dipped to 8,200. 20% of this would be 1,600 plus points, or 9,800. Look at the chart.

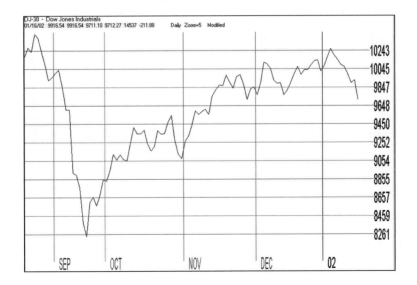

Wow. Look at the resiliency of the American Marketplace. In fact, the DOW recovered within a few hundred points of its pre-9/11 level in about a month.

So now the question—is this bull over? Read on as we explore new opportunities and new possibilities. The American Dream is far from over. May you trade well!

TWO BAD YEARS, AND UP WE GO

We find ourselves in a very unusual situation. Not only unusual but very rare. In over 160 years of tracking stock market movements, only eight times have we had back to back years of a down-trending market. If you combine the four years of 1929-1932 as one period, these eight two-year periods present an interesting future potential. For example, what happens in the year following two consecutive negative years? Is there continuity in outcomes?

The answer is yes. The year following two down years has not been incredible, but it has been credible to the upside. Look at the chart by Jeremy Siegal of the University of Pennsylvania's Wharton School:

First Year		Second Year		Next Year
1841	-17.9%	1842	-1.4%	57.6%
1853	-5.4	1854	-24.3	7.3
1876	-14.4	1877	-3.3	16
1883	-5.5	1884	-12.8	28.9
1913	-5.1	1914	-5.9	31.1
1929	-14.6	1930	-28.4	-44.4
1940	-7.5	1941	-9.5	16.1
1973	-18.7	1974	-27.9	37.4

Let's put this in perspective. We've now passed the period which would represent two down years, 2000 and 2001. It has been a murky mess. Second, we had unprecedented growth—a rampaging bull market, if you will—through 1998 and part of 1999. The Feds' comments, like, "irrational exuberance," started a process. Next followed a march to raise interest rates, and then the burst of the dot.com bubble. Also put into place by the

SEC were new reporting rules called, "Fair Disclosure." This caused corporations to "bad-mouth" their own stocks in ways heretofore unseen. The markets reeled.

Now, expectations are lower. That's a good thing. Gone are 25% to 50% year over year earnings or sales growth projections and hopes. Gone are thoughts that, "It can go on forever." Good companies will make it. P/Es are getting back into line. A tax cut has been implemented, but hasn't had the economic impact that it will have in 2002 to 2006. The Fed has lowered rates eleven times this year alone—to 1.75%. This bodes well for the future.

Recently in the Wall Street Journal, there was an article using a study about research of these two-year down markets and the year following. They warned, and rightly so, "lush" returns are not on the horizon, but good returns can be had if people choose stocks wisely. Again, note the rarity of two back to back down years. In the following year, stocks climbed an average of 18.8%. This rate is not sustained in subsequent years—it is about half of this amount. This could be a preview of the future. Obviously, the market will do what it wants—there are no guarantees. This is just one viewpoint.

With America now heading into a new era stemming from the September 11, 2001 tragedy, we will all see changes. The market doesn't like too many changes—uncertainty and confusion breed inaction. To me, it breeds opportunity. Money will move to one sector, then another. Move it will, so the new system is to figure out the direction. Please read Doug Sutton's new book, *The Beginning Investor's Bible* for details on how to play these movements.

Look at new opportunities. Here are charts of a few security companies. We started these the week before the terrorist attack.

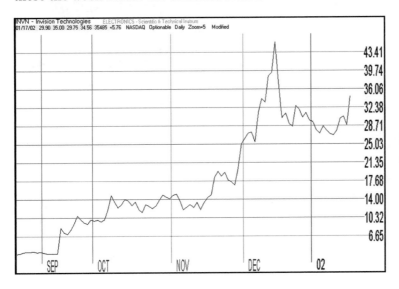

INVN: This is an airport security company

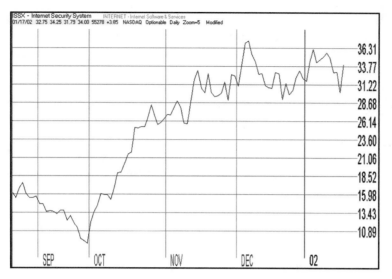

ISSX - Internet Security System   INTERNET - Internet Software & Services
01/17/02 32.75 34.25 31.79 34.00 55278 +3.85 NASDAQ Optionable Daily Zoom=5 Modified

ISSX This is an internet security company.

18

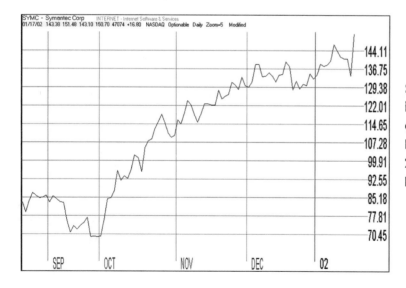

SYMC - Symantec Corp   INTERNET - Internet Software & Services
01/17/02 143.38 151.48 143.10 150.70 47074 +16.80 NASDAQ Optionable Daily Zoom=5 Modified

**SYMC is another internet security company.
NOTE: Symantec did a 2:1 stock split on February 22, 2002.**

Volatility is potential. New skills are needed. What worked yesterday might not work today. For example, option prices shrank as we headed into the Fall of 2001. It seems the option market makers are putting options on sale to generate business. Maybe the airlines should take a lesson from this. I know our company has instituted serious tuition discounts to fill up our seminars. The answer is to market your way out of problems.

Lately, I've been big into "compelling reasons." With these changes, I simply do not see enough good reasons right now to drive the market back up to the highs of the past few years. It will take time—say two to three years. We need real, good and sustained earnings from numerous companies, notably the biggies, to get the market going. One key to success is to follow earnings and earnings growth. Follow earnings now more than ever, because good earnings just may be the only thing that drives the market up. It may be the only compelling reason to move stocks back up. Make sure each trade you do—up or down—has a compelling reason to back it up.

> *If money is your hope for independence you will never have it. The only real security that a man will have in this world is a reserve of knowledge, experience, and ability.*
> ~Henry Ford

Top 10 Reasons Why We're Heading Into an Uptrending (Bull?) Market

NEWSFLASH!

In addition to the foregoing comments, which were taken from a few lectures I gave over the last few months, I want to add the following as a way of proving a point. A lot of Americans are *not* in a recession and they're willing to do whatever it takes to succeed.

1. Productivity was *up* for the three months following the terrorist attack. How can this be if America is in a recession, and if we were all beaten down by being attacked by an outside force? Not only is American resolve strong, but Americans are willing to work harder in times of stress and distress and to make good things happen in their lives.

   This productivity increase speaks to some companies laying people off, and those people then getting absorbed into other jobs; but, many companies are learning how to do the same amount (or even more) work, with fewer people.

   It also speaks to the fact that we're getting better with our technology and our equipment. The bottom line is a resolve of many Americans and American companies to do well in economic hard times. We are the "Rocky Balboas" of economic enterprise.

2. As we come out of any recession and any bear market, there are going to be individual trades worth pursuing. Though the economy may be recovering, each company within the economy will recover at its own pace. For example, some companies are very news-resilient. They do well in spite of bad news. Other companies need a host of good news; ie, news about other companies and in their sector in general for their individual stock to rise. Other companies' stock prices

will continue to weaken in the American recovery in general, because their particular recovery has not happened yet. It behooves all of us to not just get good at playing the news, but to realize that each company's stock price reacts to the news in it's own individual, unique way.

3.   In the current environment, news happens so fast that it's tough to get a handle on it. Obviously, the press searches out the negative and has a really tough time reporting on any positive news. This simply means, if the news is moving too fast on a company and you cannot catch the direction of how a company's stock is going to move, it might be better to sit on the sidelines and wait for the news for this particular company to settle down.

A good example of this would be pharmaceutical companies going through phase three of their drug testing. The news happens so rapidly that it's tough to figure out which way to play some of these stocks. My old adage, "I would rather miss a trade than lose on a trade," holds true here.

4.   Politics is getting very ugly. The current talk of the stimulus package, now being shut down by a bunch of liberal-minded thinkers, is not going to help this economy. Now, the economy seems to be recovering on its own, but from this writer's personal point of view, anytime you reduce taxes it will encourage savings and investments, which is good for the economy.

Expect the negative news to take precedence. The reason for this, is that there are basically two political parties. In one political party, they seem to be so much better at the machinations of government. A big part of this is the manipulation of the news. So, while the press may report on the negativity of things out and about in the country, the *people* who are out and about in the country, making the country work, are still very positive and upbeat.

5.   Not many of us have ever traded in this type of marketplace. The only year of recent memory that the marketplace was kind of flat and murky (which is the type of market I'm projecting for this next year) was 1994. It was easy to make money if you were good at trading in a sideways moving market. Remember, stocks are always moving up, down or sideways. I believe we can make as much money in a sideways moving market as we can in either of the other two.

In each type of marketplace there are certain strategies and formulas that work, and other formulas that have a tough time working. I have taken my 13 Cash Flow Strategies and have not only included them in this book, but have also written a critique beside them. This gives insight on which strategies work well today and which ones would probably not work well today. The point is, each of these strategies has a "Time to every season." (Ecclesiastes 3)

If you'll bear with me as I use another scripture to prove a point: just because a strategy exists does not mean it is a right strategy for the current marketplace, or that it is right for you. *"All things are lawful for me, but all things are not expedient: all things are lawful for me, but all things edify not."* (1 Corinthians 10:23 KJV) Throughout the book, I repeat that you not only need to find a trading style that works for your lifestyle, but that you need to find a specific formula you can become an expert in and work that formula repetitiously for ongoing cash flow.

6. The whole final chapter of this book speaks to the point of attitude controlling everything we do. Just because the market has been in a recession does not mean that we personally need to be in a recession or a depression. In fact, we can do everything possible to avoid it. If we can keep our head on straight and face the challenges of this current murky marketplace, figure it out and learn to trade from this viewpoint, I think we will have greater fruit from our endeavors. We literally need to set aside our past ways of thinking.

There is a quotation by Everett Dean Martin which I think speaks to this whole process. When you read this quote, ask yourself this simple question, "Am *I* willing to take my chances with the truth?"

> *The man who strives to educate himself—and no one else can educate him—must win a certain victory over his own nature. He must learn to smile at his dear idols, analyze his every prejudice, scrap if necessary his fondest and most consoling belief, question his presuppositions, and take his chances with the truth.*
>
> ~ Everett Dean Martin

23

In the Fall of 2001 I hit the road. My message: We're heading into a Bull Market. It happened. Look at this S&P 500 chart from 9/11 to 12/31/01. It's amazing:

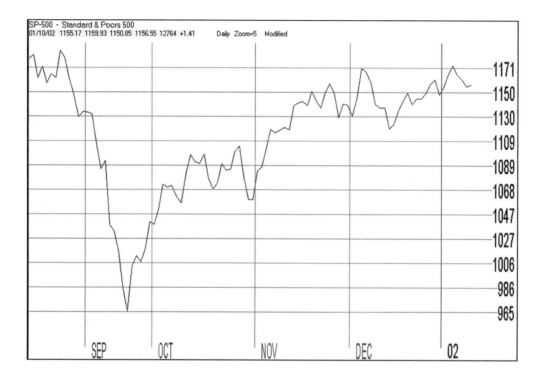

Now the question is: is the run-up over? Yes and No. It's been a great run and it's going to continue up—in a volatile pattern, with fits and jerks, huge up days followed by bad down days. Funny, this marketplace will give ammunition to the bulls and the bears. Even after the upcoming "corrections," which are inevitable, I still see an uptrending market.

My take? Read this quotation by B.C. Forbes:

Optimism is a tonic. Pessimism is a poison. Admittedly, every businessman must be realistic. He must gather facts, analyze them candidly and strive to draw logical conclusions, whether favorable or unfavorable. He must not view everything through rose-colored glasses. Granting this, the incontestable truth is that America has been built up by optimists. Not by pessimists, but by men willing to adventure, to shoulder risks terrifying to the timid.

Top 10 Reasons Why We're Heading Into an Uptrending Market

I believe in optimism. It works. America works. Our workplace is full of the people Mr. Forbes mentions.

Here now are my Top Ten Reasons why we're heading into an Uptrending (Bull?) Market.

10. Because the American Spirit is alive and well. Americans are starting to invest in American companies again. It's a sign of patriotism and it's a sign of taking advantage of the American Dream. We as Americans want it to be a Bull Market, and we're going to make it happen. Just because the *economy* may be in a recession, many *Americans* are not. They'll work hard to overcome all obstacles. American ingenuity and Yankee pride are alive and well.

    Along with point number ten is that fact that as we head into the New Year there is so much retirement money that will head back into the marketplace. You see 401K's, Corporate Pension Plans and even IRA's get stopped out. People put aside their $2,000, their $7,500, their $15,000 into their retirement plan, and towards the end of the year people can't put anymore cash into those plans. But, once the New Year starts in, there will be literally billions upon billions of dollars heading back into the people's pension plans, and a lot of this money will find its way into the stock market.

    Again, it's the old law of supply and demand. There has been a lot of supply, but now the *demand* is starting to pick up.

9. Because, even though income rate reductions haven't taken effect yet, we have lowered our income taxes. The reduction in income taxes over the next year or two will start affecting the middle income and lower-middle income people. There will be a lot more money to spend and to save and all this will stimulate the economy.

8. Because inventories have gotten so low. Truly, all across America inventories have been reduced, which means the companies who have lived off of their inventories the last year or two will need to start reordering things and beefing back up again.

7. Because retail sales are "starting back up again." Walmart® has just reported 5 and 6% gains for this last Christmas Season over the one a year ago. It's so amazing because, on the news they're talking about how horrible this Christmas Season (2001) was, but Telecheck just announced a 2 to 3% increase over the year before. It's amazing that the news reports keep talking about how negative it is, but some stores keep saying how well they're doing. Pretty amazing isn't it?

6. P/E ratios are getting back in line. Companies are starting to earn more money. More important than the P/E ratios getting back in line is that our expectations for the P/E ratios have also become more reasonable. For a few years, investors were expecting 25%—50% year over year, and sometimes quarter over quarter, earnings increases, and it was just unsustainable. Now that the expectations for earnings growth is back down in the 5%—10% a year range, a lot of companies can meet those targets. So, as investor expectations are met, the stock prices, while not shooting ahead, will at least start inching back upwards.

5. Companies have shed bad debt. They're refinancing debt. Let's deal with this another way—the fifth reason why there's going to be a Bull Market is because interest rates are pretty much at a historical low right now. The Federal Reserve has lowered interest rates and adjusted the discount rate *eleven times* over the last year.

   Now, just because they've lowered interest rates doesn't mean there is automatically going to be an increase in borrowing; ie, companies expanding, companies borrowing money to build new factories, etc. When there is talk that there is going to be a downturn or a recession or anything like that, a lot of companies, even though they can get loans at a lower rate, do not do so. They just do not get the loans and do not grow. But, that is changing. It might take a year or two for the lower interest rates to feel its way into the marketplace, but it *will* do so and the economy will go up. A lot of companies are refinancing bad debt.

4. Many companies have been shedding, not just bad debt, but bad investments. There have been so many one-time charges, one-time expenses and write-offs. Company's actual book-values are getting back in line with their market capitalization value. What the companies break-up value is, on a lot of companies, is getting closer to what the stock should go for (what the stock price to Book Value ratio has historically been), and that bodes well.

3. Because most of the Bears are out of the woods. You see, you need a whole bunch of negativism. Bears *have* held down the marketplace. These Bears *have* had their way for the last couple of years. Every time there's good news, they pounce on it with fifteen items of bad news. They're out. But, we need this negative sentiment to permeate the entire marketplace. The market will never, ever turn around, the market will never, ever recover, until the negativism captures the moment. Now, not only are the Bears out, but the Bears are tired. Their time is up, and I think even they realize it. You're seeing oscillators in the stock market changing. They point to a good market ahead.

2.   The number two reason why *I* say the market is going to go up is because, rarely in the history of the stock market have we ever had two bad years in a row. It happens about every twenty or thirty years. In 160 years of tracking the stock market, only eight times has the stock market been down two years in a row.

   Then the obvious question is, "What happens after that?" And the answer is, historically, the year after two bad years (and there's only been *one time* when there's ever been a third and a fourth bad year, and that was 1929 to 1932, and there were a lot of extenuating circumstances then) the market on average, has gone up 18.8 percent. Now that's an incredible increase for one year in the market. And, by the way, it does not sustain itself at the 18%. After that, it goes back to the historical 7% to 8% a year in certain indices.

   I think we really are going to see the market take off, slowly. That is, of course, my personal opinion. I do not think it will rush back up, but that it will be a slow, up-trending market.

1.   Because we all want it to become a Bull Market. If enough Americans want it, is it going to happen? Seriously, if enough people start buying stocks again in anticipation that the market is going to go up, it becomes a self-fulfilling prophecy, just like negative talk became a self-fulfilling prophecy.

As the market takes off, the question everyone has to ask is this, "Am I going to get ready? Get prepared? Start nibbling at opportunities now? Am I going to start paper trading and get ready to go?" So, as the market turns around, I'm in a profitable position to benefit. By the way, I have to tell you that we're now at the beginning of 2002. A lot of people have been to my seminars in the last couple months. I have been talking about the new "Bull Market" ever since the terrorist attack on September 11th. The DOW, right after September 11th got down to *8100*. And it's at *10,000* today. It's already a Bull Market, by the historical definition of a market that increases 20%. It's already gone up 20% in the last three or four months.

Let me tell you another angle to this, what it means to me. The market is *resilient*. It bounced back. We were attacked by an outside force, now we are engaged in a new type of war. Do you not feel a certain pride in America? Did you not see a certain rallying around the firemen and the policemen? Not just in New York City, but all over this country. You saw sports teams; you saw concerts; everywhere you go you see the flag waving. We're saying the Pledge of Allegiance again. We're seeing God Bless America signs everywhere. And, by the way, I think that God truly will bless America.

So my number one reason, that overshines every other reason you see here, is that we are a blessed people. We live in a great country and God, I think, wants to pour out his choicest blessings on all of us. Not just in America, but all over the world.

America will not only lead the world this time, in our own Bull Market, but we will lead the world economies. Remember the expression that says, "When the tide rises, all boats rise, both big and small"? Well, as the American tide rises, all countries, all over the world will rise. People need what we, as Americans, have. They need our Yankee ingenuity. They need our products and our services and that speaks well for the future. As our country grows and expands, and lifts all boats at the same time, our economy will continue to do better.

The question, once again, is simple. "How do I take advantage of this?" Well, I know one answer. You sure can't take advantage of it sitting on the sidelines. You cannot. You have to be involved some way. If you want to play in the stock market or real estate, how do you take advantage? By learning; by experiencing; and by doing. I pray that the American Dream becomes real for you.

Low P/Es Spell Value

Earnings

Before we look at historically low P/Es formed in the market place right now, we first should discuss earnings and earnings per share, or P/E. The earnings of a company are its bottom line—they are the profits (after taking out dividends to shareholders of any preferred stock and after taxes).

To figure the earnings per share, we take the number of shares outstanding and divide it into earnings—hence we get earnings per share. Earnings are very important and are that which the company uses for dividend payouts, for investment in growth, for excess debt reduction. This figure is most often used by lending institutions for calculation of new debt paybacks.

Earnings should be from sales, and not from one-time phenomenons like the sale of a division, or a bad investment charge off. Many sources list earnings per share: Barron's, Investor's Business Daily, most local newspapers with financial information, and most computer on-line services.

In determining your stock purchases, you'll not only want current figures, but you'll want to know where the company has been. Does it have a history of increasing earnings? Did they increase, then slow down? We need to understand why the earnings per share are what they are.

The P/E is a very important number. I teach this from coast to coast. "When in doubt," I say, "follow earnings." Yes, the other measuring sticks are useful, but not as important as earnings. Think of it. Some companies just don't need a lot of assets to produce income. Some need a lot of assets and other forms of overhead.

The P/E is stated in terms that let us figure how much each dollar of our stock purchase is making. If the company's stock is trading at $80 and it earns $8 per share, it has a multiple of 10. If it's making $4 per share, it has a multiple, or P/E of 20; 20 times $4 equals $80. Another way would be to divide $4 into $80 and get 20, or a P/E of 20. In this case, what we're saying as investors is that we are willing to accept a 5% cash flow return (even though we may not actually receive the $4 or the $8); 5% of $80 is $4.

As I've said, P/Es are very, very important. We need to understand how to use them—and how to keep them in perspective. Let me give you a cab driver's take on this. A P/E stated as dollars just says how much your paying for each dollar of earnings. If a company has a P/E of 42, you're paying $42 to get at one dollar of earnings. Likewise, if the P/E is 8, it means you're paying $8 to get at one dollar of earnings.

To decide if a P/E for a particular company is good, we need to: (1) pick a number we're happy with—say, "I'll buy any company with a P/E under 24," or (2) compare it to the market as a whole, or (3) compare it to stocks in the same sector, say high-tech or pharmaceuticals.

Let's look at (2), as (1) is self-explanatory. Standard and Poors has an index of 500 stocks. It's called the S&P 500. The combined P/E for these companies is in the thirties. You compare your company to this number and get a feel for how well it's doing.

You could also look at a smaller picture and compare your stock to other companies in the same business. There are so many variables in trying to get a handle on this information. One problem is that different reporting services use different time periods. For example, one newspaper may use "trailing 12 months" numbers to figure a company's P/E. It could be accurate to the last decimal, but is it appropriate to make a judgment solely based on where a company has been? Are we not buying the future—what a company *will* earn? Some figures are on projected earnings. If we only used this number, would that be complete—as if anybody knows what a company will actually earn? Yes, analysts (for the company or independent) can make their best guess, but they often fall short or overstate earnings.

Probably the best gauge would be to take a blend of the "trailing" and the "projected earnings." Many papers report it in some combination: say, trailing 12 and future 12 months. Many use six months back and six months future.

A couple of thoughts:

1. I have been such an adamant proponent of caution in buying stocks. So many investors get caught up in the hype of it all. Yes, I agree we all have to recognize the sensational and buy into it a little—but very little. "Follow earnings, follow earnings,"

I shout. People who have attended my seminars and even some of my employees have drowned me out. Let me give an example by way of a story.

Iomega (IOM) is a high-tech software company. Years ago, the stock reached new highs and kept going up. They announced a stock split (I really like stock splits) and the stock soared. I got in at $14 and $16 and sold out at $30—a really nice profit. The stock went to $50. The hype was still in the air. I bought some $40 options, even though I knew the stock was way overpriced. I got out in days with a double on some and a triple on others. The stock went over $60 and headed for $80.

Everyone was getting in—in both stock and options. I stopped. These numbers put the P/E over 100. I think it hit 120 times earnings at one time.

At my seminars, in my office, and on W.I.N.™ (our Internet subscription service) I shouted, "I am not playing," "the bubble has got to burst," and "it's way too high." Yes, I might miss out, but this high price can't be sustained. Also, I had been following Iomega for some time as a nice, little, volatile, covered call play, and this time around I wasn't going for it. This all happened between the spring of 1996 and the fall of the same year.

It's hard to buy a stock at $50 when you were buying it for $14 just months before. Yes, it's earnings were up a little, but not that much. The price was not justified.

It did another split. It was a 2:1. The stock split down to the $30 range and went back up to $40. This is when it was at 120 times earnings.

I held no positions, but everyone around me did no matter how hard I tried to stop them. I calculated the stock (based on earnings and a little hype thrown in) ought to be around $23 per share. I was throwing in about $10 per share for the "Internet hype" value. It was really a $12 to $15 stock.

This next part will seem like a joke, but it's true. When the stock was way up there, analysts for the company were trying to justify the high price. They actually made comments like: "The price isn't so high based on projected earnings three years from now." That's right, three years. Talk about hype. But tens of thousands of people bought into it.

Guess what? It fell to $30, then to $24—almost overnight it was at $16. Then it trickled on down to $13. It rebounded to $13½ to $14½ and I started jumping back in. I bought stock, options, and sold puts. I loaded up. I sold out within weeks, before and when it hit $27.

I'll play this type of stock a lot, but not when the price is too high. One of the questions you must ask is this: what must the company do to sustain this price? The hypesters that run up a stock are gone; and it could take years to recover from buying too high. Be careful! Follow earnings!

2. The market is crazy, and if not totally wacky, at least hard to understand. This example has played out recently in scenario after scenario. Here's a typical example: a stock is at $60. An analyst (someone with what kind of education? What kind of real-world experience in running companies? What kind of motivation?) projects that in the next year the company will earn $3 per share. He/she calculated this by taking numbers supplied by the company, et cetera, et cetera and putting the numbers through some kind of filter—possibly what other companies in the same field are saying or doing, and comes up with the $3. This is a P/E of 20 and not bad for this sector. He/she recommends the stock as a buy. Not a strong buy, just a buy, and thousands of investors and funds start to buy. The stock goes up to $62 on this recommendation, but within weeks it's back down to $60.

Let's thicken the plot a little with more information. Last year the company earnings were $2.90 per share. For this type of business this was a nice profit. The year before it was at $2.40 per share and the year before that it was $1.50 per share. It's had a nice increase. Time passes and the actual earnings are $2.97 per share. The analyst was off 3¢ and the stock falls to $52, dropping $8 off its value. You think I'm joking, but I can show you a long list of this same story played out repeatedly.

The company is profitable, it's growing, it's earning millions—more than the previous year—but alas, the stock gets killed.

More thoughts on P/E:

1. To make sure you're not overpaying for a stock, watch the P/E in changing markets. In a bull market the P/E can be higher. In a bear market you would expect a lower P/E.
2. Certain industries have different P/Es. Banks have low P/Es—say in the 5 to 12 range. High-tech companies have higher P/Es—say around 35 to 60. Check the sector to see what you're paying.
3. If your bank P/E is at 15 and the average is 18, you are paying a premium for the stock. It's okay if you expect higher earnings. If your food sector P/E is 16 and the company you're considering has a P/E of 12, then you're getting it at a discount.
4. A low P/E is not a pure indication of value. You need to consider its price volatility, its range, its direction, and any news you think worthy.
5. You may want to check the historical level (P/E) of the stock. If the current P/E is above the 5 or 15 year historical P/E, the movement of the stock may be about to drop back into line.

Important: The activities or news of a company—that which has driven the P/E to its current level—does you no good prior to your stock purchase. This is why you also need to look at, consider, and take into account the future earnings estimates. Yes, be careful, but remember, you make your money after you buy the stock, so it is the future that will pay you—in dividends and in growth.

P/E Ratio Study

In late September 2001, we collected a list of stocks for companies with low Price to Earnings (P/E) Ratios. We were trying to show that many large, well known and well run companies had reached very low valuations just after the events of September 11th. We updated that list on October 9, 2001. After the market run-up of the last few months of 2001, we went through the list again at the end of January 2002. We found that several stocks had healthy increases in both stock price and P/E Ratio. Some, however, stayed at about the same level as October. Some P/E Ratios changed because the company increased earnings in the last quarter of the year. You might make a case that those stocks that did not increase may not have attractive fundamentals, but do your own research on that idea. One stock, Ford, actually had no P/E Ratio at all after reporting a large loss in the last quarter of the year, wiping out the previous 3 quarters of profit. Here is the list of stocks with side-by-side numbers from October 9, 2001 and January 30, 2002.

List of P/E Ratios

COMPANY	10/09/01		1/18/02	
	P/E	CLOSE	P/E	CLOSE
Alcoa (AA)	18	$31.61	32	$33.70
Adobe Systems (ADBE)	22	$28.83	42	$34.58
American Express (AXP)	18	$29.00	29	$37.02
Bank of America (BAC)	12	$52.15	14	$60.80
Bank One (ONE)	14	$29.36	15	$38.14
Boeing Co. (BA)	10	$36.00	15	$38.14
Citigroup (C)	15	$42.70	10	$39.15
Disney (DIS)	21	$18.92	19	$49.96
Du Pont (DD)	20	$38.04	63	$40.68
Exxon Mobile (XOM)	15	$41.06	16	$38.40
Ford (F)	12	$17.55	n/a	$14.50
General Motors (GM)	9	$40.81	26	$49.77
Intel (INTC)	20	$21.45	64	$33.48
IBM (IBM)	20	$97.14	25	$114.25
Minn. Mining (MMM)	21	$98.44	29	$106.80
Sears (S)	9	$37.14	23	$52.63
World Com (WCOM)	11	$13.53	n/a	$12.78

Now let's revisit some of these stock prices and look at a $50,000 investment spread out evenly among these companies.

Company	10/09/01			1/18/02		
	Closing Prices	Number Shares	(Value) Cost	Closing Prices	Value at Close	Gain/ Loss
Alcoa (AA)	31.61	88	2,777.78	33.77	2,967.59	6.8%
Adobe Systems (ADBE)	28.83	96	2,777.78	35.95	3,463.79	24.7%
American Exp. (AXP)	29.00	96	2,777.78	37.16	3,559.39	28.1%
Bank of America (BAC)	52.15	53	2,777.78	61.12	3,255.57	17.2%
Bank One (ONE)	29.36	95	2,777.78	38.62	3,653.88	31.5%
Boeing Co. (BA)	36.00	77	2,777.78	38.33	2,957.56	6.5%
Citigroup (C)	42.70	65	2,777.78	49.90	3,246.16	16.9%
Disney (DIS)	18.92	147	2,777.78	21.24	3,118.40	12.3%
Du Pont (DD)	38.04	73	2,777.78	40.51	2,958.15	6.5%
Exxon Mobile (XOM)	41.06	68	2,777.78	38.64	2,614.06	-5.9%
Ford (F)	17.55	158	2,777.78	14.70	2,326.69	-16.2%
General Motors (GM)	40.81	68	2,777.78	49.77	3,387.65	22.0%
Hewlitt Packard (HWP)	16.72	166	2,777.78	22.61	3,756.32	35.2%
Intel (INTC)	21.45	130	2,777.78	33.48	4,335.67	56.1%
IBM (IBM)	97.14	29	2,777.78	114.25	3,267.05	17.6%
Minn. Mining (MMM)	98.44	28	2,777.78	106.80	3,013.68	8.5%
Sears (S)	37.14	75	2,777.78	52.63	3,936.31	41.7%
World Com (WCOM)	13.53	205	2,777.78	12.78	2,623.80	-5.5%
			$50,000.04		$58,441.73	16.9%

Interesting results, are they not? Is it over? Not by a long shot. Recently, in several classes, I gave the students, now split up into teams, an assignment to find three companies with P/Es below ten. It was amazing. Within 30 minutes, each team (6) had 5 to 10. Some with P/Es at one to five. You can find these in the paper, online, your broker and in many other financial publications. It's just not that tough.

Now remember, P/E's are part of the "health" indications of the Company. Debt, dividends (yields), book value and sales (to book) are other measuring sticks. P/E's are just one component, but I think the most important one.

At the time this book was published, we found these companies with low P/E's. Prices of stocks change so this list of ratios is already old. But it's a start. Check them out, do a lot more research, pick your trading style already and see if any of these fit.

Low P/Es Spell Value

Short Name	Ticker	P/E	Closing Price 1/31/02
Phillips Pete	P	9	58
Conoco Inc	COC	10	28
Wash Mutual Inc	WM	11	34
El Paso Corp	EP	11	38
Boeing Co	BAC	11	41
Exelon Corp	EXC	11	49
Natl City Corp	NCC	12	28
American Electric	AEP	12	42
Philip Morris Co	MO	12	50
Sears Roebuck	S	12	53
ChevronTexaco	CVX	12	84
Duke Energy Corp	DUK	13	35
TXU Corp	TXU	13	49
Household Intl	HI	13	51
Suntrust Banks	STI	13	62
Bank Of America	BAC	13	63
Cigna Corp	CI	13	92
Allstate Corp	ALL	13	32
Burlington/Santa	BNI	14	28
PNC Financial Se	PNC	14	58
Dominion Res/Va	D	14	59
Lehman Bros Hldg	LEH	14	65
Albertson's Inc	ABS	15	29
Cvs Corp	CVS	15	27
Bb&T Corporation	BBT	15	35
May Dept Stores	MAY	15	37
Bank One Corp	ONE	15	38
Verizon Communic	VZ	15	46
Wachovia Corp	WB	16	33
Honeywell Intl	HON	16	34
SBC Communcatio	SBC	16	37
Safeway Inc	SWY	16	40
Gen Motors Corp	GM	16	51
Union Pac Corp	UNP	16	62
Freddie Mac	FRE	16	67
Fannie Mae	FNM	16	81
Metlife Inc	MET	17	30
Exxon Mobil Corp	XOM	17	39

4

Top 10 Ways to Trade
Right in a Recession

RECESSION?

I have a quote by Thomas Edison. Whenever I see a quote by Mr. Edison I think that he, along with only a few other people in America, have the right to tell any of us what to do. If you want at a person who walks the walk, a person who has paid the price, a person who lives his life in the second mile, it is Thomas Edison. Where did all of his inventions come from? Not just from a brilliant mind, but from incredibly hard work. He said this: *"Opportunity is missed by most people because it is dressed in overalls and looks like work."* There are many other people who want the results, want the good things without the effort that goes behind them.

I would like to use that to remind all of us that trading in the Stock Market was never designed to be easy. It's just like any other business.

I talk about treating the Stock Market *like a business.* To me that means, just like any other small business, it is a lot of work and you have to keep your costs under control. You have to go out and market and sell things. Now, the hope of a small, family-run business is to make enough money that you can continue to keep the business alive and, hopefully, take enough home to pay your bills. If you go to work for someone else, you get a paycheck. If you run your own little family business, you also need to take home a paycheck. That's the whole purpose of being in business. If you get rich at the same time, that would be wonderful. Most people, however, don't get rich at running their own business—they have a glorified job, like working for someone else.

Why would that be different in the Stock Market? Whether you buy or sell stock, whether you buy stock and write covered calls against it, whether you sell puts against stock to generate the cash, whether you buy call and put options to play the up and down movements on the stock on a leveraged basis, it takes a lot of study, a lot of work. I hope that no one ever thinks that making consistent profits in the stock market is easy.

When I say 'easy' in my books and my tapes, I mean that it is *functionally* easy. You can do it on a cell phone; you can do it in your back bedroom; you can do it on the Internet; you can call a stockbroker—you don't have all of the normal expenses of a business. *However*, easy to make money? No. It is *tough* to make money consistently. I hope to take some of the edge off of the process and get people through the learning curve very quickly.

I keep using the convenience store metaphor, because it works as an effective example. In a convenience store you could purchase and stock your shelves with all kinds of items you like, but guess what? Maybe the public doesn't like what you like. When it's time to sell, nobody wants it. Likewise, in the Stock Market you could buy a stock that nobody else wants. "Oh, I like this little company," but nobody else likes it. You go to sell and there are hardly any buyers out, so the price goes down because there's not a big demand. I have repeatedly said, even from my earliest Real Estate days, "The way to get wealthy is to own what other people want." Is that a big revelation? I hope it's not. By the way, the way to get wealthy is to own a whole bunch of things that a whole bunch of other people want. I don't care whether it's barrettes for your hair, or women's shoes, or food. If you have what other people want, you can consistently make money.

I remember clear back in high school, 1967, my economics teacher said, "If you want to make a lot of money, if you want to get rich in America, sell food or women's shoes." I will never forget that. That was an interesting statement that taught me a lot. One of my first jobs out of high school, while I was working my way through college, was selling women's shoes at Leed's Shoe Store. With around 23 sales people, I was number 1, 2 or 3 in sales on any given month, in that store. At that point in time (it's probably more now) the average woman owned 26 pairs of shoes.

I'm sure there are a lot of other ways of making money, but I have been in the restaurant business and in the shoe selling business and I understand both of them to a certain extent, and that teacher was right. The gist of what he was saying was to have what other people want.

So, as we go through this information, I'm hoping that everyone at the end will say, "Wow! I'm going to be a better trader today." I'm not here for your health or my health—I'm here for our *financial* health. I have quite a few comments to make about recessions in general, about trading in a recession or in a down market—one of economic malaise. I believe there are certain things people can do to better their results?

I could re-title this event "Trading Right." You know, doing the "right trade", the "right thing" at the right time. Because 2002 is not going to see a rampaging Bull Market like 1998 and 1999. If you know all about it, do you know how to trade (even one of my 13 Cash Flow strategies), in a downturn? Do you have stocks which just can't seem to get off the bottom? They just sit there?

I'll give you an example. I was looking at some call options on a stock to sell out in February—a covered call to generate income. With the stock at $8, I was looking to sell the February $10 calls against my position. My stockbroker was scrolling through page after page to get to the $10 call position, and it was taking a long time. He said, "Well, I'm just scrolling past the January $300 calls." This was an $8 stock! Now, if it's an $8 stock, there'll be the $5 calls in February, the $7.50's, the $10's, the $12.50's and maybe the $15's. If it's a new option to be sold for January or February, the option market makers are not even going to write the $17.50 or $20 calls. The strike prices will be two or three increments away from that particular stock price. What does that mean, then, if he was scrolling past the *January $300 calls* on an $8 stock?

They were the LEAPS®, the Long-term Equity Anticipation Securities, from a year and a half to two years ago. LEAPS are written out up to two and a half years in the future. So, a couple years ago, that stock had to be in the *$300* range and the *$300* calls (LEAPS) existed at that point in time. Here we are a year and a half or two years later and the stock is at $8. I bought it at $7 and it's at $8 going on to $9 or $10 and I'm hoping to write a covered call. A lot has changed. Today, you can buy stocks for what we used to pay for options which expired.

Some stocks have a hard time. How would you feel if you had bought that stock at $300 and were sitting holding it at $8 saying, "What do I do now?" Do you think there is anybody in America who bought stock at $300 who is now holding it at $8 a share? I think so. You hear about them all the time.

We're talking about trading right and when I go through these today, I want you to think about the "why" behind everything I'm saying. That's what this seminar is about: "Why?" "Why, why, why?" Keep asking that question. I often quote Diane Ravitch: *"The person who knows 'how', will always have a job. The person who knows 'why' will always be his boss."* I love that quote. More important than the "how to's" are the "why to's."

Manager or Leader?

Speaking of trading in your own account and treating it like a business, what's the difference between a manager and a leader? Are you a manager in your life? Or are you a leader in your life? What is the difference between them? Does a company need managers or leaders? I read a definition awhile ago that is quite pertinent. A manager is a person who does things the right way; and people who know how to do things the right way are invaluable. But a leader is a person who does the right things. There's a world of difference. A leader who sees the direction, the overall picture, the mission and the ins-and-outs of a company, can to hire managers to run the company the right way. In your own life, are you a leader or a manager? You need to be both. You need to be the leader in your life, and from time to time you also need to be the manager.

I suggest to you that you will make a lot more money if you're a leader. You can hire a stockbroker to do things the right way. If you're doing spreads or trying to buy an option at the right price, if you're trying to look at support and resistance levels—you do not have to be the one sitting at a computer. People who sit at a computer, to me, are people who do things the right way, and even though they may be doing things the right way, they may not be doing the right things. Their account might not be moving in the right direction. They're adept at getting the trades in, they're adept at the transactions, but they are *not* adept at the leadership qualities to run their life, or to run their business enterprise.

A lot of our customers and our students are running their own businesses. They're trading in their accounts and they're supporting their families. Along with doing things the right way, they are doing the right things. When I hear Diane Ravitch's comment about the person knowing how always having a job and the person knowing why always being the boss, it comes back to the manager/leader correlation. The person who knows "how" will be a good manager. The person who knows "why" will be a good leader. There is a major difference.

Let's talk about the differences now. We'll use this as a segue into differences in recessions. This discussion is not just about how to trade in the recession and trading right, but it's about various strategies. Before I give the ten ways to trade in a recession, some of which will be actual formulas which people can use, let's talk about this particular recession we are in.

Recessions usually weaken the American dollar, but, over the last ten months, our dollar has strengthened against almost every major foreign currency. The German Deutschmark, the Japanese Yen, the French Mark, the English Pound—our dollar has strengthened. That is unusual.

Timing of recessions: a recession is defined as two quarters in a row where the major economic indicators are down. Those indicators vary, by the way, but generally, according to the government, they are the unemployment rate, the money supply rate, the inflation rate, etc. They refer to how much money is in the economy. If those indicators are down for two quarters in a row, we are said to be in a recession.

Now, the problem with this is that most of those kinds of indicators are what we call lagging indicators. You don't know what they tell you until three to four months after it's over.

For example, I was just upstairs editing *Red Light, Green Light*, as we're getting ready to go to press. Most of you don't know this, but I started writing the book *Red Light, Green Light* and several of the special reports that became chapters in the book, clear back in 1999. In the year 2000, I updated a lot of this information. We thought the book was to come out last Fall, and now have held off the printing until now. It was so amazing. I read my reports, which I wrote in the Spring and early Summer of the year 2001. I decided to leave my two year old remarks in the book. People will have to look at the dates in the book and when it was written to determine whether I was prescient or not. I said in May or June of last year (2001): "We're in a recession right now. It's a mild one, but we are in a recession." The official government record on the recession did not come out until right before Christmas of 2001, when they said, "We have been in a recession since March."

I'm going to quote from James Grant in *Forbes* magazine. He said, *"No recession has never not ended."* In all of his study of economics involving hundreds of years, no recession has never not ended. He also said, *"Since the early 1950's, no recession has lasted over 16 months."* according to the two-quarters rule of economic indicators.

Here we are again, this January 2002, in what has officially been called a recession since March. We're ten months into this one. Let me tell you a mistake I made. I forgot that averages are averages. Before, when I talked about Bear and Bull Markets, and how the average Bear Market is nine to eleven months, and then we hit our eleventh month, I said, "This is it, it's over." I forgot the law of averages. *Averages.* Sometimes a Bear Market can go two or three years and sometimes only three months. They're both figured into the averages. When they say nine to eleven months, that's an average. I jumped in, the positive, optimistic person that I am, and lost quite a bit. I should have waited. Now, Bear Markets are not recessions and Mr. Grant's figure is *not* an average. *No recession* has lasted longer than 16 months since the early 1950's.

I need to discuss a bit more about these indicators. There are three types of indicators: 1) Future Indicators, or what are called leading indicators. 2) Coincident Indicators, things that are happening right now, today, and 3) Lagging Indicators, and that is what we have been talking about.

Future indicators say, "The future looks like this." Coincident indicators say, "We're in this kind of a market right now." Lagging indicators say, "Nine months to a year ago, we were in this kind of market."

How many of you have heard something like this? Each time the government puts out a report that says something like, "Housing starts are being adjusted by this amount," or "Retail sales for last month are this," and then a month or two later they'll come back and say, "We're revising our statements. The jobless rate was not really 5.4%, it was 5.2%." Or, "Sales in the month of December were not really down 2%, they were only down 1%." Things like that happen all the time. Lagging indicators are *usually* a bit more truthful, because they do not deal with estimates or wishful thinking. They deal with *real* events, *real* happenings.

Let's talk about some weird things involving leading, coincident and lagging indicators. Here's a weird one – we're in a recession, but since the terrorist attacks on September 11th, our stock market is up quite a bit. As a matter of fact, if you were to take a chart for the whole year and just take out September 10th and 11th through the 21st when the stock market opened up again, and put the chart back together again, guess what you would see? Pretty much that it picked up right where it left off. We were *on* an inclining market through part of this year, and that terrorist attack slowed us down for several

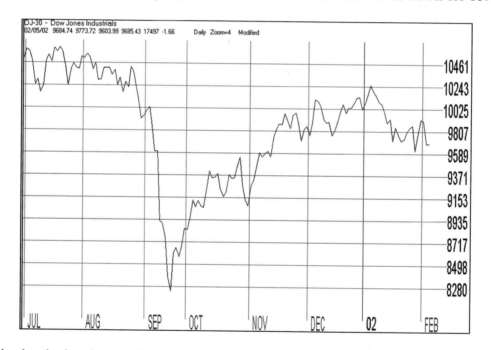

weeks, but look at how resilient our market place is. Do you see that we're right back up to where we were before the terrorist attack, and all this within two months?

Stock prices have been up. Usually in a recession, the money supply shrinks. Over this last year, 2001, our money supply *boomed*. We have so much more money available in the credit market, so much more money available in what is called the M1 and

M2 supply of money. Now, a lot of that was controlled by the Fed lowering interest rates, but the point is that there is a lot of money in the economy.

Another thing that usually happens in a sustained recession is that unemployment keeps going up, but even in two or three months after the economic downturn because of the terrorist attacks, we are hearing all kinds of strange things. In one state, unemployment is going up, but overall in the whole country, for two to four weeks in a row, unemployment claims were going *down*. This came after three weeks of bad unemployment claims. But then, what is usually reported in the newspapers? The good reports or the bad reports? It's always the bad. They thrive on the "fire" syndrome. Somebody has to be shot dead on the front page, or newspapers will not sell. They're always reporting the negative.

Here in the state of Washington, we had huge layoffs because of Boeing, but unemployment went down and there were more people at work week after week. We had huge dotcom companies here the last couple of years, laying people off, and yet the employment statistics, which measure the need for employment over the next few years, say that we here in the state of Washington are going to need 240,000 more employees for our high-tech industry.

Will you agree with me that sometimes a pink slip, getting laid off, may be painful at the time, but could turn out to be the best thing for your family's economic health? Often, when pink slips are delivered, people say, "I'm tired of this, I'm not going to go to work for any other company, I'm starting my own business." They start up a small business and hire people. It's a boon to the economy.

I don't want to be just a good-news newspaper. I'm not going to just report good news, but I'm hoping to keep things in perspective. We've had huge layoffs, but then why haven't unemployment claims gone up that much? It's interesting, isn't it? Overall in the country, unemployment claims have been down, like the couple weeks before Christmas.

How can this be if there is all this talk of recession? Are we out of this recession? That's an interesting thought. We just might be. I'll tell you why I think so in a minute. If we don't know for three to nine months that we've *been* in a recession, how do we know when we're *out* of a recession? If you're looking at the lagging indicators, guess what you need? The answer: proof.

Here we are in January, coming up on February of the year 2002. We will not really know if we are out of the recession just yet. If we are, it would have been about a nine month recession. We might not get the official word until July or August, when all of the lagging economic indicators will say, "We were out of the recession clear back in the Winter or early Spring of 2002."

43

HOLD THE PRESS. It's happened. People are already saying we're out of the recession. Read the following:

John M Barry in The Washington Post:

WASHINGTON – Powered by soaring auto sales and a sharp increase in government spending, the U.S. economy resumed growing in the final three months of last year, albeit at a meager 0.2 percent annual rate, the Commerce Department reported Wednesday.

The unexpectedly strong number, a first estimate that will be revised in coming months, suggests the U.S. recession that began last spring may have already ended. If so, it will have been the mildest on record.

"The worst is over. We're on the road to recovery," said Bill Cheney, chief economist at John Hancock Financial Services in Boston.

"Signs that weakness in demand is abating and economic activity is beginning to firm have become more prevalent," the Federal Open Market Committee, the policy-making group, said in a statement announcing its decision. "With the forces restraining the economy starting to diminish, and with the long-term prospects for productivity growth remaining favorable and monetary policy accommodative, the outlook for economic recovery has become more promising."

The announcement appeared to lift spirits on Wall Street, which rallied from losses earlier in the day. The Dow Jones industrial average rose 144.62 to close at 9762.86, while the Nasdaq composite index climbed 720.45 to 1913.44. The Standard & Poor's 500 index increased 12.93 to 1113.57.

Alan Greenspan of the FMOC (The Feds):

U.S. Federal Open Market Committee Statement: Full Text Jan 30 2002
Washington, Jan. 30 — The following is the full text of the statement released today by the Federal Reserve:

The Federal Open Market Committee decided today to keep its target for the federal funds rate unchanged at $1\frac{1}{2}$ percent.

Signs that weakness in demand is abating and economic activity is beginning to firm have become more prevalent. With the forces restraining the economy starting to diminish, and with the long-term prospects for productivity growth remaining favorable and monetary policy accommodative, the outlook for economic recovery has become promising.

The degree of any strength in business capital and household spending, however, is still uncertain. Hence, the Committee continues to believe that, against the background of its long-run goals of price stability and sustainable economic growth and of the information currently available, the risks are weighted mainly toward conditions that may generate economic weakness in the foreseeable future.

Fed Saw 11th Rate Cut as 'Insurance,' December Minutes Show

Federal Reserve policy makers lowered the benchmark interest rate by a quarter percentage point on Dec. 11 as "insurance" against "prolonged economic weakness…"

"Several members viewed an easing action as a measure of insurance against the potential for greater or more prolonged economic weakness…"

Anirvan Banarji, Special to TheStreet.com:

The long-awaited U.S. economic recovery is now at hand. That's the clear message from the array of leading indices maintained by the Economic Cycle Research Institute that first warned of recession 16 months ago and signaled its inevitability 10 months ago, right when the recession began. The latest data show that employment and industrial production, two key components of the USCI that are used to date recessions and recoveries, kept falling through December. In fact, the USCI itself declined in December, implying that the recession continued at least through that month. But we believe a recovery is imminent.

The WLI bottomed in October 2001. Since then we've become increasingly optimistic about the economic recovery. It's now clear that the WLI has risen in the pronounced, pervasive and persistent manner that marks a cyclical upturn. Thus, it's highly likely that the economy will begin to recover by the first quarter of 2002.

…in four decades, the lead of stock prices at business cycle troughs has never exceeded five months. If the September low in stock prices holds, as we expect, the economy will bottom by the first quarter of 2002.

Kristen French in RealMoney.com

"Fourth-Quarter GDP Shows Gain in First Print":

War abroad and cheap auto financing at home combined to create a slight increase in fourth-quarter gross domestic product, the government said in a preliminary report.

The unexpected 0.2% increase confounded economists prediction of up to a 1.1% contraction in the quarter and made it increasingly likely that at least one definition of recession — two consecutive quarters of GDP contraction — would not be met in the current downturn.

Weekly jobless claims and consumer confidence numbers suggest the consumer ought to be in pretty good shape. After peaking at 506,250 in mid-October, the four-week average dropped to 404,250 in the week ended Jan. 19, the last report on record. Consumer confidence has risen to 97.3 in January from 85.3 in October.

The question is this: Can you still play this market? Are their profitable plays to be made? Is this a good time? The answer is yes.

One more comment before we get into the ten reasons.

This is a comment by Tony Dywer out of *Real Money*. He said, "Typically, after the initial surge off the low, the market enters a period of low volatility." Let me explain what that means. For a lot of us at the Stock Market Institute of Learning, we like leverage-type investing. Leverage-type investing means that we can buy an *option* to buy a stock and put up far less money than it would take to buy the actual stock. If Cisco, for example, were at $18 and we really like the future of Cisco, it would cost us $18,000 to buy a thousand shares. Now, we can use margin, where the broker will put up half the money and we would have $9,000 of our own money tied up. That might be really good. Now, if Cisco moves to $19 or $20, it was a good decision. If Cisco goes down to $17, $16, $15, it was a bad decision, *but* we still own the stock.

Another way to play Cisco is to not buy the stock, but to get an option to buy the stock. Options in this price range go in $2.50 increments. An option is the *right* to buy the stock, not the *obligation*. You could put up far less money and have the right to buy the stock. You're not really buying the stock, you're paying for an option to buy the stock.

Your broker says, "When do you want the right to buy it, and at what price?" You ask, "What's it going for?" and he says, "Well, do you think it's going to go up?" If you think it's going to go up, you want to buy a call option. The $17.50 calls (remember, the stock is at $18) are going for $2. The $20 calls are going for $1. So, for $1, you can buy an option, or the right to buy Cisco for $20 out two or three months. Now, if Cisco goes to $19 to $20 to $21 and you have the right to buy it at $20, depending on how much time is left before that right expires, your $1 could become $1.50. It could become $1.75. That would be quite interesting. You call your stockbroker, thirty seconds later you sell your option. You didn't buy the option to actually buy the stock—you bought the option to make money on the *option*. With your right to buy Cisco at $1.75, and you have 1,000 of those rights (10 contracts), your $1,000 turned into $1,750, or a $750 profit (minus commissions).

Think this one through with me. $1,750 after commissions may produce $650 or $680 in profits. You would have made more money with the stock. You would have put up $18,000 and sold the stock at $20, that would have been $20,000. That's more than $650 profit. It's a $2,000 profit, but what's the point? The point is how much *cash* you have tied up. This is a form of leverage. It's not like a down payment in real estate. It's an option to buy the stock, and that option can expire, you could lose all or part of your $1,000.

If you own Cisco and were in a recession atmosphere and there is no big news or no good news, then nothing is going to happen. Could you not then, if you own the stock, whether you bought it at $24 or $13, sell that same $1option, giving someone the right to buy your Cisco stock away from you at $20? Well, if you *sell* the option, you now take on an obligation. You would take *in* $1,000. Whoa. $1,000. Is that your money? Yes. You sold it and have taken in $1,000. Somebody has the right to take this stock away from you, but the only way they're going to take it away from you is if the stock goes above $20. If it stays at $18, $19, you keep the stock. It's not going to get purchased. Now, if you could sell it for $20 you'd be happy, right? You bought the stock at $18, you sell it for $20, you made $2. For 1,000 shares, that's $2,000, but you also get to keep that other $1,000 from selling the option.

What I just explained is called "Writing a Covered Call." "Writing" means to sell, "Covered" means you actually own the stock, and a "Call" is a call option. This time, instead of gambling and betting that the stock is going to go up, and *buying* the call option, you *own* the stock and you *sell* the call option against your stock position for *cash flow purposes*.

I think most of the people who are attracted to us want *income*. We keep talking about treating the stock market like a business. Well, for $18,000, or $9,000 on margin into this Cisco trade, we just pocketed $1,000. If the stock goes up, we pocket another $2,000, which would be pretty neat. If it stays the same we keep the $1,000 and after the expiration date, we sell the next month's call option and generate more income. If the stock moves above $20, we sell the stock (electronically) and make $3,000, $2,000 in capital gains, $1,000 in option premium.

This covered call strategy is a way to work the stocks that you own that have gone down in value. It's also good for stocks that are not lurching forward. It's a monthly income formula. What if you could do that with three or four stocks a month?

There are many people who have sick portfolios. They are waiting, and think they are at the mercy of the marketplace. For example a person calls his stockbroker and asks, "I bought this stock at $80. Its down to $18, what do I do?" The broker says, "You don't need the cash so why don't you just wait it out?" Then along comes Wade Cook and he says "HOLD IT!" Instead of just waiting it out and being a victim of where the stock has gone, why don't you fight back? Why don't you learn things you can do to start building back the value? Why don't you sell the $20 call and generate a dollar? The stock goes to $18, then to $19. If it is not at $20, you are not going to get called out, but if the stock is at $19.50 on that third Friday, or the expiration date, and you don't get called out (or the stock is not bought away from you) what do you still own? You still own the stock! Then what could you do? Sell the $20 call out the next month.

The next month the call is going for $1.50 because the stock is higher, it is more valuable. Whoa! A $1500 potential! Are you fighting back? Either it gets bought away from you at $20 or not. Then the next month you do it again, and so on. You fight back! There are a lot of people who need to fix their portfolios.

The Ten Ways to Trade Properly in a Recession

#10 Manage the Downside

Far too many people have not taken care of their downside. For example: if someone came to our program and had 1000 shares of an $80 stock, we would teach them about stop losses. Most Americans don't know about stop losses. This stock has gone from $40 up to $80. We teach students in our seminars to ask a question: Can this price be sustained? It is on an all time high of $80—usually, the stock is going to back off. They should know how to capture the profit, to protect the latest run-up in the price of the stock. It doesn't cost anything to do this! They would call their stockbroker and say, "Place a stop loss order on the stock at $65." If the stock drops back down to $40, they would already have an order in to sell it at $65 or $70. Most people who own stock in the stock market do not know how to do this.

Next, they could buy a Put option. A Put will go up in value if the stock goes down. They could buy the $75 Put or the $70 Put. That would have protected them. If the stock backed off from $80 to $70, the Put would have gone up in value from $7 to $9 per share, which could equate up to $9000. They would have protected themselves.

My point about a recession is that it makes us all stop and manage our downside better. Why? Because there is not much potential for a big run-up in a recession. No stock is going to go flying from $40 to $80, at least I haven't seen very many of those lately! I have seen a lot of stocks go from $80 to $40 in a heartbeat! I saw one recently go from around $14 down to $3, because the FDA approval did not go through on their phase-three testing. It bounced up a dollar today, but down $11 in one day! How would you have liked to own that stock? You bought it at $3 and it has gone clear up to $12 in the past five months. Now it is back at $3. All that profit lost!

If these stockowners had come through our educational system, we would have taught them about a stock's sustainability. We would have made them think about this: what if the FDA approval doesn't come through? If it does come through, that $13 stock could go to $23 or even $33. But what if it doesn't? Then the stock will probably go down. They should have learned to buy Puts; they should have learned to place stop loss orders. Everyone needs to learn to manage his or her downside better.

#9 Opportunities Abound!

There are compelling reasons to buy stocks. Stocks have been hammered, but a lot of those companies are still very profitable. The last couple of years, especially in the dot.com era, many stocks were racing ahead. They had lavish expectations, with earnings growing at 50% and 100% a year! Has anyone ever run a business before? If you have a business that made $40,000 this year, what are the chances that, without major increases in some area, your business is going to make $80,000 next year? Highly unlikely.

Most business at $40,000 will go to $44,000 or $48,000 in a year. We saw some companies that were expanding on the Internet so rapidly that we were constantly expecting 50% or 80% growth rates or even 100% growth rates in their earnings, and in sales. We were expecting companies' growth rates to be 30% or more per quarter! Not even year over year! Expectations became so high.

This current marketplace is a rolling-recession type marketplace and it is a pretty interesting place to be. Why? Because these stocks, that were at $80 and are now at $8, mean those exaggerated expectations are gone! Now we are getting back to reason. We are now expecting companies to grow 5% a year, or 8% a year. A lot of companies can sustain that. Some can even sustain a 10% growth rate. The stock at $8 or $9 is a good price. It will grow slowly. Now the play is different.

Here is a problem that occurred when a stock went from $20 to $80 based on huge projections of what the growth rate or earnings rate would be. The analysts would say the over exaggerated price was okay, based on the *projected earnings* in three or four years. They were justifying today's price based on these huge ridiculous estimates of future earnings. That is why the bubble popped for the dot.com industry. It wasn't because they couldn't sustain their price; it was because they could not sustain their *earnings projections*. They could not sustain their earnings growth rates. Something had to give. Everything returns to the norm.

Historically over the last 80 years in the marketplace an average P/E is 15.5. A typical New York Stock Exchange (NYSE) stock is at 20 times earnings. A typical NASDAQ stock is 40 or 60 times earnings because NASDAQ is composed of many high-flying companies. As a general rule, 15.5 is the historical price earnings ratio for all stocks. This means that you would pay $15.50 to get at one dollar of earnings. If you are paying 30 times earnings for a stock you are really over-paying, based on the historical average.

Here is my point. Everything returns to the norm. Here is an example. Krispy Kreme Donuts (KKD) is a really good example to use. At the time of this written entry the stock was around $40 per share. Its P/E is in the 80's, which means that at this stock price you are paying $80 to get at $1 of earnings.

If you have a stock trading at 87 times earnings and the stock is now $40, what has to happen? If everything returns to the norm, what has to happen to Krispy Kreme stock? One of two things. Either the earnings have to increase to justify the price of the stock, or the stock price has to come down. If the earnings don't go up, sooner or later the stock price will come down.

Why, then, is a P/E of 87 possibly okay? Because Krispy Kreme is in a major expansion mode. Almost every quarter earnings increase. This company constantly beats their earnings estimates. Revenues are growing and so are net profits. If this continues, the stock price will stay up.

I want to encourage everyone here to use a little triage. If you watched M.A.S.H.*** you know the word triage! Every time the bus or the helicopter landed with patients, the nurses or doctors would go out to greet them. Triage, in a medical sense, means you must screen and classify the wounded, sick, or injured patients to determine priority needs and thereby ensure the most efficient use of medical equipment, staff, facilities etc. Who are the ones who are going to die if they do not receive immediate attention? They are first. Then there are those people that need help quickly, but they can wait a bit, or be taken care of by medical staff other than the surgeons. Then there are those not as serious that can be taken care of last.

In the stock market people think that any deal could be the right deal. We need to do a financial triage and ask ourselves questions like: Is this opportunity immediate? Do I need to do something right now, or is this trade going to be around a bit? Can it wait for a couple of weeks, or will it be around for a few months? The answer will either be, now, never, or later.

In Chapter 6, I present the topic, *Compelling Reasons*. I explain that every trade must have a compelling reason in order to work. If you don't have a compelling reason or impending event then you should get out of the way. It is better to miss a trade than to lose on a trade.

For example: Yesterday the market (the DOW) went down almost 210+ points. Do you know what started it all? It started with Intel (INTC). They had incredible earnings. They beat their estimates by .05 cents. They were awesome! Go INTEL! The news is screaming that the economy is in a downturn and here company after company is coming through with these better than expected earnings, they're making money! You can't go broke making money! But Intel said… *"We are going to slow down our capital expenditures."* The stock and several other stocks related to this industry got clocked!

What is the difference between a capital expenditure and any other kind of expenditure? A capital expenditure is a purchase of things like capital equipment and machinery. Intel manufactures chips. The companies that supply the machines to do the manufacturing just got slammed in after market trading and all through the day! It was tough on the market. The only way we are going to come out of this little bear market or recession is when we start having great earnings. I am not saying good earnings! Good earnings are almost met with disdain. Yeah we beat estimate, making money, but everyone is saying, "No, we need *great earnings*."

The stocks are not in a runaway mode right now. Intel might go up with the news of beating estimates, but it could just as easily go down depending on the comments they make about their company. What value does the marketplace on earnings going up? IBM closed right under $120. If IBM goes up, it isn't going to go up very much. $122 or maybe $124. That is a small percentage on a $120 stock. If it goes down, it is not going to go down very much—it is not that volatile. If they had killer earnings of say $4 a share versus expectations of .85 cents a share, the stock could go up maybe to $150! But the earnings today do not justify a runaway stock.

Opportunities are everywhere to make small chunks of change! You can watch the patterns. Have you missed out on the last opportunity? Don't worry! If IBM goes to $122, in a few days or so it may move to $118 again. It will roll. There are plenty of times to make a play.

#8 Negative Beta in a Down Market

Even in a negative marketplace you can find stocks that perform. Let's explore this and use a stock option-measuring device to hunt for stocks which perform well under adverse conditions.

The "beta" is a measuring stick. A stock's return is in direct correlation to the returns on some market indices, known as beta. A stock with a high beta responds strongly to variations in the market, but a stock with a low beta is somewhat less sensitive to market variations. Depending on what strategies you use, you want to pick stocks with betas relative to your trading style. For example, if the market is moving down, and you do not want to play stocks to the down side because you are a bull, then chose a negative beta down stock. This means that the stock is not moving in the same direction as the market, hence perceived as negative, but it is positive for you! Stocks may have different betas depending on whether it is an up or down market. Chose your beta based on your bull or bear trading style and the current market conditions.

If you are going to trade options, the following brief discussion on "delta" may help. We do not want to over-pay for our options. Use a delta formula to avoid mistakes.

Delta measures how the option performs as compared to its stock. For example, you have a stock at $18 and you look at the $20 call option out for two months. You find the option is a dollar. If the stock goes up one dollar to $19 and the $20 Call option goes up in value to around $1.50 that would have a delta of .50. The .50 cents represents a percentage. If the stock went up $1 and the option .50 cents, this represents a 50% ratio, or a delta of 50%. If the stock went up $1 and the option went up .80 cents that would be a delta of 80%. You want to buy stocks that have a high delta of 60 or greater. Every stock-broker can give you a delta on a stock option. If a stock has a delta of 10 and the stock goes up $1, the option will go up .10 cents. Your $1000 is now $1100. You would barely break even on that trade. Delta is a measuring stick to keep a lot of people out of trouble, so as not to over-pay for options that have a high likelihood of not making you any money.

Back to beta: in a negative beta down we have to divorce ourselves from just the option designation, or the option comparison. Negative beta indicates a stock moves in the opposite direction from the general market. As the market goes down certain stocks go up. Usually 1500 to 2000 stocks of the 30,000+ stocks publicly traded in America, go up when the market goes down. Look for stocks that do well in a recession, or when the market goes down. You can scan for these, or ask your broker.

#7 Select Stocks that Perform Badly

In a recession these stocks are easy to spot! The market is going down, so individual stocks are going down. Remember there are bearish strategies and bullish strategies. For example, in a bearish marketplace, IBM may come in with fairly good earnings, but the stock is not going to go that high.

There are stocks that are not going to perform very well because they do not have huge news to sustain them. We can play bearish strategies if we don't think a stock is going to go anywhere. We could buy Puts. We could do Bear Call Spreads. We could sell the stock short. There are all kinds of strategies we can use.

For example there are huge Internet companies making a lot of money. The ones consistently making big money today, the ones that have earnings even though the stocks are down from what they were, include Juniper (JNPR), Cisco (CSCO) Extreme Networks (EXTR), etc. Instead of being a retailer of the Internet they provide all the Internet companies with equipment. Like the gold rush of the 1840's. Who made money no matter what, whether they found a vein of gold or not? The answer: the suppliers! The people selling the picks and the shovels and the food and the tents. The gold miners were the risky ones. Some of those people did get rich, but very few. Who is going to make money in this industry?

These types of negative trades are too tough for me! As good as I am at some of these kinds of trades, I hardly ever start looking for bad stocks. It is not in my personality. I found out that if I play too many Puts, I find myself thinking about airplane crashes and hoping someone gets sick at a restaurant so their stock will go down. I don't want to be that way. Your personality can change because of this way of thinking. I am a Bullish kind of person. Stocks in a recession can take days, weeks, and months to climb up and with just the slightest bad news they just crash back down. The people who get good at buying Put options on stocks can make a lot more money faster than waiting for the Call options to go up.

#6 The Good Stocks Do Act Better

(53)

Medical stocks and food stocks act really well. There are some stocks that are definitely tied to the recession. For example, energy stocks. They have been hammered this last year because oil prices have gone so far down that their profits have shrunk and yet they're still making billions of dollars. Other recessions have been due to energy prices being so high, but this recession is not caused by energy prices!

Oil and gas are a big part of our economy, from the local truck driver delivering bread to the trains running across the country, to the airplanes and ships that cross the oceans. Everyone needs oil and gas. Right now there is a glut.

Do you remember a year ago when there was all the talk about high-energy prices? Oil stocks at that time were incredibly high. But energy prices have become so low. I know this! I own parts of several oil wells and my checks that were at $8,000 and $10,000 a month are now at $2,000 or $3,000 a month.

You saw gasoline go from $1.80 to $1.20 a gallon. For a 20-gallon tank of gas at .60 cents less per gallon, that is $12 less per tank. If you fill up your gas tank once a week, multiply that $12 by 50 weeks, it's $600 a year. That is $600 more a year for you to do other things! Multiply this amount for a company that has dozens of trucks. Do you think

Federal Express and U.P.S. are doing better? What are you looking for? Companies that will do better when energy prices are down.

There are other companies that will do better no matter what. Like health care companies. They will get through a recession. Do you think that a recession is going to stop people from eating at McDonald's or Burger King? Not really, people still eat out!

#5 The Law of Leverage:
in a recession there is a tendency for money to seek higher and better uses.

One of the ways to get your money working better is to use the law of leverage. In almost every business opportunity, including ships sailing out of ports hundreds of years ago, leverage was and still is the key. The highest leveraged money will always seek out opportunities. When investors look at stocks in a recession, they know they need to become better at picking winners and making trades with the least amount of cash tied up, but with the highest likelihood of success. If an investor buys 1000 shares of an $18 stock for $18,000, versus buying the $17.50 call options for $2,000, the risk is $18,000 vs. $2,000.

People get tighter with their money; therefore they use the law of leverage. I am going to suggest that options in a certain way are even less risky than stocks. Hopefully this good news to a lot of people. Stockbrokers may not understand options and how they work, they may even badmouth them; but you can do your best homework to determine if you think a stock is going to go up. It's coming up on earnings, the earnings expected are going to be good. These things point to a good trade. You buy the call option for $2. Again, an option is the *right* to buy; but not the *obligation*. You buy a thousand shares, (which would be ten contracts) for $2,000. If the stock goes to $19 or $21, your right to buy the stock at $17.50 could easily become $3. You sell it for $3, and your gross return is $3,000. You went from $2,000 to $3,000—netting $1,000 in cash. If you owned the stock, you would have $18,000 tied up. The return might be larger, but the *rate of return* is better with options.

Let's go the other way. If the stock goes down to $16, your right to buy at $17.50 is only $1.00. Your $2,000 becomes $1,000. You would lose $1,000 if you were to sell the option at that time. What if it goes down to $12? You are going to lose, but you are only going to lose that initial investment of $2,000. Here is the irony. The stockbroker might bad mouth options because they are risky, and I will grant you that they are risky because they have that added element of an expiration date. The stock has to perform before a certain time or you are going to lose. But what about the *stock* you would have bought at $18, which is now $13? If you sell now, it's down $5, a $5,000 loss. Most stockbrokers I know don't think anything bad about that at all. They don't think anything about a *stock* going down $5, but they call a $2 *option* risky. To a certain extent that is the reason I like options. You have unlimited upside potential, but limited downside risk. If that stock goes up to $38, you have the right to buy it at $17.50. Your $2 option becomes worth maybe $15, which would be worth $15,000.

Again, where else do you have a limited upside potential with limited downside exposure? This is one of the reasons why options have become so popular. Making consistent money is not as easy as it might sound, but anyone can go through a learning curve and learn how to buy options and protect themselves at the same time.

#4 A Service Economy

One of the reasons that recessions have been so short (the longest recession being 16 months) is because only 20% of the American workers are involved in farm or industrial work. About 80% of American workers are involved in service industries, white-collar positions. The industrial companies are the first to get hit: the steel industry, the coal industry, and/or the farming industry.

In Detroit, even though it's the home of several major car manufacturers, there are more people working in insurance companies or retail establishments. There are more people involved in *selling* and *servicing* cars than people involved in *manufacturing* cars. These types of service industries are less effected by energy concerns. When 80% of our country was in farming and heavy industrial, a downturn affected everybody.

I think we are heading into a 90/10 factor. By 2010 or 2015, 90% of workers in America will be involved in some sort of service industry, including sales. From shoe sales to car sales, our economy has changed; our type of work has changed. That is one of the reasons why this recession will be short. You may want to avoid industrial companies in a deep and prolonged recession.

#3 Recession: Breadth and Depth

Whenever You Enter a Recession…. Ask the question "Is this recession short and shallow or is it deep and long?" The answer will definitely affect your investments and how well you trade. A recession could be short, 9 to 15 months, and shallow (it doesn't affect every industry). An example of shallow would be home building. How would you like to be in the home building industry in our country right now? Many sectors have turned down, but the home building industry is incredible, it is strong. It is leading the way.

I just read a report. It said the construction business is a bit down, yes, in some types of office building. But they included housing with the report. Separate housing out from the whole, and you will find it has been up every month. That means that there are people still buying homes. People are refinancing their homes and/or buying new ones. If the interest rates go back up, which I don't see happening in the near future, then the housing industry will slow down once again. But right now, interest rates are low.

Usually high interest rates cause a recession. I don't think that was the case this last time. I really think it was the dot.com bubble. It was a weird situation. My own commentary on this is that the stock market usually is a foreteller of events. Sometimes a recession can sneak up on people.

About two years ago, everyone was saying "These dot.com companies are so high priced, these stocks cannot maintain these levels." Stocks were priced at $400 a share when they should have been at $20 per share. The bad mouthing spread. It was started by the phrase "irrational exuberance." We talked ourselves into this bear market, and the downtrending stock market caused a bit of panic, which exacerbated the recession.

The SEC through this time changed the rules. In November of 2000 they changed the rules in regards to what a company has to say. Companies' simultaneous bad-mouthing and good-mouthing their own stocks has become an institutional enterprise. It literally works like this: under the new SEC guidelines, corporations who know things about their company, any negative thing at all, have to get it out to the investing public as fast as they can. They used to tuck away these negative things in their SEC filings. They came up with a new word "guidance." How often did we hear the word 'guidance' a year and a half ago? We never heard it. But now, every day, 15 times a day!

When you hear, "this company has lowered their guidance," it means their projected earnings. They are going to make .32 cents a share, their guidance. No one wants to be in violation of the SEC guidelines. Many companies are doing an incredible amount of bad-mouthing about their own stocks.

What kind of an effect do you think that has on the marketplace in general? You may hear them say, "We're doing okay," but tucked somewhere in their statement is "Well we might not do okay in the future." What does that mean? As Intel said, "We think we might not spend as much on capital expenditures." Every company around them tanks because one specific company made a cautionary statement. In real life they are doing well. They are going to continue to do well, but they are all bad-mouthing their future. The marketplace has changed.

By the way, I predict now that in the next couple of years the SEC will change their guidelines again. When this marketplace is not going anywhere, the administration will put all kinds of pressure on people to tell the truth about their stocks. They will have to tell the truth such as "we think we are doing okay, we made really good money and we will probably be okay in the future." Just like they used to say! Today they are saying "We beat our estimates, we are making good money, we think things are going to be okay in the future, but we must lower our sales forecasts." The stock gets clobbered.

Even though I believe this recession is shallow and short, it will be exacerbated, or aided by this continual bad talk. It is similar to when you are trying to get out of the lake when your kids don't want you to! My kids just love me to be in the water with them. As I try to get out of the water they are wrapped around my legs dragging along. That is the way this recession is. We are trying to get out of the water, but we have all these little negative comments dragging us back in.

#2 All Recessions End!

We don't know when this one is going to end. The irony is, it could have ended already. We may not know until much later. At some time, things will pick up! This one is shallow and rather short. I would call it murky because no one can see through it. There is no clear light at the end of the tunnel. Everyone knows it is going to get better, but in the mean time there are not a lot of companies out getting new loans.

It's interesting that interest rates are at historical lows, but, in spite of lower interest rates companies are not going out to get new loans to build new factories. Here is why: there is talk about the future. They are saying, "We don't want to expand or hire new employees or open up a new factory because if we truly are in a recession then why borrow now?"

The good news is that people *are* refinancing their homes. If you have a $1500 per month mortgage payment, you could easily knock it down maybe to $1100. That gives you an extra $400 to spend. That bodes well. With taxes lowered, as a fiscal policy, it means more money in the hands of the consumer. Consumers will lead the way out of this recession.

#1 Play the Talk

Watch the forecasters. Watch what the commentators are saying because the bears are everywhere, the bulls are hard to find. Watch what analysts do. For example, yesterday when Intel (INTC) made that incredible announcement that they had beat earnings, their stock backed off two dollars! How can a stock that just beat its earnings back off?

In theory it should go up. It comes back to the old adage, "buy on rumor and sell on fact." Buy on anticipation of news and sell on the news. The anticipation of the news the last couple of weeks drove Intel stock from $31 to around $35. When the news came out and was better than anyone expected, the stock backed off by $2. (It recovered .60 cents today). The *market* went down around 211 points.

When this happens, what do you think all the forecasters are saying? They are starting to voice the opinion that it is time to get involved again. One of the major financial firms came out and upgraded Intel to a buy today. So all their clients start buying INTC. When IBM made its announcement today, one of the major financial firms put a buy recommendation on IBM with a price target (usually meaning one year) of $140. Play the talk! It is the easiest way to get good at the stock market. Find out what the forecasters are saying about any particular stock.

Talk about forecasters! I think all of us realize newspapers and talk shows are very negative, slanted in everything they say. For example, from November all the way through this last Christmas (2001), there were all these people saying "This is going to be a bad Christmas, there is no money out there."

Right in the middle of that bad report, they said "Wal-Mart just announced it had a 5+% increase in sales in the month of December. How can this be? The worst Christmas ever and Wal-Mart increases sales? Fifteen minutes later I was listening to a business radio station talk about the "Worst Christmas ever," yet they said TeleCheck had just announced a 2+% increase in processing in the month of December.

How can the news commentator be so negative, while the real results from many stores are so positive?

Here we are a couple of weeks after December. After all the garbage talk, the semi-official government statement is that sales were down 1% in December. That is so much better than what everyone was led to believe. We had been hearing that sales were down 5% and 10%!

I think in a couple of months when they revise their numbers, they might come back and say that sales were actually *up* 1%. It will be a surprise because things were not as bad as "everyone" said. Now who is "everyone?" Wade Cook didn't say it, especially when I had to stand in long lines in three different malls to buy Christmas gifts. Everywhere I went the stores were packed. I was in Wal-Mart trying to buy a Harry Potter game; I could have had a heart attack and would have been unable to fall over due to the volume of people around me! It was packed.

How are you going to play this kind of market? We have a dichotomy. For example, there are 4.3 trillion dollars in cash in the marketplace and yet we have had a pretty bad downturn. It doesn't make sense to have that much cash available and to have a downturn. These are opposite ends of the spectrum.

Let's look at another example: we have a slight slowing, or a decrease in capital spending, but consumer spending is at an all-time high. Imagine that—consumer spending leading the way out of a recession! Instead of companies investing in equipment, which is not helping much, the consumers are spending; therefore the economy is not that bad.

Here's another dichotomy; we have a 10% spike in the money supply in this country, which usually means a weak dollar—but our dollar has gone up.

There are so many mixed signals! Some states have unemployment going up but the housing starts in that state are going up as well. That doesn't make sense! If unemployment is going up, more people are out of work, housing should be going down, but it is going the opposite direction.

I wouldn't ignore all of the bad and I wouldn't play into all of the good. The answer is to find the compelling reason on *each trade*, not to play the marketplace in general. Play specific stocks and specific options, after you know all there is to know about a stock; and then only play it on a specific compelling reason.

One last thing about the professionals and what they are doing. There has been a huge influx of money into the marketplace as of December. There is every year. In December there are so many financial professionals who wanted to get their money in the way of the movement. They all realize that we, as the small investors, will enter last. They want their money to be in front of us. They may take a stock like Intel (INTC) from $28 to $34 and we (the consumer) will take it from $34 to $36, but they are usually out by that time. Then the stock falls back to $32. Think like a big trader would when using your small amount of money.

Every three or four days there will be many mini-signals that will drive the market up 200 or 300 points. Guess what will happen? A few negative comments and that will drive the market down 200 or 300 points.

If you look at the Wade Cook way of trading, this is the kind of marketplace to be in. The market is going up down, or sideways, and which is my favorite? Sideways! The old rolling stock idea.

<u>Bonus comment</u>: Just because the economy has been in a recession, does not mean that we need to be in a recession! We do not mentally need to be negative. It is so easy for people to start thinking negatively when everyone else around them is negative. So look at the marketplace and figure out how to play it! It is almost like "What Monday and Tuesday giveth, Wednesday and Thursday taketh away, and then Friday giveth to us again"… etc.

Many people look to me for the wrong reasons. "Do you want a hot stock tip?" "Do you want to get rich?" Then you are talking to the wrong guy! Do you want to build up $6,000 or $9,000 a month so you can spend more time with your family? Then I want to help. Let me share a rolling stock formula, or teach you how to write a covered call. People in this marketplace want the next hot stock tip, that is not what I do. That would be giving them fish. I want to *teach* people *how* to fish.

We trade in the stock market and the market teaches us many things we need to know. We are all just fellow students. The stock market will humble us and teach us how to make money, if we learn our lessons properly. It provides the perfect part-time business opportunity with the relative ease of conducting a trade to hopefully make an ample amount of money, so we can live the lifestyle we want.

This is a great marketplace for us. This is the type of market we sit up at night dreaming about. A couple of days up and a couple of days down, over and over. It gives us plenty of buying opportunities and plenty of selling opportunities. That is the key.

Trading Formulas Revisited

**Wade Cook's Street-Tested
Cash Flow Formulas**

**Trading in the New Millennium:
A Critique of These Formulas**

Strategy #1
Semester Investor
(Right-Term Hold)

What: Use fundamentals and technical analysis to find great stocks in companies with likelihood of going up for your future. May be used for Writing Covered Calls. Sold when profitable for extra cash. Many of these may pay dividends.

When: Anytime. My other strategies are more income generation oriented, so you can pay off debts, pay the bills and then invest in these good solid stocks. Don't be afraid to clean house. Build your own "Mutual Fund."

Comments: Ample buying opportunities. P/Es in line on many great companies. Many have cut expenses, shed debt and restructured for greater profits.

Who: Start young. Add to positions as you go. Monitor your account to make sure you have the best choices. Great for gifting and donations to your church.

Strategy #2: Rolling Stock™

What: A system of buying and selling less expensive stocks that trade in a sideways pattern—buy at $2 (support) sell at $3 (resistance) in repeated waves.

When: In a flat market, or sideways moving stock. Even in good markets, many stocks move in rolling patterns.

Who: Beginners. Those who want little risk, and not huge, but consistent profits.

Comments: Too many to mention, these roll from technical moves, not fundamentals. Look for 5 to 7 week patterns.

Strategy #3: Options

What: Use small amounts of money on low-cost, limited risk options to control large blocks of stocks. A movement in stock from $84 to $88 could see the $80 call option move from $6 to $8, i.e., $6,000 to $8,000 in hours, days or weeks. Upside potential is huge, loss limited to premium paid.

When: Use calls on up movements, puts on down movements. Risky, should be practice traded. Huge profit potential—available and workable in all markets. Added risk: option expiration dates.

Who: People who do research, understand connections and the power of news and potential news (rumors). People who want large, quick profits. Note: only use small "risk" capital.

Comments: More traders today. Volatility is not great. Seems option market makers are not expecting big moves up or down. Still good for "compelling reason" trades.

Strategy #4:
Writing Covered Calls

What: Sell options (generate income in one day) against your stock positions—agreeing to sell stock at a

Comments: Could be effective way to fight back with stocks which have lost predetermined price (profit). Nice monthly cash flow machine—10%-15% cash income—per month. More, if stock is on margin.

When: Used on large stocks—with options. Used anytime to pick up cash and then sell stock or keep it depending on the strike price—"Do you really want to sell the stock?"

Who: People who want income. $100,000 in stocks will produce $10,000 to $15,000 of extra income. Many beginners buy stock just to sell calls for income.

value. Option premiums are not high, so it's not as easy to get 20% monthly returns, but 12% to 15% monthly cash returns are not uncommon.

Strategy #5: Stock Splits

What: Many companies split their stocks when they get pricey. If the company is good, company stocks have a tendency to go back up to or above price before split. Sometimes in two to five years. Sometimes in three to nine months. Look at the charts on Page 9 for examples.

When: Five times to get in and out. Build a portfolio of these stocks. Use options within limits for quick-turn profits. Options trading on these enhances potential and reduces risk.

Who: Anyone needing profits. Easy to practice on and master before using real money. Many one-to three–day trades available.

Comments: This has been slow, but is starting to pick up. Currently 64 companies have announced—some big ones. My favorite is strategy #4, rally into the split.

63

Strategy #6: Selling Puts

What: Generate income by agreeing to have a stock sold to you at a price you like—on a company you like. Nice income, plus potential to buy stock wholesale. Seems risky to naive stockbrokers, who, ironically, will sell you risky stocks in a heartbeat.

When: Use in bullish situations. Stay above strike price and consider your margin requirements. Note: a variation of this is the Bull Put Spread to elimi-

Comments: My favorite. Good on dipping stocks, or stocks expecting good news. This is a bullish strategy, so be careful in "Red-Light" months.

nate much of the risk and lower your margin amount.

Who: People who want cash flow. Can be as safe as someone wants, depending on stock choices and option strike prices.

Strategy #7: Bull Call Spreads

What: Similar to Writing Covered Calls, but use purchase of call option (much less money) rather than stock. Limits risk, and by selling upper calls you limit profits. Spreads are created when you buy a call and sell a call on the same stock at different strike prices.

When: Can be done repetitiously. Good in any market— works best with uptrending stock. Huge profits (more risk) in high flying stocks.

Who: Good for cautious people. Could generate 15% to 30% cash, three to four week returns.

Comments: Still available, but now is not a great time. Try Bull Put spreads instead.

Strategy #8: Bull Put Spreads

What: This is one of my favorites. It's a credit spread which means you get paid to put it in place. You sell a put (income) and buy a put (outgo) below the price of the stock in a Bullish situation. Stock stays above strike price, and you keep the cash.

When: New definition of Bullish: the stock goes up, or at least stays up above a certain strike price. Used when stocks hit support, or on bounce (dip). Note: use a Bear Call Spread on opposite—downtrends

Who: People who want monthly income. 20% to 40% two to four week actual cash returns are very common.

Comments: Good for cash flow and safety. Plenty to do. Great if you can't sell uncovered puts (#6). Harder today to unwind.

Strategy #9:
Rolling Options™

What: Same as Rolling Stock, but on more expensive stocks. As a stock hits support and starts up, buy a call, then at its peak sell the call and buy a put; or do bull put spreads on upswings and bear call spreads on downturns.

When: These are available every day. You must grasp option volatility and pricing. You need at least $5 to $10 swings in the stock.

Who: People who have extra time to monitor positions, or get adept at placing sell orders. Good money-maker.

Comments: Option volatility is low, so these options are cheap, but they don't move that much when the stocks move. Consider finding less expensive stocks and avoid the options.

Strategy #10:
Bargain Hunting, Turnarounds
And Bottom Fishing

What: Buying low priced stocks on serious dips; check fundamentals and buy stock or options on stock. Try for doubles and practice, practice, practice. Use extreme caution with penny stocks.

When: When stocks fall out of favor, take on new management, company comes up with new products, ends lawsuits, or is a takeover candidate.

Who: People should use limited money here—profits are spectacular, but few and far between. Expertise can be developed.

Comments: Values everywhere. Low P/Es. IPOs gone amuck. Avoid companies with low or no profitability.

Strategy #11: Range Riders

What: Similar to Rolling Stocks, but with upward trend. Use trend lines (and/or support lines) for entrance points. Place sell orders to exit trades with 20% to 40% profits. Use stop loss to minimize losses (risk).

When: Many stocks follow this pattern. Can be played with stock or options. Spreads are also effective here.

Comments: Many stocks performing this way. Too many to mention.

Reverse range riders can be used when stock moves in opposite (down) patterns.

Who: People with time to monitor positions. Nice two to three day trades available. Also, trader should subscribe to charting service for support lines, trend lines and moving averages.

Strategy #12:
Initial Public Offerings (IPOs)

What: Invest in stocks in a PRE, on OPEN, or POST IPO formula. Each has concerns and definite exit points. Tough to do on open—consider 25 day IPO rule (quiet period) and jump in there. These stocks are highly volatile. There are probably better times.

When: Obviously, when a company is ready to go or is going public. Watch local newspaper. Many times to get in. Don't let ads (fads) on TV affect you. Difficult to make money with IPOs.

Who: People who like a challenge and added risk—must do extra homework and be above the hype.

Comments: Not that many good ones. Wait awhile. These will return.

Strategy #13: Spin-Offs

What: Good opportunity to get in on a company with a market niche, good management and a lot to prove. Great examples abound. Best play is on the company being spun-off (baby), not the parent (unless parent is generating a lot of cash).

When: This is a rarely-used strategy because there just aren't that many available, but great when available. Buy stocks, options, or do spreads.

Who: People who like a lot of safety—even then, one must be careful. There are many ways to play these. Often options aren't available for several months.

Comments: No. Not now. There are just not that many to play, so it's tough to build expertise.

To work cash flow strategies in the market, we need movement, or volatility. The market moves up, down or sideways. We all want it to go up, but certain strategies work better in different circumstances. See my new book, *Red Light, Green Light* (WSMM Volume 6) due out in the Spring of 2002. Fit the strategy to the market at hand.

I started this book with the title, TWO BAD YEARS AND UP WE GO. Not so fast, though. For years, I've concentrated my efforts on helping people generate monthly cash flow. With the last Bull Market, and the ease of making money, some people made money even with bad companies. Now it's time to get back to enhancing the quality of your life by focusing on strategies that work to produce income on a *monthly* basis. So, whether it's a Bear Market or a Bull Market, let's work to get our assets producing the income we need to live on, so we can quit the 9 to 5 grind. It's the right way: assets which produce income.

These skills can be developed through learning, practice, understanding and experience

This has been my mission: to help people build skills to enhance the quality of their lives. So…get ready, get learning, get practicing, and trade with the correct tools.

67

Compelling Reasons

Momentum. Position Trading. OMFs (Other Motivating Factors). Stock Splits. Earnings Reports. Share buy backs. Red Light, Green Light periods.

As I instruct people to get their money in the way of movements, I've frequently camped awhile on the notion that a stock moves for a reason. I've asked my students in seminars to write down in big bold letters — *What compelling reason does this stock have to go up (or down)?*

If you are playing a stock for a two to three day trade, and you want it to go from $62 to $66 and then plan to get out of the option at that point, you should be doing so for a reason. If it's just hopeful thinking, you'll probably be disappointed more times than you like. If it's because it's a few days before earnings are to be out, and whisper numbers are looking good, or it's bounced off of a support level, and rumors are that the company's management is to announce a stock split, chances are it will move upward.

First, check the surrounding news. Are there other bad earnings forecasts? Is the whole marketplace on an uptrend or a downtrend? Ask yourself, what can go wrong? What can stop or hinder this up movement?

Here's the point: If there is no compelling reason for the stock to move, you should stay clear. Remember, no news is death to these stocks. Bad news has a tremendous downward pull. Even good news, if it's tempered with negative forecasts, can spell defeat for this trade.

Remember, remember, remember — current stock prices, and price movements, are based on the *anticipation of future earnings*.

With the stock market being as topsy-turvy as it currently is, I am constantly looking for specific trades that have momentum — either up or down. These are trades that have what I would call a "compelling reason" or what I call the impending event. One of those trades right now would be to play companies that are rallying into a split. The second trade would be to buy put options on the stock at the split time. Fundamental analysis and technical analysis are designed to measure ways to justify stock prices and to determine which way prices are heading.

In the open air marketplace, today's stock price reflects all kinds of information made available and the anticipation of future earnings. This is why you may see such a high concentration of attention on what the Federal Reserve is going to say. In short, if the Fed is going to raise the interest rate, and in nine to twelve months corporate earnings will go down because of the high cost of borrowing money, and there will not be much in profit and earnings, the stock price will come down now. The stock market reacts today based on what a company will be earning in nine months or twelve months or even in the next one and a half years.

Let's take a brief look at three ways to analyze or look at stocks. Then, we'll take a look at options and see the connection.

Fundamentals

One way to look at the value of stock is to take a "fundamental approach." The "fundamentals" system primarily looks at the earnings of a company. This is often stated as a P/E, or price to earnings ratio. Simply put, the P/E states how much each dollar of earnings will cost you. A P/E of 32 means you will pay $32 to get at $1 of earnings. For a clearer view of P/E, let's look at some selected excerpts from *Wall Street Money Machine, Volume 5*:

One caution: when you get the P/E you don't necessarily know if it's past tense, or "trailing earnings;" or if it's future tense, or "projected earnings," or if it's a blend of both. Projected earnings are someone's guess at what the company will earn over the next year. The projected earnings are usually higher than what happened last year so the P/E will be lower. You see, a lot of people like low P/Es. You are buying the future earnings if you buy the stock today, but it's also more honest to look at what the company has done in the past. A blended P/E would give us the best of both worlds. I like it best when the company — or a news article — bases their P/E on six months back and six months forward. It is a better reflection of where the company really stands.

I believe earnings are a key to stock movements. I've shouted it from the rooftops. Follow earnings, follow earnings. Is the company profitable? Are they (and the earnings) expanding or contracting? Are their sales growing? What are they doing with their money? Are earnings growing because they've acquired another company? Will this acquisition slow them down? Are earnings growing from cost cuttings (sometimes good, or can contraction be bad?). Learn everything you can about a company's earnings.

Technical Viewpoints

Technical analysis uses numbers to help us determine movements. These technical measurements help show when a stock will turn up, or go higher, and when a stock will decline, die or turn around. This study uses moving averages to show when a stock gets in a buy or sell range. Other technical viewpoints use call and put volume increases. Some technical analysts like gaps, when a stock price gaps up or down to show the direction it will go thereafter. Others use money flows to see if money is entering the stock or leaving. There are many more, including some way-out planetary models. A fun technical is when the NFC or AFC wins the Super Bowl. The market goes up or down, they say.

Many people, like me, are busy. I know of these measuring sticks and I have three good stockbrokers who love the technical aspects of all this. I listen and use their advice sometimes. I'll say, "I want to buy 200 shares of Microsoft." They'll say, "Wait one or two days, it should drop a dollar or two." I question and get an ear full. I wait. They are often right. But Microsoft at $67 instead of $64 is not a big difference if it does a split and you sell 400 shares at $50 a few months later. That's a $6,600 profit. At $64 I would have made an extra $600. Like I said, not a big deal, sometimes.

Now, when it comes to option trading — especially quick turn trades — every dollar is important. Technical analysis tells us when to get in and when to get out. Let's spell it "technEEcal" analysis. The "EE" are for Entrance and Exit points.

Other Motivating Factors

Now the fun begins. Once we start to use fundamental aspects and technical entrance and exit points, then we realize that newsy items or other motivating factors also drive the stock or option. Earnings reports drive stocks up and down. So does the anticipation of good or bad news. Watch for patterns. Look for good buying opportunities.

Spin-offs and IPOs are news events. (See Chapter 6, More Red Light, Green Light Cash Flow Strategies, for more information about how to trade on these.) So are mergers, take-overs, and stock splits. Lawsuits — either instituted or ended — play into the picture, as does a management change.

One other major factor in the Red Light, Green Light movements, are the positive or negative movements of the whole marketplace. If we see a flat market like 1994, or a boom market like 1996-1998, or even a disastrous market like the year 2000, it's almost as if all contrary news has only a minimal impact. The company has great news, but the marketplace is going down. Your stock's good news (a squirt gun) is drowned by the torrent of negative news (a fire hydrant) on the news wires every day.

Some thoughts:

1. If the market is on a tear and momentum players are everywhere, and it gets to the point that otherwise "non-stock market" people are pouring their money into the market, it seems that negative warnings from companies are sloughed off. Seriously, we saw companies in 1998 and 1999 not making money — saying that they were not now and that they would not in the future make any money. People were paying 2000 times earnings for their stock. They were second mortgaging their houses to get the money to do so. It was ridiculous. The news and the warnings existed, people just forgot logic and propriety and jumped in.

2. On the other side are companies with decent earnings, nice growth, but in a year like 2000, all the good news couldn't outweigh the continuous stream of negativity. Actually, I thought there would have to be a correction all along. One of my rules is this: "Everything Returns to the Norm."

   Yes, there was a flight to quality during these times but even the quality stocks got caught in the downdraft. Remember the old market maxim: "Don't try to catch a falling piano." It was sure true in 2000 and throughout 2001.

It's time for a time out. At the end of the Vietnam war, I found myself in the Air Force as a Chinese linguist. The classroom study areas were being taken over by new Vietnamese language trainees. Seriously, the German, Chinese, Russian, Korean, etc., students were being pushed out for more Vietnamese students. These Vietnamese language study programs took over whole buildings. I kept thinking, "But the war is over. It's been over for two years, and they're still coming." A peacetime military machine is difficult to maintain at peak efficiency levels. You see, they scheduled needs, in this case thousands of linguists, up to two years or more in advance. It was hard to stop the flow. We were in California shouting to the East Coast, "Hey you guys, the war is over!"

Now, you have to be wondering what this has to do with the Red Light, Green Light, news/no-news periods? There is a connection here. In my Red Light, Green Light seminar (now wonderfully reproduced in a Home Study Course), I mention how many company bigwigs have fallen into a reporting rut.

Here's how it has played out. Stocks shot up. They entered never never land. Even the company's boards, management and others knew their stocks were too high for their current earnings. You heard analysts (trying to justify their recommendation) saying things like this: "The stock at $260 is not bad, based on earnings projected in three to five years."

I'm sure they didn't want their stocks to tank, but they did want a reprieve — or at least an end to the wild run-up. Politicians got involved. Other government officials weighed in.

Remember, "Irrational exuberance?" These new players set the tone and again, like lemmings, corporate heavyweights read from the new script.

Virtually every day, but especially in the pre-earnings season and as their SEC documents were filed, press releases, news conferences, interviews flew out the door — with a twist. "Oh, we're earning money (then under their breath — "hundreds of millions more than before...") but we see a slowdown in revenues, sales, growth, etc. Again the driving sentence: Current stock prices are based on the anticipation of future earnings.

Left and right — companies beating their estimates, making untold millions, had stocks dipping $2 to $22 overnight.

Now, it's time for a new rut. Yes, honesty is the best policy, but they don't need to overplay the negative. Those remarks have been tucked away in their filings, that is where they should stay. They need to honestly state their direction, profit potential, future earnings — in less harsh terms. It's time for a change. It's been two years and more Vietnamese language students are coming. Enough already.

3.   The streets of San Francisco must be one of the best places for car chase scenes. The views are beautiful as the cars go up, and then shoot up, literally flying through the air at the top of hills. Then the downward chase, hitting everything in sight, spinning around corners, and then, yep, back up with another airborne police car chasing them.

     This, I feel, is a good depiction of the stock market of late — at least of many stocks in the hi-chase (tech) arena.

They shoot up the hill like a man shot out of a cannon, but then gravity takes over. Airborne, there is no where to go but down. Their stock prices cannot be sustained. They're not only airborne, but the air is mighty thin. Their flight is brief. Airsickness sets in.

The lead car and all the others in the chase pack come crashing back to earth. That would be okay, but the earth right there is not flat. It's downhill. These cars need good brakes, or even parachutes — but most crash into other barriers. Many things go down with them. Carnage.

The car is the stock price. The hill up or down is the marketplace. The marketplace can hinder or help the movement, but after all the hype and hoopla, these two, the car and the hill, blend to become one with the universe.

I try to point out these things in my constant talks at my seminars. Watch out! It's all hype! Check earnings. Lately, I've felt like Chicken Little. The sky is not really falling, I know, but stock prices are. Learn from it. Get better at using effective measuring sticks. Don't fight gravity or any other natural financial laws. If you do, you'll be moo goo gai pan in a San Francisco Restaurant.

This current "rut" will change as two things happen:

1. Corporate leaders quit bad mouthing their future.
2. Everyone quits their 25% to 50%, year over year, earnings growth rate expectations. The party was good while it lasted, but as of the beginning of 2002, we need to get back to the norm. 4% to 10% revenue growth and slightly higher earnings growth are historically feasible. Hold management to these reasonable growth expectation levels and stock prices will be easier to measure and more stable.

Compelling Reasons

Listed below are news events which would constitute a compelling reason for a stock to move up or down.

1. A stock being added to the S&P 500, or DJIA 30; other major indices, or groupings of stocks held in trusts (Spiders, like QQQ, SPY, MDY, DIA, FFF, etc.). Why? Because many funds buy all the stocks in an index. They are widely followed and widely owned.
2. A stock being taken off one of the lists mentioned in #1. Stocks like this trend down, unless there is other good news. Why? Some funds and other trusts must sell these stocks. Note: not all stocks which discontinue trading in an index are officially dropped. Some merge with other companies, moving, for example, the S&P 500 to 499 companies. They need a new entry.
3. Mergers. In many stock swap deals, there is a period of arbitrage. There is a ratio merger; say two shares of X for one share of Y. At the time of the actual merger, the price/ratios will be in line, but at the announcement and until the actual merger, there could be a discrepancy and a chance to buy the stock or option on the stock which you think will move the most. Each situation is so different that you need to get the details and put a pencil to it. We put as much as we can on W.I.N. at www.wadecook.com. Mergers with a lot of expensive new debt will have a tough time. Excessive debt is a killer of business.
4. Share buy backs are good if the company actually goes through with the purchase. Many programs end with unpurchased stocks. Some stall as the current price of the stock has risen above their purchase price authorization. A share buy back can add strength to other good news — especially a profitable, well-run company.
5. Spin-offs. I like spin-offs. This is where a company spins off a subsidiary company, or a division. If the parent company is raising cash (through an IPO spin off) it could bode well. This news is usually brief. Soon, the baby company has to make it on its own.

74

6. Lawsuits. Starting lawsuits is a bummer. Ending lawsuits is seen as good. The news is brief. It plays out fast. Remember the media have to get out new editions tomorrow.
7. Seasonal events and weather: hotels, cruise lines, airlines in summer; fuel, clothing, Christmas shopping in winter.
8. Catastrophes, like a Presidential assassination, an earthquake, a nuclear accident, or a Terrorist attack can be played up or down; insurance companies, energy companies, etc.
9. Government news: mergers, buyouts, enterprise zones, government tax increases or reductions, lawsuits, etc., all add to the mix.
10. Government Agency News: Crop reports, housing starts, CPI (Consumer Price Index), PPI (Producer Price Index), and a host of other reports. Note: you may see moves just as big in anticipation of these reports as you do after the actual report is given. Remember: Buy on rumor, sell on fact.
11. January Effect. There is a flight of money in January to the stocks with the most potential. January is usually an up month. The move into equity starts in mid-December. I call it the year-end rally. Why? Many big funds want to own great stocks for window dressing and get their money in the way of January in-flows of money.

    You see in January, there are millions of dollars once again pouring into 401K, IRAs, pensions, new budgets, etc. The pension money deposits peter out in July and August as many people hit their maximum contribution level. For four to five months these funds go on a diet. January is here and the new year brings new money.

    Did you catch my statement: They want to get their money into these investments in advance of our, or should I say, "the little guy's" money. They get in. We get in and push the stocks up, and buy at higher prices. They get out. We sit there with our lower-priced stocks, wondering what happened. Where have all the flowers gone?

Compelling Reasons — NOT

Let me share with you what are not compelling reasons.
1. Stockbroker recommendations, even though thought-out, are not a reason to drive up a stock. Now, however, if the stock broker knows what you're looking for, has current information on news, support lines, gaps, or a host of other factors which could end up helping you spot movements, then GREAT!
2. Friend's "hot tips." Enough said.

3. Wishful thinking is not a compelling reason. Base your decision on events which can make a serious move. Remember, if you're playing options, the stock has to move and move it must in a timely manner.
4. Weather, catastrophes, earthquakes, etc., are usually events which happen and then the markets rebound before you know it.
5. TV news interviews play out fast. Almost too fast to play. You'd have to be a magician to consistently make money.

Compelling Reasons Recap

Now, let's put this all together with some more timeless wisdom from Wall Street Money Machine, Volume 5:

Fundamentals / Technicals / OMFs

Fundamental Analysis	helps us know	WHAT to buy or sell
Technical Analysis	helps us know	WHEN to buy or sell
OMFs	help us know	WHY (to buy or sell) NOW

That's it. Use all three. Don't ignore any of this. With the use of all three methods, you'll make better and quicker decisions. Your "meter drop™" cash profit potential should take off.

Let me reiterate the statement that I make constantly in my Red Light, Green Light Home Study Course. It is simply this:

1. The stocks move in anticipation of a news event.
2. Stocks move at the news event based on the quality of the news.
3. Stocks also move in tandem with the marketplace in general.

Here is a W.I.N.™ update I did on Krispy Kreme. Please read every line. You'll see converging news events (seven total) dog-piling on this stock in a two to three week period. Then in a few months, you can go back, check the W.I.N. archives and see how well I did.

7

The Upcoming Bounce
(It Happens Every Year)

It's a New Year. We are heading into our first full week of the Stock Market. Coming out of January 1st last Tuesday and then on through January 2nd, 3rd and 4th, things went well in the Stock Market, and who knows what's going to happen in the future. As I've traveled the country in the last couple of weeks, a lot of people have asked me, "Where are we heading?" "Will there be a bounce?"

There are ten reasons why I see a bounce. I hope the bounce can be sustained. These ten reasons are given in a countdown method.

10. A lot of hope enters the picture. It's the New Year. There is a lot going on psychologically to lift people's spirits.

9. At the end of December and on through January, people start to move their money in the way of the American Dream. Big investors especially realize that new money flows into the market from the "little guys" and they try to get their money in before this happens.

8. The tax-loss selling in December is out of the way. At the end of the year there is a lot of tax-loss selling, because, even in really, really good years, there are still some company stocks which have gone down. If you have a stock that has gone from $90 down to $30, (even though you may want to keep it because you think it's going to go back up) your tax accountant might say, "Unload it by the end of the year." Why? Because, then you can book a $60 loss against other profits. There is a lot of this type of selling, which happens at the end of the year.

These last two years have been so bad, though, that there has been *an excess* of tax-loss selling going on, even up to the last day of the year. It used to take five days for a transaction to clear your accounts. Now it takes three days, but with computers being so fast, your transactions are now reflected almost instanta-neously. You will see selling still going on right up to the Market close on New Year's Eve.

7. We are past the year-end Window Dressing. I will explain this briefly, and then explain what it means as we move into the new year.

A lot of mutual funds will start loading up on the bigger-name companies towards the end of the year, even though these bigger-name companies have already had their run. They're not expected to go up *that much* in the New Year. Fund managers know there are probably better prospects in other, smaller companies going up in the next year, but how do they want their books to look at the end of the year? Mutual funds are in the business of managing people's money. They want you to put your money with them. They want to show Disney, 3M and AT&T on their books, because these are familiar and easy-to-understand. They feel you will be more comfortable putting your money with them if you are famil-iar with the companies they own. When they produce their really nice big port-folio books, which show all of their holdings for the year, they do not want to list Acme Waste Management or any other small, no-name company.

The fund may have made all of their money in Acme, and it may have gone from $8 to $28, but it's a no-name company and they're going to get rid of it at the end of the year, even though they may turn right around and buy it (or other similar companies) again at the beginning of the next year. This creates an effect on a lot of these lower or no-name companies in December. Their stocks go *down* a bit, and the big companies' stocks go *up* towards the end of December.

Now, there's an interesting sidelight to this. Let's say this mutual fund has a stock which was at $8 and has gone to $28. Throughout the year, the stock has done very, very well. This mutual fund owns a million shares of the stock. When they unload the stock in December, for the sole purpose of *not* having it in their portfolio, this sale can have a dramatic impact on the stock's price, because a million shares being sold can be a huge determinant to an up stock movement. Now, this mutual fund company turns right around in December and buys a big-name $80 stock with the same money. How many shares can they buy now? Not nearly a million shares. Maybe a third of that. So you see, there's an impact; an upward movement in December in big stocks; a downward movement in small stocks.

Then the opposite happens in January. Mutual fund companies will sell, say, a million shares of an $80 stock, or $80 million and then have that money avail-able for purchase of stocks with a greater near-term potential. To summarize, they'll *sell* a lot of the big-name companies in January, and *buy* a lot of the no-name companies.

6. People are willing to take more risk. Sometimes the only aspect of the new year mentality that people know about, is the movement *out* of these high-quality stocks *into* stocks that carry a bigger risk, but have a greater potential. There are a lot of funds and people willing to take a risk in the first part of a year, who are not willing to take risks at other times of the year, especially at the end of the year. That is one of the most important points. The *willingness* to put their money into riskier, no-name stocks—high-potential stocks without much of a following—helps with the upward momentum of this bounce.

5. Picking up on the movement of big money in front of new money entering the market: as of late, this movement even starts in December. Caution: we're little guys. We wait until the end of the year to see how much cash we have available. We little guys hold out whatever we're going to need for Christmas. But the mutual funds and the great big pension funds are sitting there with all this money. They know that January has historically been a really good month, so, about the middle of December—even if they have a lot of cash in their cash accounts—they start moving their money back into the Stock Market.

December has become a big month for money moving into the market and it continues into January. Why? The big money has already moved, remember? One of the things I have taught in a lot of my seminars is that we're always the last to know. We're buying into these stocks, the stocks have gone from $56 up to $70 and boy it looks like the momentum is just going to keep going. But what pushed that stock from $56 to $70? Was it all of the money that moved in the stock from the middle to the end of December? We then, as the last to come to the dinner table, start jumping in. The big money, the money that wants to play the January bounce, is already in there. This new money might now push the stock from $70 to $74 or $75, but the big movement has already happened.

For example, if you saw me on WIN, I was trying to scrape together every bit of money I could. If we had even $2,000 in one account, we were trying to get that money fully invested in December. Historically, almost every year there *is* a Santa Claus rally the two or three days before and after Christmas.

Lucky for us, everybody knows that the month of January has historically been a great month, so, starting in the first week or so of January, a lot of the other big money drove up the market. We joined the first crowd.

Isn't that what you would do? If you think of the stock market like a surfboard, wouldn't you want your surfboard in position to be *in the way* of the next big wave that comes; not *after* the wave has already gone, and not *as* the wave is upon you, but in *advance* of the wave?

If you know historically that a new year has been a good time, and you're sitting there with $800,000,000 in a fund, what would you do with that money? You would get it in front of those stocks that have the highest likelihood of edging their way back up. You worry about February when February comes. Worry about the rest of the year when it comes. Right now, you want to get your money in the way of movement.

4.   A lot of companies, who had wanted to do their IPOs (Initial Public Offerings) earlier in the year, finally do them in November and December. Throughout any previous year, there always seem to be a lot of IPOs that hit the marketplace in the summertime and in the Fall. The irony is that a lot of these companies *wanted* to go public in January, February or March; but if you have ever studied the IPO process, whatever the absolute, last, lock-down, drop-dead date is, it's going to be six more months before anything happens. Any normal human being would think: We're going to get this IPO out on March 31st, then the accountants and the attorney's take over and what happens to almost every deal? If it even stays alive at all, it is going to happen six to eight months down the road.

Don't get me wrong, even though everyone was talking about how bad the last year (2001) was for the IPO market place, the average number of IPOs in any given year is 900, there were 891 last year. Even though IPO's have been down, we were still real close to the annual average for IPOs. Not however, as high as 2000 IPOs in 1999.

Let me tell you a couple of other things. Last year, in the year 2001, there were a couple of firms that raised money. They're what are called Venture Capitalists or Investment Bankers. Sometimes, with the acronym "VC" for Venture Capitalists, they call them "Vulture Capitalists", because they try to scoop in and take advantage of every deal they can. Just a few big VC firms raised over $100,000,000,000 (one hundred billion dollars) to put into new IPOs for new start-ups, and only $25,000,000,000 (25 billion dollars) of that money had been spent—or committed—at the year-end. Which means, they have $75,000,000,000 waiting to go into IPOs. *Then*, I read in the same report that there was more money just *sitting* and waiting, which had been raised in the previous year, the year 2000. This money is also waiting to go into deals. Seemingly, the IPO marketplace had dried up in the year 2000 and there were not many IPOs. All of these people had cash to put into the IPOs and they did not do so. This year will be different. This money, at least much of it, will be put to work.

Here is another aspect of IPOs that should be taken into consideration. We need to discuss the lock-up period and the twenty-five day rule. We'll go over them briefly here.

When a company goes public, there are 25 days when nothing can be said. From the day a company does its "new issue", the day it does its IPO offering to the public, nothing can be said for 25 *business* days, or 25 *trading* days. These companies enter what is called a "Quiet Period". The underwriters, the companies that took the company public, all of their analysts, their stock brokers, basically everyone, has to *hush up*. The IPO is definitely out there and on the first day there was a lot of fanfare, a lot of hype and hoopla, but then they enter...the "Quiet Period".

If your stockbroker were to call you about this company, they would be in violation of their company rules and probably some SEC regulations. They cannot hype the stock for 25 days. No one can PR the stock, they cannot put their President and CEO on CNBC—*nothing,* for at least 25 days.

Now, if it's a big firm and they have good underwriting and a good PR department, they will blast out with all kinds of good information about the company at the end of this 25 days. Can you see them, after 25 days, coming out with a news report that says, "Oh, we messed up, we don't like this company any-more"—after they just raised $80,000,000 for this company? If they're going to do any PR at all, is it going to be good PR or bad PR? It's going to be good, of course, and they're going to support the stock for quite awhile.

Now, the lock-up period is this: When a company goes public, there are a lot of founders of the company—these are the people who started it, who can register their stock through the offering. Let's say you own stock in a company and it's registered in the IPO. You own a million shares. Would it be unfair to the investing public if, on the day the company goes public, you sell your stock right away? Could your million shares have a huge effect on the marketplace? Yes. So, number one, they (the underwriters) might make you hold that stock for six months or more.

My point is, if a company went public in the middle of the year, those lock-up periods end in January or February. You might think that a lock-up period is negative. It's not. As I study lock-up periods, at the end of the six or nine or twelve months, the stocks usually go up. Do you know why? Because hardly anybody ever sells their stock at the end of the six months. Now think this one through. All of the anticipation, the thinking that the founders might sell, has been holding the stock back. It's gone from $18 to $30, and it's just kind of hanging around $30. Why? Because, there is a lock-up period, which has the stock of the nine original founders of the company on hold, and that period is going to end, let's say on January 12th.

Just because the lock-up period is over on January 12th, does it mean that you and all of your eight buddies are going to run out and sell your stock? No, it hardly ever happens. As soon as the lock-up period is over and the public realizes that all of the founders, the original people, are not going to sell their stock, the stock usually moves from that $30 to $35 to $40 very quickly.

I'll give you an example: Krispy Kreme®. Do you know Krispy Kreme has only been publicly traded for about a year and a half and they've already done two stock splits? Their lock-up period was during the same time. There was so much fear that the stock was going to go down when they hit the end of their lock-up period. The stock had been right around $60, and this after two 2:1 stock splits. But, within three to five days after the lock-up period, people realized that all of the founders and the insiders were not selling their stock, and the stock went from $60 to $75, then up to $80 in a matter of days.

Below are two charts for Krispy Kreme Donuts (Ticker Symbol KKD). They both cover the same time periods—the initial trading day to the present. There were two 2:1 stock splits. See explanation (below) of why the charts look differently.

This first chart is rectified to adjust for the splits. See the stock at $40 on the IPO date. A 2:1 split would

put the starting price at $20. A second 2:1 stock split puts the starting price around $10. Your 100 shares would now be 400 shares.

The IPO was 4-4-00. The lock-up period was not six months, but one year. In fact, the lock-up period ended between the two stock splits. The stock continued to go up.

This chart is rectified. See A & B (the two lines going down), about March 3 and June 3.

Once again, if you would have purchased 100 shares on the IPO, for $40 each, or $4,000, today you would have *400* shares at around $40 each, or $16,000.

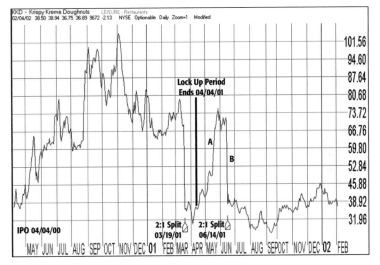

This chart allows you to see the stock split, climb back up, then another split and the upward trending stock throughout 2001. This company is still expanding.

The lock-up period had no downside affect on this company's stock price.

I've studied a lot of these lock-up periods and you would be amazed. Not all of the time, but *most* of the time, the stock has a nice upward move *after* the lock-up period, which defies logic. You would think that if they *can* sell, they *would* sell. I'm sure that some people do, but it doesn't happen all that often.

3.   Bargains are everywhere. This is in regards to the tax-loss selling and to the fact that a lot of money *has been* sitting on the sidelines. Towards the end of the year, October, November, December, a lot of money doesn't move into these smaller companies from the big funds, even on some of these newer IPO companies. In fact, the price of these beat-up stocks even goes down further, with the year-end selling.

Here's another unique thing happening this year — there *have* been quite a few failed IPOs and a lot of companies that *could* have gone public but didn't. Do you know why? Because a lot of the firms that take companies public—the incubators, the venture capitalists—have lost their nerve. They have been beaten up so

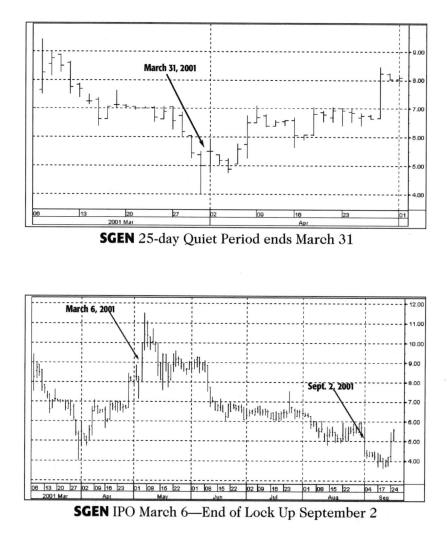

SGEN 25-day Quiet Period ends March 31

SGEN IPO March 6—End of Lock Up September 2

badly, yet they're sitting on top of the assets of 30 different companies. I have been reading a lot of reports, and right now there are a lot of *other* venture capitalist firms that are going through the rubble, like vultures, if you will, picking up these assets. What do you think they're going to do with them? They pick up this technology over here, and pick up another technology over there - they pick up a company's technology that *was* going to go public and changed its mind, but

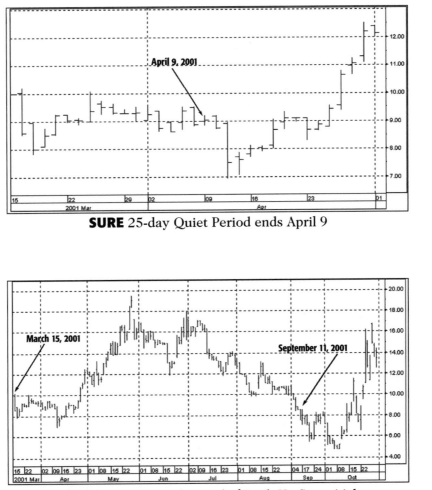

SURE 25-day Quiet Period ends April 9

SURE IPO March 15th—End of Lock Up Sept. 11th

they sure still had good technology. They were going to go public at $200,000,000, but now others can pick up all the rights for their widget, their gadget, whatever it is, for $20,000,000. These bargain shoppers don't pay $200,000,000, they can just pay a fraction of it.

If they're out there buying valuable assets for $20,000,000, what are they going to do? They're going to put them up for sale. What is the best way to do this?

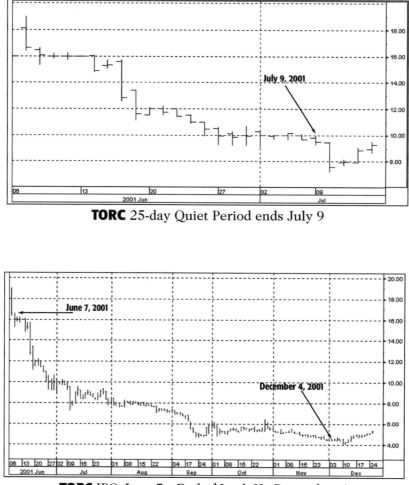

TORC 25-day Quiet Period ends July 9

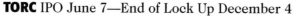

TORC IPO June 7—End of Lock Up December 4

Pay $20,000,000 and sell for $25,000,000 or $30,000,000; or, take a $20,000,000 asset / business plan, get it out there, get it making money, and then take it public at 20 or 40 times projected earnings? Where do you think the money is? The money is back in getting at this $20,000,000 worth of assets, reconfiguring it, and then selling it for $200,000,000 or $300,000,000, *not* $25,000,000. Now *we* can learn about these moves and tag along and try to make some money as some newly reconfigured company goes public. I like to buy stock in those incubators. In fact, to a certain extent, this is how I want to spend a good part of my future. I can't go out and buy $20,000,000 in assets—I don't think too many people can. But, we *can* tag along with $25,000 or $50,000 here and there and latch on to some of these companies who are doing just that?

I'll give you a couple of magazines in which to look these companies up. You'll find some of them in *Forbes*. In a magazine called *Red Herring*, you'll find more information on IPOs than in probably any other magazine. *Red Herring* has a lot of information. Almost every issue has information about companies that are going public and assets that are being reconfigured. They have a website as well, at www.redherring.com. If you want to tap into the IPO market place, that is a good magazine that will get you the information you need.

Now, once you hear about a mutual fund or a grouping of investors who are doing this type of play, you have every right as an investor to call them and say, "Do you need any more investors?" "Yes, yes, we are looking for 300 investors to put up $25,000 each." You may get a prospectus from them and then *you* can determine whether you want to play along and be a part of it.

By the way, if I *had* a million dollars, I would rather put it into twenty $50,000 deals instead of *one* $1,000,000 deal. I would rather diversify my money. There are so many bargains out there—not just bargains in terms of companies, but bargains in terms of assets—that it is easier to diversify.

2. I think the number two reason why stocks go up in a bounce fashion in the first part of the year is because money starts moving back into Pension Plans and IRA's. Most Americans realize that they can put their money into their IRA on January 2nd, the first business day of the year, but how many Americans make their IRA deposits for the year 2002 on April 14th of the year 2003? They wait until the very last minute to put aside their $2,000. If they really thought it through, isn't this kind of silly? If you have the $2,000, would it be best to wait 15 months until the year 2003, or would it be best to put the money aside as soon as you possibly can? If you put it in your 2002 contribution on January 2, 2002, you have another 12 to 15 months of tax-free earnings in the account.

Now let's go the other way. There are a lot of people with 401K's and people with corporate pension plans. They can put aside $7,500, $15,000, sometimes even more into these plans. If you're one of the top earners in the country, you can put aside a lot of money into a defined benefit plan. But at some point in time, the amount of money you can put in for the year tops out. That is usually, even for high income earners, in June or July. The month of August and the month of

September have a big drought in the pension industry. Here's what happens. People will contribute a lot of money and donations out of their paychecks, but all of a sudden, in the middle of July it ends. That's it. That's their maximum allowable contribution for the year." So, what happens till the end of the year? Not much. No new money goes into these 401K's or into pension plans. They've capped out.

Billions of dollars goes into pension and IRA-type accounts through the first part of every year. That money starts pouring back into those accounts at the beginning of a new year. A lot of people want to invest in the Stock Market in their pension-type accounts with no tax ramifications. All of a sudden in January, they start contributing all kinds of money. You can even put money in on January 2nd, based on the *whole* contribution that you *think* you're going to make for the year.

Billions and billions of dollars start pouring into pension accounts. Not all of it goes into the stock market as some of it ends up in Credit Unions or in bank accounts, but, a lot of it finds its way into the stock market. That addition of money, I think, is a significantly great reason why the market starts to turn around and go up.

1. The first reason is more personal to me, and I hope it will be personal to some of you. I like hanging around positive people. The optimists always seem to come back in January. The American Dream is alive and well. The glass is half-full people start to move. The big pile of manure with the kid jumping in means there has to be a pony in there somewhere. Those kinds of people seem to come out of the woodwork.

Now, when I say that America is back, I also mean that this particular year is different as well. Patriotism is alive and well. Let's take a look at our holidays. The next three holidays we celebrate are basically secular: Martin Luther King Jr., Valentine's Day, and President's Day. The holiday after that is a religious one. The two big religious holidays of the year being Christmas and Easter.

The three holidays after Easter, I think are going to be very, very patriotic. Memorial Day, July 4th and Labor Day. Those are our American holidays, all about America.

By the way, I'll submit to you that within a year or two, September 11th is going to become a holiday. It will be a day off. Whether it will be a National Holiday or a State Holiday, I don't know, but I definitely think New York State will make it a holiday. It may or may not be a Stock Market shutdown day or a bank closedown day. They might consolidate a couple of holidays. The only problem with using

September 11th is that it is too close to Labor Day. It's about one week later, and they like to spread out holidays. I think September 11th will be a new Memorial Day for this country.

Those three holidays, and let me say then the fourth, September 11th, are going to bode well for this country. You're going to see the American Dream, not just by American's, but by American companies, come alive. American companies are going to continue to do well overseas, because the world still needs so much of what America has. If you look at the indicators, America is still leading in so many areas. You're going to see a big resurgence in stocks in America.

Here's an interesting example: not only is foreign money coming here, but this weekend (first week in January, 2002), a big European company just announced that it is going public. The company is in London, Harrod's Department Stores. They're not only going to go public, but they are going public on the New York Stock Exchange. Is that strange? They're going to leave certain shares on the London Stock Exchange (good for them), but they're going to go public in America. Does that tell you something? One of the icons of the commercial freedom in Britain is Harrod's, and they're going public on the New York Stock Exchange. What does it tell you?

So, point number one is, *America is here!* The flag is going to fly, the optimism is coming back, not only this January, but I think for the whole year and beyond. There you have the ten reasons. We are heading into a good uptrending market. If you look at the chart history, NASDAQ, the New York Stock Exchange, you would really have to look hard to find a down-January. They are there, you can look back several years and find them from time to time, but almost every time it happened, there were wars and rumors of wars, the depression, etc. January has been good, because it has all of these compelling reasons and market forces working towards a good month. Look at the chapter, *Trading on Company News*, for four other great times to trade.

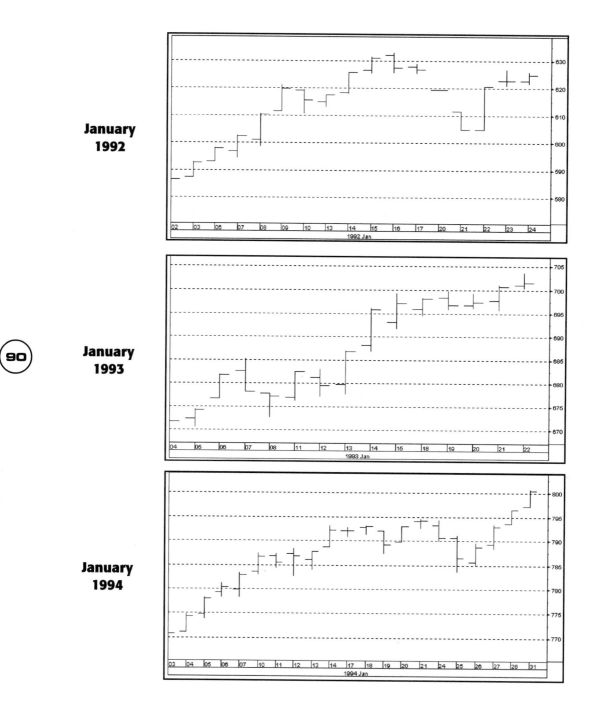

January
1992

January
1993

January
1994

The Upcoming Bounce

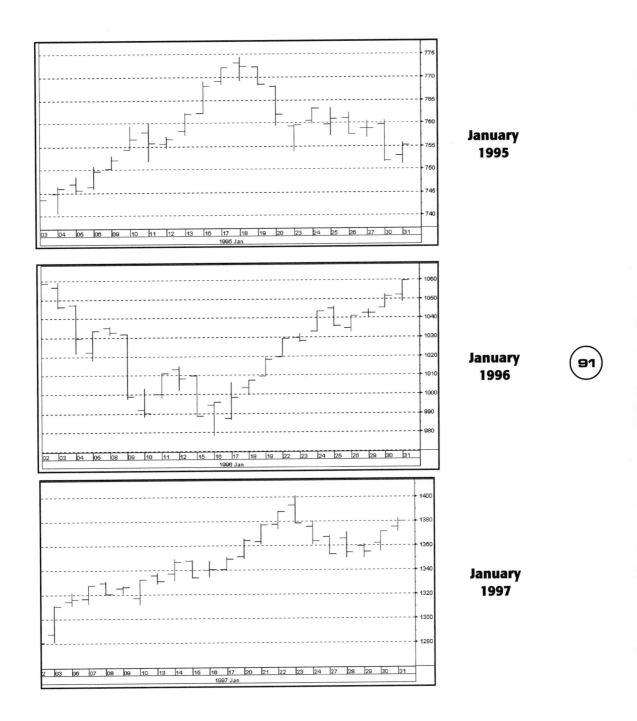

January
1995

January
1996

91

January
1997

January 1998

January 1999

January 2000

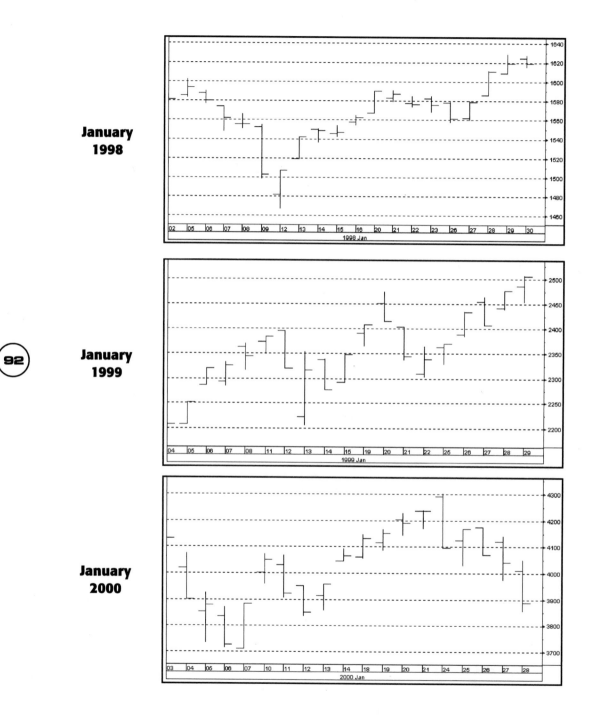

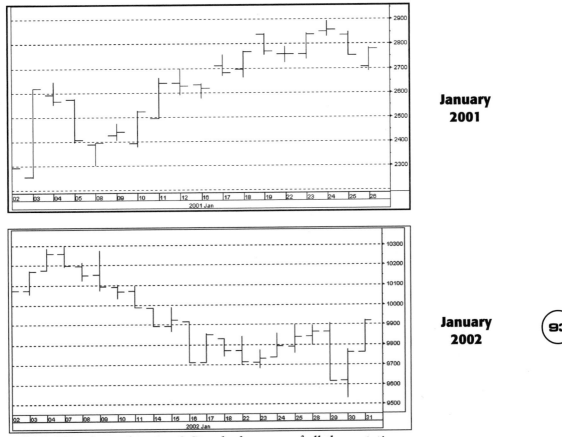

January 2001

January 2002

2002: Why down this time? Simple, because of all the negative talk—Enron, Tyco, Government leaders and Corporate Earnings Forecasts.

Wade Cook—Financial Education Coach

Note: The staff at Lighthouse Publishing's sister company, the Stock Market Institute of Learning, Inc. thought you should know this about Wade Cook.

Wade Cook—Possibly the most controversial man in America.

Okay, then why should you get to know this man? And more importantly, what can this man do for you? It's simple—most people end up broke or have to seriously reduce their standard of living at retirement. Most people don't develop wealth-building skills. Most people live paycheck to paycheck. Most people think they can get extraordinary results from ordinary actions. Peter Drucker said, "We should base our decision on conflicting opinions." Wade Cook will give you conflicting opinions.

May we introduce Mr. Cook to you. He was a cab driver, now turned multi-millionaire. He is a cash flow specialist. He discovered a whole new way of thinking: the key to potential wealth accumulation and income growth is in repetition and duplication. He discovered a way to compound profits in his taxi by going for the "meter drop™"—short, numerous runs instead of waiting all day for the big run.

He made so much driving a cab, he started buying fixer-upper houses. Everyone else at the time was into buy and hold (rentals). Wade learned that the meter drop style also worked in houses. He would buy a house, do minor fix-ups (clean-up) and then sell. Oh, he sold these houses quickly, because he took the buyer's down payment and provided owner financing—carrying back the paper with all those monthly checks coming in. He retired at age 29. His books, *Real Estate Money Machine, Real Estate for Real People, 101 Ways to Buy Real Estate Without Cash* (Bob Bruss, the syndicated columnist, gave this book a "10 out of 10" and called it "excellent") and *How to Pick Up Foreclosures*, are hailed by beginner and advanced real estate enthusiasts alike as easy-to-read, under-standable—but more importantly, achievable.

Mr. Cook's real passion, however, is not limited to real estate. Real estate was merely a means to an end—the end product for him was an insatiable passion to help people better the quality of their lives. To him, this means parents spending more time with their kids; family dynasties being built; more donations to churches and charities. Wade wanted to teach. He simply loves helping people. He sells no investments. He gets nothing out of what his students do. He gets people excited with knowledge.

Next, he turned to the stock market because, unlike real estate or most traditional businesses stock market trading (NOT day trading or the harmful S.O.E.S. trading) cre-ates a more accessible and safer environment for the average person to build potential cash flow. Trading in stocks and with a limited exposure to riskier options, beginners—busy executives, stay-at-home-moms, career professionals (in short, the butchers, bak-ers and candlestick makers) could, with proper skills training, treat the market as their own cash flow business. His book, Wall Street Money Machine, is a huge business best-seller. It was literally on every type of best-sellers list in existence. He has appeared on over 1600 radio and TV talk shows. He has keynoted some of the greatest conventions in America. Mr. Cook also wrote *Business Buy the Bible, Brilliant Deductions and Success: American Style.*

Now, Mr. Cook is the President and CEO of a publicly traded company. (Ticker: WADE) This experience has helped him "connect the dots." Never again will you view the stock market the same way. You'll learn from Wade how to spot mistakes; how to position trade; strategies about getting your money out of harm's way; and how to succeed in life where others fail. Success is about following rules—most people don't even know the rules.

I found this (information) extremely beneficial. I am a financial planner who works primarily in mutual funds and life insurance. Any financial professional who criticizes Wade's strategies is simply speaking out of ignorance.

—Christopher M., OH

You'll realize a hallmark of Wade's style. He has nothing for sale. If you want more in the way of books, videos or home study courses, you'll have to buy them from us. Re-member, Wade gets people excited with knowledge. Then, and only then, can you decide. You are minutes from an in-depth discussion of these methods, techniques and strate-gies. Your retirement is too close, your family's finances are too important to leave it completely up to chance. Here you'll learn, not from an Ivy League General, but from a foxhole Sergeant. This next quotation by Wade summarizes it all: "Our purpose in life should be to build a life of purpose."

Wade Cook is truly an American Rags to Riches story. His mission is to help you write your own success story. We hope you enjoy this special report and we stand by ready to help you achieve your financial dreams.

Wade Cook—Financial Education Coach

When Martina Navratilova was at her best game, I think she was one of the greatest woman tennis players of all time. Before every match she worked with her coach. Joan Sutherland and Beverly Sills were two of the greatest opera singers of all time. They both had voice teachers. Why? They're the best. Nobody could beat Martina consistently. Why did she need a coach?

Think of Phil Jackson, coaching in Chicago and then L.A. Yes, he had great players, but look at the results—results brought about by great coaching. In the financial arena, that's what I want to be—one of the country's most effective educators. I want to help people accomplish more than they have ever thought possible.

Let me give one example. Here are two testimonials from students. Note that I get nothing out of what they did. I don't even know which particular stock they were rolling or using. Remember, I coach the basics. The stocks change, but the strategy is the same.

I just wanted to let you know, that I was able to play one (rolling) stock over a three week period, seven times, and was able to realize a $7,000 profit from a $500 investment.

—Thom A., TX

When Thom came to our Wall Street Workshop we didn't promise him this kind of profit, but he did it anyway.

I've made $100,000+ in five months starting with $5,000.

—Ricky I., VA

Who is on your team to help you make money like this? I am not promising you that you'll make this kind of money, but you know what, I didn't promise Thom or Ricky that they would make this kind of money either. All I want to do is give my students a fighting chance—to learn how to play the game better.

$500 to $7,000. Wow. Can your financial professionals show you how to do this? I don't think so. Ask them. Oh, they'll criticize me, but stick with this thought process. They don't have the tools. Many of them do not know that these types of trades even exist. Let them place the trades, but you learn the process. You need to grasp these simple formulas.

97

I want to be your coach. I'm in the game. I'm doing the deals, but more importantly, I study the coaching process extensively. I'd rather be better at helping students than doing the deals myself.

Let's reason together. Can a coach see things you don't see—even about yourself? Can a coach, based on experience and real-world events, bring to the table aspects of the game you might overlook? Can a coach know strategies that may help a particular player shortcut the long process of learning and achievement?

I think you know the answers to the above questions. Effectively coaching a player or a team is key to success. Show me one great player or winning team who has made it big...who has done so without help? Now, let me ask the question—why me? Why Wade Cook? Simply put, I am a student of the teaching process. That sounds weird, doesn't it? I want to study and learn, then implement ways to help you quickly and effectively get through the learning process. You want results. I help people get results.

One way to coach is to lead by example. One is by writing. Another effective way to educate is to develop home study courses—manuals, CD Seminars, and videos. Yet another way to coach is to get on the field with our students, like at the live Wall Street Workshop and BEST events. Another aspect is to hire, train and use great assistant coaches—our wonderful TEAM WALL STREET. But the most important characteristic is an overwhelming desire to be a great coach. My results are measured in the improved quality of the life of my students.

Finally, effective coaching means to go where our students are. Play to their strengths, correct weaknesses, develop skills and push them to be better. Why does anyone think the financial arena is different than sports? With our education company you get a company dedicated to being the best coaches in the country. You benefit.

Semester Investor

"Long-Term Buy and Hold" is Flawed

My momma told me "If you can't say anything nice, don't say anything at all." I will live up to what my mother expected and tone down my comments here about a very significant and widely used "theory" in the stock market. I'll also include a bonus. At the end of this chapter, I'll give a method of solving or overcoming the problems we'll explore here.

You see, for years I've tried to treat the proponents of bad advice with kid gloves. However, the time has come to reevaluate this position and shed light on one of the most destructive ways of investing ever foisted on the American public. I'm taking off the gloves.

Investing should be done for one reason and one reason only—to make money. Now, making money can take several forms. One could be an increase in asset value. To you, the value exists on paper. Another form could be real cash, even if the cash is posted in your account. This cash is easy to get at and easy to use. Cash is good. Cash will always have more opportunities. We'll explore this cash aspect later. Another form of wealth or "money" is tax savings. Tax savings are real. Companies with tax credits, deductions, write-offs, have more cash to spend on building for the future. You too. If you're in a 31% tax bracket, a $10,000 tax deduction means $3,100 that doesn't have to be sent away. It's cash now.

These are the three benefits of ownership: Income, Growth, Tax Savings. Each of us needs these three benefits at different times and in varying degrees. In all of my books and seminars I have placed income or cash flow first. Even now, I'd like to break out and show you some simple cash flow strategies, but I must forego and get back to beating up on an age-old, yet very moldy investment concept.

"Buy and Hold" with all of its cousins is an idea whose time is past. It needs to be scrutinized, picked apart, analyzed and then used sparingly; and even then, only under certain conditions with strict guidelines. Put simply, "Buy and Hold" alone as it is being promoted by so-called "financial professionals," just doesn't work in today's economic marketplace.

In fact, "Buy and Hold" has gotten me into so much trouble. For example: recently, I did thirteen awesome position trades on a few companies doing stock splits. I was detailed, focused and knew my exit point and "compelling reason" on each trade—in short, what makes each trade work and how I would define and conquer my profits. It was a great two weeks. I made $23,000. Wow! But in the same account, one of my "Buy and Hold" investments went from $50,000 to $20,000. I bought 1000 shares at $50 and then paid little attention. In the same two weeks or so this stock tanked. It went down to $20. I sold it with a $30,000 loss.

It got worse. If I would have continued to hold that stock, I would have seen that $50,000, now $20,000, shrink to $6, or $6,000. Then it went to $3. Then $1.60. A few days ago it was at 20¢. That's $200 for the 1000 shares. This was _the_ best stock. It was supposed to sit nicely in my account. My future was to benefit. Humbug.

As I've traveled the country lately, stories similar to this have played out in thousands of people's accounts. Ironically, most of these people need more income—doesn't everyone? Funny how we keep expecting a plow horse to run a race. "Buy and Hold" doesn't produce current income. "Buy and Hold" doesn't pay the bills. "Buy and Hold" doesn't help your tax situation—except in deferral. "Buy and Hold" barely works to accomplish that which it was designed to accomplish: to produce wealth over a long period of time. There has got to be a better way. The problem is most people's needs occur long before "Buy and Hold" bears fruit.

SEVEN REASONS "BUY AND HOLD" DOESN'T WORK

There are seven major reasons and numerous minor reasons why "Buy and Hold" is a flawed strategy. As you read these I ask that you ponder your own situation. Yes, at the end of this chapter I give a great new way to succeed at all of these methods, but you need to find yourself. You need to figure out what you're going to do with this new information. You need to find a better way for you. My general comments have to filter down to your specific situation. The seeds of your future success will be found in the soil of the problems I'll introduce.

1. SELLING INVESTMENTS FOR THE FUTURE. I've always had a problem with people selling things which they don't own or use. Stocks are the same. We're always getting sold the next "hot stock." Once the brokerage company's allotment is gone, they're on to the next deal. That's the way they operate. They get commissions and can't pay their bills without selling. We should be careful not to buy into the hype.

Let's buy their $14 IPO and get out at $20—not wait for it to go to $100, because most of them don't.

OR, let's sit it out. They are selling an investment that will do its thing out sometime over the rainbow, when they won't be around to be responsible for it.

"It's like the Wizard of Oz. You learn that the Big Wall Street Guys are hiding behind the curtain, peddling a contraption to generate enough noise and sound to be convincing enough to keep you afraid and away from the truth."

—Tim W., VA

Think of it. They sell a stock to you at $60. It goes to $65, then sits for years at $40, with dips down to $30. They do damage control: "Remember, George, this is your hold position. We have a 25 year horizon on this stock. Oh, and it's for your retirement."

Let me get my cash flow jab in here. You can pay the bills, buy a new home, and buy all the "Buy and Hold" investments you want once you have built up your income. Concentrate on developing a system of cash flow enhancement first. One simple opportunity for example: write covered calls on existing stock positions. Many of you with a few hundred shares or a thousand shares of stock are leaving untold thousands of dollars on the table every month. You could sell calls against your covered stock position, and generate cash.

2. THEY DON'T PRACTICE WHAT THEY PREACH. We're asked to follow people who do not do what they tell us to do. The average mutual fund—you know, the ones with dozens of their managers traipsing on and off of CNBC—changes 30% of its stock holdings every year. They want to get their money in the way of money flows. They want to get a few of the next hot rising stocks. What about you? You could hold an investment way past its peak. Its start up and then rise to higher values is past tense. The person who sold you the stock has probably sold their position two years ago, and has been in and out of three other positions during that same time.

Every company exists somewhere along the road to oblivion. How many of the current Dow stocks (The Dow Jones Industrial 30) were there at the beginning? Only two, and they are substantially different companies. If indices change their components all the time, why don't you?

Current companies last about 40 to 50 years. They are taken over, or sold. They sell off parts (spin-offs). They mutate. They change. They become obsolete.

Many great companies have a four to five year growth span. Some companies find that the only way they can keep growing is to acquire other companies. Sometimes it works.

In the dot.com era this was the case. From Amazon.com to Cisco; from VeriSign to Microsoft; companies grew their revenues by acquiring other companies—nevermind the fact that they were acquiring another "stupid business" idea. Lately, we've seen huge "charge-offs," or one-time expenses. Companies carried these purchases on their books as an asset and now expense it—move it to their income (profit and loss) statement. Tax savings are good, but earnings suffer and their stock prices go down.

Again, a cash flow note: these earnings surprises (one time, out of the blue charge-offs) create bounce opportunities. Play stocks or options on the bounce.

However, on a more somber note: great leaps in wealth, especially leaps founded on a dream or on a thought that double-digit growth will continue forever, are usually followed by a major correction. Call it a bear market if you want. If all of these stocks surrender back part of their growth because of the "talk," and there is a lot of bad-mouthing going on, these companies, while already negative, pile on their bad investments, write them off, adding more fuel to the fire. It gets to be a self-fulfilling prophecy. _It will get better when a bottom is hit_.

Some stocks will never recover. Others will take years. Yes, earnings rise and fall, retreat and rebound—or not; and generally, stock prices follow earnings. From now on, I want to chase earnings, but even more importantly, I'll look for at least a three year history of earnings. I want to see earnings improvement. I'm also going to pay more attention to the Feds interest rate and monetary policies. If they raise rates, stock prices fall. If they lower rates, stock prices rise slowly and sporadically. Internal and external forces all have a certain power. The real question then is this: is the power real and is it sustainable?

3. OUT OF CONTROL. For years, I've said, "You can't get rich being out of control of your money." Then I take my cash and buy Apple Computer stock and I'm out of control. A purchase of stock in Apple (AAPL) in 1989 at $19 would have seen the price go up shortly and then down and not recover to $19 until 1997. During this time, the market rose a lot. This is one of the greatest brand names in the world. It is also a classic blue-chip, "Buy and Hold" type stock.

J C Penney is similar. The stock was $20 in 1988, and $18 in 2001. Xerox (XRX) was $8 (adjusted for splits) in 1988 and $5 in 2001. Polaroid was over $20 in 1988 and 50¢ just recently. That's right, 50¢. Even Eastman Kodak, a great company, had stock in 1988 at $40 and is now just above $30. Wow, can we afford to keep following the advice of these so-called financial professionals?

And, think about dividends, a share of the company's profits. We also have no control over these. Up or down, paid out or held by the company—we're not in the Boardroom making decisions about dividends.

If you choose investments wisely and baby-sit them, you might be able to stay rich by being out of control, but you can't get rich being out of control. Wealth accumulation is a straightforward concept. I call it "cash to asset to cash." Take whatever cash you can get together, put it into an asset and get it back to cash as fast as you can. Money into cream and sugar into ice-cream and back to cash. If you don't do this well yourself, invest in companies that do it well. Far too many of us go cash to asset and forget the third step. Then we sit and wonder what happened? We make it in our business and lose it in their business.

Now the third step can be of a different nature. We hope it will be small amount of cash into the asset and a big amount of cash back out. However, sometimes it could be payments—or small monthly "cash flows" when we sell.

In stocks, it could be dividends—a slow working choice; it could be monthly option premiums we received by selling covered calls. We put our investment to work harder—making each dollar earn its keep so we can personally quit working at some time. We need to control and direct our own financial destiny.

4.   INNOVATION CREATES OBSOLESCENCE. The rapid addition of innovative improvements and the introduction of whole new hi-tech gadgets has seriously shrunk down the life of many companies.

In the hi-tech arena, names come and go in two to three years, not 30 to 40 years. Improvements have come at a dizzying speed. There is always some kid in a garage wanting to upset the status quo. We benefit as a society—our workplace and methods increase our output—but the particular stock we own in HI-GROUP INC., might get pummeled by a new start up.

Many years ago, a good friend and fellow real estate instructor spoke of getting in the way of progress. He showed how downtown areas, once the busy and exciting part of the city, gave way to close-in building programs. Then the suburbs sprang up and became a life unto themselves. Some suburbs expanded and became cities of their own. His point was that the excitement is always on the fringe—like a fire set in the middle of a field. The fire burns outward and the heat is on the edge, usually way away from where the fire started.

Not until a new development, a sports arena, or hospital, or mall/condo complex is built in the central city will there be a revival. Then the whole process starts over.

Corning (GLW), the old "bowl in the oven" company is an example. It's an "old economy" company. A new fire was lit with "glass," or fibre optics. It got widely profitable again, but even now, with so much competition, and a slowdown in the hi-tech (speed of light transmission), its stock is having a tough time.

IBM has remade itself. Microsoft is into Internet Service, games, banking and too many other divisions to mention. In other places, banks are selling insurance and investments. Everyone is trying to rekindle their fire.

Our job is not that tough. We can read about and watch the new developments. We can see industry leaders emerge, buy into it, but sell when the tides change—in six months or two years. We need shorter term horizons, because, just as companies peak, so do our investments.

5. MANAGERS CHANGE. We'll explore the changing nature of investments from two angles. The first, in regards to a particular company (A), the second in regards to mutual funds (B).

(A) I've constantly espoused the investment philosophy of betting on the jockey, not the horse. An "A" management team, a team from the trenches, with experience and foresight, can take a "C" level product or service and make it a winner. If not, an "A" team will find a new product, fix the old problems, gather good people around them and make it better.

A new team, hired on after a company has been devastated, could be just the fire needed to re-ignite a company's prospects. The problem is, most fixes take time, and often just as the problem is getting fixed, they move on. It's the cycle of life—from a stock market point of view. But note, it is a cycle and *change is the only constant!*

(B) For years, I've shown how mutual funds change the character of their make-up. A growth fund mutates into a small-cap fund. A bond fund starts with overseas debt, then convertible debentures, then ends up with stock.

Usually, changes in mutual funds happen when there is a management change. Each person has his/her own personality, and the fund will eventually take on that personality. The question is, is it right for you? Tax ramifications are a concern. Do you want long-term growth (or attempts) as compared to high yield investments? What are your needs and will your needs change?

I suggest you build your own mutual fund. One benefit is to avoid fees and year-end surprises. If in doubt, consider buying SPIDERS® like SPY, DIA, QQQ and MDY. These are trusts which own stocks. Fees are relatively low and you can choose the sector, or general area of investments which you think will do the most good. Note that even these stocks form rolling patterns. You can better your portfolio by buying on dips and selling at peaks. Also, you can sell options on some of these stocks to generate cash against your stock position. That's cash in your account in one day.

The concern we should have is to better monitor our investments. Get rid of the losers. Let the winners run. Don't hold an investment past its prime. Now you must be thinking that this statement is an irony: Wade is criticizing change, yet telling us to change. Yes and no. I'm not criticizing change. Trust movement. I am criticizing people who advertise for our money and then do different things with it. I like corporate changes. We just have to figure out if the change is good or bad. But, if the pros are constantly trying to better their hand, then why shouldn't we?

6. NO "GREAT COMPANY" IS SAFE. Investment dollars always flow. Today, as always, money is looking for innovation. It doesn't mean that a $90 stock can't go up to $180, or a double, but what about a $9 stock that goes to $90? Look for great potential.

Debt also flows to its best use. Sometimes companies issue debt and so be it—people are happy with 4% of 14% returns—other money though wants a piece of the action—or equity.

The good ol' boy network of even 20 years ago has a whole new group of players. Mergers, acquisitions, buyouts and takeovers have new players. Money has always flowed to the bold. Little *Capital Cities, Inc.*, buying out the giant *ABC*. If you think your big solid blue chip company is immune from these attacks, it's time to rethink. Go for the bold.

Here's our problem: as small investors, the money moves behind our backs. We're the last to know. Big money is fickle and most big money investors are impatient. We finally hear about the great deal and jump in just as others are jumping out. Have you ever thought that the major brokerage firms' big advertising push to sell out a certain stock could be its way of unloading their position? There is no substitute to study, reading the news and watching trends. (For great information on money movements, see Doug Sutton's book, The Beginning Investor's Bible.)

> As a general rule the most successful man in life is the man who has the best information.
> ~ Benjamin Disraeli

7. LONG-TERM CAN BE TERMINAL. We are not long-term people. Our personalities don't work like that. We move homes. We change jobs. We drive different cars, buy new clothes, and change hobbies. Just as we change individually, the whole country changes.

Popular products come and go. Styles change. New cars are introduced. Vacations are different. Food is different. And everything I've written about in these two paragraphs provides products or services sold in publicly traded companies.

We can invest, but we can also trade in change. Invest means to gain ownership—again, for the most part we're out of control. Trade (not day trading) means to capture profits by getting money in the way of movements. I call this position trading.

SOLUTIONS

Let me share briefly why I like position trades:
(1) Formulas/techniques can be identified and studied.
(2) Movements and patterns, say the five times to trade as a stock goes through a stock split, can be learned. (Darlene and Miles Nelson's new book, *Stock Split Secrets,* has detailed information about these stock split patterns)

(3) You can practice, or simulation trade before you use real money. (See David Hebert's book, *On Track Investing*)

(4) It works or it doesn't. You don't have to wait years to build wealth.

(5) These trades develop real profits—to let you retire or better your retirement. The profits are cash, not someone's guess about value. It's cash to pay the bills.

(6) This cash can be used to buy other, longer-term (four months to 48 months) positions.

(7) Virtually every investment position, once you understand my 13 formulas, has a purpose—a beginning, a middle and an end.

(8) You can live a better lifestyle. My aim has always been to help people fit a trading style to a wonderful lifestyle, not the other way around.

The strategies become the workhorses. I've long said, "I teach formulas and then find stocks which fit the formulas." Here's a back-up statement. I was watching a football game, and the commentator said, "The coach's methods are proven, some of the players are not." So it is with stocks.

SUMMARY

To sum up, "Buy and Hold" doesn't work as it's being promulgated by the so-called bigwigs. It is an ineffective way to build wealth. Even real estate peaks. You could buy an apartment complex, live off of it, take care of it, and watch it grow. At some point, though, with your basis low, and more "deferred maintenance" needing done than you have the inclination for, it might be time to move on. Let new money fix it up.

To everything there is a season. A time to buy, a time to sell. A time to dump losers, a time to capture profits. This time is a season, like a semester in school—a beginning, midterms, and an end.

I propose you look at investments with a new "term" outlook. Become a SEMESTER INVESTOR™. Think in terms of months, say four months to 48 months. Pay more attention to your holdings. Make your money work harder and be prepared–totally without emotion–to move on.

A SEMESTER INVESTOR does the following:

(A) Knows what is wanted from each investment.

(B) Position trades: gets money in the way of movements—both up and down.

(C) Uses leverage (options) to advantage.

(D) Learns and uses selling positions, calls and puts, to generate income.

(E) Weeds the garden better, unloading stocks past their usefulness.

(F) Learns cash flow formulas to the "T." Precision produces profits.

(G) Avoids fads—sticks with fundamentals like earnings, low debt, increases in revenues.

(H) Diversifies into formulas.

(I) Does not "dollar cost average" down. He/she waits for support levels, and then trades on timely upswings.

(J) Knows the quarter "news-go-round" and measures not only the quantity but the quality of news. (See the *Red Light, Green Light*™ Home Study Course by Wade Cook)

(K) Questions everything. The "why is more important than the "how."

(L) Keeps increasing his/her skill level. Education is a way of life.

> *If money is your hope for independence, you will never have it. The only real security that a man will have in this world is a reserve of knowledge, experience and ability.*
> ~Henry Ford

(M) Is self correcting—always improving.

> *Discipline yourself, and others won't have to.*
> ~John Wooden

(N) Surrounds himself or herself with like-minded winners.

> *Keep away from people who try to belittle your ambitions. Small people always do that, but the really great make you feel that you too can become great.*
> ~Mark Twain

"Buy and Hold" *can* work if given 30 years or more, but I feel that there is such a better way. Yes, position trading is more work, but the results are definitely worth the effort. The hold period must be appropriate. It must fit your risk tolerance, your own particular stage in life and your own cash flow needs. You can get your money to work harder as you learn to deploy money like you would in any other business. Position trading is a business that can support your family. All you have to do is change your expectation level and learn how to "work" your money better. The current correction in the marketplace, seen as risky by some, provides great opportunities for others.

10

People Who Walk the Walk

I am pleased to introduce you to Darlene Nelson (and her husband Miles), Doug Sutton and David Hebert. These are three of my fellow instructors at the Stock Market Institute of Learning, Inc.

Read carefully their words. They are in the arena everyday, walking the walk.

THE POWER OF STOCK SPLITS

Excerpted from *Stock Split Secrets* by Darlene Nelson & Miles Nelson

When we first started trading stock splits Miles asked our broker if many people used this strategy. The broker replied, "There is no reason to buy a stock just because it was splitting. In fact," he went on, "the split actually dilutes the stock and can reduce the perceived value of the stock."

Many stockbrokers may tell you that a stock split has no real impact on the value of a company. You might hear someone say, "When a stock splits, the share values are adjusted with no actual change in shareholder equity. A stock split is no reason to buy that stock."

Brokers have to pass a licensing examination on SEC rules, stock market basics, and legal definitions. As a result, most brokers learn what a stock split is, but not how to profit from one.

When a company splits their stock they simply issue more shares of stock and distribute them to current shareholders. In a two-for-one stock split, a stockholder with 100 shares of stock would receive an additional 100 shares. Before the split, if 100 shares of ABC stock are worth $10 each, the value of this holding would be $1,000. After a two-for one stock split, ABC issues 100 more shares of stock to the shareholder and the value of all shares is reduced to $5. Multiply 200 shares by $5 it's still $1,000—the result is no change in shareholder equity.

Although there is technically no change in value, there can be a substantial change in perceived value in the market. If a company splits their stock they are usually doing very well; business is growing and profits are improving. Because of the great news, share prices are climbing. Stock splits are often done to increase affordability by lowering the share price, to increase the number of shares on the market, and to reward shareholders. Some companies pay dividends of stock rather than cash.

After well-known stocks have split, they tend to continue increasing in value until they have returned to the pre-split stock price. If you purchase shares in a strong company that has just split, you have the law of averages on your side. Chances are, if you purchase today and it splits two-for-one tomorrow, that stock will probably increase in value. Eventually it could be selling at a price equal to the pre-split price.

Let me give you an example: If you own 300 shares of Home Depot, Inc. (ticker symbol HD), selling at $70 today, and the stock is split two-for-one tomorrow, you would end up with 600 shares worth $35 each. Wait for a year or so and as Home Depot continues

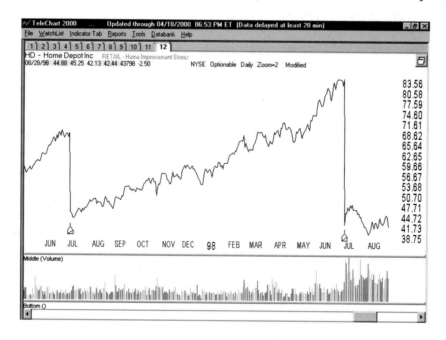

growing, expanding, and profiting, your shares will probably have increased in value until they're worth close to $70 again!

Stock Splits Are Magic

There is something magical about a stock split. Investors get excited and stock prices jump. In many cases this jump in price is based not on fundamental data, but on pure emotion.

This kind of emotion can create high demand: more buyers than sellers. The law of supply and demand says that if you have people buying more than selling, the price must go up. How far? How long? Who knows? However, if you know that it is going to happen, you have the ability to make a profit from it. Applied knowledge is money!

If you knew the future, you could use that knowledge to make millions of dollars in the stock market. Imagine knowing about the crash of 1929 a month early. You could sell everything and have cash under your pillow. Then, in the months after the crash, you could buy stocks in big companies for pennies on the dollar.

You may not be able to tell the future, but you can predict the likely performance of stocks based on scheduled events. A perfect example is what happens to a stock when it is being added to the Standard and Poor's 500™ (S&P 500™). In order to match the movement of the S&P 500, index funds need to purchase shares of any stock added to the list. As a result, within a few days of an announcement that a stock is being added it becomes a hot target for index fund managers.

This creates a situation where there is more buying pressure on the stock than owners willing to sell. With this pressure the stock price goes up and it can become like a feeding frenzy. If you knew beforehand which stocks would be

added to the S&P 500, you could purchase before the buying delirium, then sell when the stock price is pushed up.

You can apply the same concept to companies that are splitting their stock. These companies tend to behave in a very predictable manner. It's almost as if the stocks are handed a script. Knowing this is like being able to see the future, and you can profit from it. If you are one of the people with a copy of the script you can read between the lines— making a profit whenever you want!

Stock Splits Are Emotional

Stock splits are emotion-based, and so is the stock market. Each business morning when the bell rings, people are faced with another day of trading. One day the market is shooting up and the bulls are taking no prisoners. The next morning, bears are in control and news anchors are declaring the end of the world. It's amazing how a bean-processing plant failure in some Third World country can signal a rash of sell orders and send the market into a tailspin. Then some analyst makes a public statement and the emotional climate changes again, with massive price shifts within moments.

Do these up and down swings really happen because of facts and figures? Could huge corporations really be so unstable that the stock price merits a 5% adjustment one day, only to turn the other direction the next morning? Not very likely! The market usually changes because emotional tides sweep through the trading floors, causing wave after wave of intense buying and selling. Of course, there are things that start the emotion, but the market seems to overreact to everything.

There are times when massive price adjustments do need to be made in a stock. Perhaps a news announcement declares that the company will increase profits by 50% the following year, or that their biggest market has been eliminated and they will have an 80% reduction in earnings. When big news announcements occur, the stock price is usually adjusted very quickly. But the emotion of the market can cause up and down swings, driven by pure speculation and rumor, not fact.

By understanding the psychology of this game you can reap massive rewards. Professionals look for specific events that can be used to predict the direction a stock will take. Stock splits are one such event—a tremendous indicator to help you predict the direction and timing of stock movement.

Professional investors use pre-defined formulas to profit from these specific events. This book will discuss many such formulas, time-tested recipes that have been refined and proven successful in stock splits scenarios. In order for these formulas to work, you need to have all of the ingredients, which is where this book comes in. By following these recipes, you can have your cake and eat it, too!

Stock Split Companies Regain Value

Experience has shown me that after a quality company has split, the stock tends to keep increasing in value. This trend continues until the price per share is nearly equal to the pre-split price. If a company were to split its stock two-for-one when it was selling for $146 per share, after the split the adjusted price would be $73. Top companies may continue growing and the stock price will slowly climb until it approaches $146 per share again. This price recovery may take anywhere from six months to three years, but the stronger companies usually reach their pre-split price within $2^{1}/_{2}$ years or less.

Stock Split Companies Perform

Some time ago I learned about a professional study that looked at two-for-one stock splits. This study, "What Do Stock Splits Really Signal?" by David L. Ikenberry, Graeme Rankine, and Earl K. Stice, discovered that these companies tend to grow at an annual rate of 54.24% faster than the general market—prior to the split. After splitting, they continue their explosion, growing another 7.93% faster than the market, for an entire year. If you look closely at the top splitters, you'll see their growth rate is even better.

When you look at the history of strong, profitable companies, you will discover that their stock price performs, on average, much better than other companies. You'll also find that most of these powerful companies split their stock on a regular basis—usually every one to five years. Stock split companies are usually the top performers in their sector and industry. This observation can become powerful when looking for stocks to add to your investment program. In the next chapter you will get to experience the excitement of developing a stock split portfolio.

Explanations And Terminology

Bears: Bears are those who believe stock prices will fall.
Bulls: Bulls are those who believe prices, either of a stock or the market overall, will go up.
Use the Formulas: In order for the formulas to work, you need to have all of the ingredients. By following the recipe, you can eat your cake and have it, too!

SECTORS

Excerpted from *Beginning Investors Bible* by Doug Sutton

One of the biggest challenges when first starting to trade the stock market is the tendency to over-shop. Beginners tend to sit at the computer until the wee hours studying charts, developing lists of potential trades, trying to pick the best trade out of the scores of stocks, and ultimately doing little if anything with all the work they have expended. They are looking for the proverbial needle in the haystack. I have found that finding the whole haystack and then looking for the stock that is most likely to move is a far better way to spend my time.

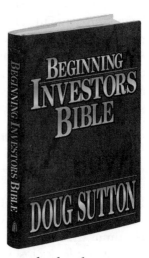

Imagine a bucket half full of water. Tip it to one side and then let it rest on the floor. The water will slosh around the bucket, leaving one side only to splash up the other and then to another side and so on. The market is not unlike a big bucket filled with money instead of water. For the most part money does not leave the market; it just sloshes around within the market. For a few days or weeks the pharmaceutical stocks will be performing well and money is flowing in their direction. They will weaken and the momentum will shift to the airline stocks. Money will slosh from the drug companies, then airline stocks will start to fly. The airlines will weaken and the banks will gain favor. Money just flows from one sector to another.

A *sector* is defined as a grouping of companies that provide the same product or service. Pharmaceuticals, banks, chemicals, software, Internet providers, and oil companies are examples of a few of the hundreds of sectors in the stock market.

Sectors are Grouped by Service and Products

The challenge is finding a way to identify and then monitor the different sectors that each individual investor is inclined to follow. It can be done in two ways.

One way is to have a charting service that has already divided stocks providing similar services or products into groups. Instead of watching thousands of stocks you can then monitor just a handful of watch groups to see which are gaining favor and which are losing favor.

If you are playing options, your chances for profit are doubled because you can play stocks in one sector to the upside and stocks in a different sector to the downside.

One charting service that does an excellent job of organizing sectors is called Telechart 2000®, provided by Worden Brothers. They divide stocks into sectors and label them as specific Watch Groups. Here are several of those groups that an investor might follow and some of the stocks that make up the Watch Group.

Listed below are some of the more closely followed sectors in the stock market and the ticker symbols of some of the most active stocks within those sectors (as of the writing of this book). If you find yourself holding too many positions in one sector or sectors that are closely related (i.e., oil companies and oil service companies) you'll want to reallocate your holdings.

Oil – XOM, CHV, TX, SC
Pharmaceutical – MRK, PFE, BMY, SGP, LLY, ABT
Retail – WMT, KM, HD, S
Clothing retailer – GPS, LTD, ANF, TJX, TOM
Automobile – F, DCX, GM, TOYOY
Entertainment – BBI, DIS
Big banks – BK, C, JPM, CMB, BAC
Medium banks – KEY, MEL, WFC, NB
Chemicals – DOW, DD, ROH, UK
Communication equip. – CSCO, LU, QCOM, NT, CIEN
Communications – T, SBC, FON, BLS
Computer 'box makers' – IBM, GTW, DELL, CPQ, HWP
Computer software – MSFT, ORCL, ADBE, PSFT, BMCS
Computer information, techs – UIS, EDS, CSC
Electric – GE, HON
Semiconductor – INTC, MU, AMAT, AMD, LSI, TXN
Personal products – G, AVP
Beverage – KO, PEP, BUD, VO
Grocery – SWY, KR, ABS
Oil service – HAL, SLB, DO, RIG, BHI
Insurance – AIG, AFL, CNA, CI
Household products – CL, PG, UN
Airlines – UAL, DAL, ALK, LUV, AMR, CAL
Brokerage – SCH, MER, MWD, BSC, PWJ, LEH
Internet – CMGI, AMZN, LCOS, XCIT, YHOO, EBAY

This is by no means a list of recommended stocks nor is it as complete as it could be. It just serves as an example of sectors that bear watching because these are companies that have a history of active price movement, and price movement is what a trader thrives on and profits from.

Please be aware that any companies included in this book, and specifically in this chapter on sectors, are used as examples only and may have changed fundamentally since I wrote this manuscript. Their inclusion does not constitute a recommendation to trade them. Always do your own homework. After all, it's your money.

The Lead Dog Turns the Team

Another way to track sector movement is to follow the dominant stock in the sector. Think of it this way. If you were a dogsledder with a team of huskies leashed single file to your sled and the lead dog turned left, which way would the rest of the team turn? Left! That is the power of the dominant stock.

If the dominant stock has great earnings, the whole sector gets a boost. If the dominant stock is in a downtrend, the sector is more than likely in a downtrend. The rest of the dogs will follow.

To identify which stocks to follow just think of which stocks are the leaders in their sector.

Money center banks – J.P. Morgan (JPM) or Citigroup (C)
Software – Microsoft (MSFT) or Oracle (ORCL)
Pharmaceutical – Merck (MRK) or Pfizer (PFE)
Semi-conductor – Intel (INTC)
Entertainment – Blockbuster (BBI) or Disney (DIS)
Insurance – American International Group (AIG)
Oil – Exxon (XOM) or Chevron (CHV)
Retail apparel – The Gap (GPS) or The Limited (LTD)
Retail specialty – Wal-Mart (WMT)

These are just a few of the dominant stocks within sectors and I am sure you would have come up with many of the same names had you been asked to identify them. Take the same approach in picking the leaders in other sectors you choose to follow.

Stocks that Flock Together Tend to Split Together

Another phenomenon that occurs within sectors is the tendency to split as a family. For example, in February 1997 Royal Dutch Petroleum (RD) announced a four-for-one stock split. It split at about $200 down to $50.

You must think of the perceived value that Royal Dutch presented to the investing public. Here was a stock that had been trading at $200 a share and was now valued at $50. Since stock split companies have a high likelihood of regaining their pre-split values, they often present a great investment opportunity after a split.

If you are one of the other oil companies, you can't have a competitor looking like a better bargain than you. Within six months nearly all the domestic oil companies announced stock splits with the exception of Chevron (CHV). Exxon (XOM) split two-for-one at $108, down to $54; Arco (ARC) split two-for-one at $140, down to $70; Mobil (MOB) split two-for-one at $140, down to $70; Texaco (TX) split two-for-one at $120, down to $60; Shell (SC) split two-for-one at $140, down to $70; and BP Amoco (BP) split two-for-one at $120, down to $60.

These prices are all approximate prices, but isn't it interesting that when all the splits were done all the stocks were once again trading in the $50 to $70 range? No single stock had a perceived price advantage over any other in the sector. An investor had to make a buy decision based on the fundamentals of the company, not its price.

Just to reinforce this point, in mid-1998 Warner Lambert (WLA) announced a stock split. Within the next six months Abbott Labs (ABT), Schering-Plough (SGP), Bristol-Meyers Squibb (BMY), Merck (MRK) and Pfizer (PFE) had either announced a stock split or had already split their stock.

The exact same thing happened to the Internet sector at the end of 1998 and the beginning of 1999.

To take advantage of the opportunity this knowledge presents, an investor must become an investigator of sorts. Do some research on companies within the sector and get answers to the following questions:

1. At what price does the stock typically announce a stock split and is the stock trading near that price? (Note: TC2000® can display stock prices adjusted or unadjusted for stock splits.)

2. At what time of the year has the stock usually announced a stock split and is it near that time?

3. What is the company's news cycle? Do they announce stock splits at or shortly after board of directors meetings? Do they announce a split at the time of earnings announcements?

4. Has the company filed a Definitive 14A with the Securities and Exchange Commission requesting the right to issue additional shares of stock? If they have asked for this with the intent of taking the request to the shareholders for approval it is a vital indicator that the company may be preparing for an eventual stock split. Check the SEC website www.edgaronline.com for details.

If the answer to all these questions is yes, then there is a high likelihood that the stock *may* split. The operative word here is "may." There are no assurances; the stock is just a very good prospect. If your intent is to buy options on the stock instead of buying the stock, make sure that you buy a lot of time and give the company time to follow through on its plans.

Some Sectors can be Cyclical

Another interesting characteristic is the cyclical nature of certain sectors. Some companies have times of the year that dramatically outperform the others.

There is something that happens every year like clockwork, like the falling of the leaves. Millions of children across the nation go back to school and when they do, all those clothes they have outgrown, worn out or wouldn't be caught dead wearing because they are last year's fashion must be replaced. I have an adage: "Follow the money." In this country there is a tremendous amount of discretionary money that is controlled by the youth of this nation and they are very selective about where they spend it. Follow the kids because that is where the money is spent.

There are several high profile stores that cater almost exclusively to this age group and are highly successful in their sector. The Gap (GPS), Tommy Hilfiger (TOM), Abercrombie & Fitch (ANF) and The Limited (LTD) are just a few of the key players that come to mind. If you were to look at their price graphs over the past few years you would see that nearly every year their stocks moved significantly higher just following the back-to-school buying season. Not only that, they often had an even bigger move in January just following the holiday season after parents filled Christmas stockings with all the things they didn't get three months earlier.

Other stocks that perform well during the Christmas season are the bookstores. Books are the gift of choice when you don't know what else to buy and millions of holiday shoppers find themselves in this position. Look at Barnes & Noble (BKS) and Borders Group (BGP) just prior to Christmas over the past few years. These kinds of companies typically do well.

Agricultural chemical companies sell millions of tons of fertilizer in the spring each year when the ground is opened for the first plantings. Not only that, you can almost see exactly when the second and third plantings for the year are started.

Begin watching the weather. What do you think happens to the profits of electric utility companies and heating oil companies when there is an unusually harsh winter? They are making more dollars for each gallon of oil pumped and kilowatt hour delivered. What happens to property insurance companies when a hurricane strikes or a major river floods? Paying out millions of dollars in claims does not enhance stock values. Watch the price of oil. When the price goes up, the oil stocks benefit. When the price goes down, the airlines benefit.

The possibilities are endless. You just have to be imaginative enough to recognize them and take advantage of them. The old saying, "A rising tide floats all boats," is never more true than when it is applied to sectors.

Playing the Whole Sector

I have talked about finding the needle in the haystack, finding that one stock in its sector and playing it. There is also a way to play the whole haystack. That is to play options on a whole index.

There is a real advantage to playing the whole index, in that your risk is spread over many stocks instead of just one. However, if you are going to play options on indices it is critical that you find those that have fairly equal member weighting. On some indices one stock out of the eight or nine represented may carry as much as 25% of the index's weight. If that is the case you may as well just play that stock because its movement biases the movement of the whole index. Your challenge is to find an index that has member weighting within two or three percentage points of each other.

There are some other disadvantages that surround playing indices. They are sometimes too broadly based to provide the big price movements that result in substantial option price jumps. That is related to another weakness, the fact that options on indices are lightly traded. This low trade volume also effects option price movement.

The last shortcoming is the execution procedure at some of the options exchanges. Some orders are still hand-delivered and are a little slow in trade execution. But, for those of you who are willing to sacrifice big price movement for spreading the risk over a broader area, trading options on an index may be just the ticket for you.

Summary

- Learn to monitor sector movement. It can greatly benefit your trading timing and profitability.
- Follow the money flowing into and out of a sector to possibly make money in both directions.
- Watch for sectors that are potential split families. Do your research on companies yet to participate.
- Pick a handful of stocks that are seasonally influenced and watch them for patterns.
- Don't ignore the power of "Mother Nature" to impact the stock prices of a whole sector.

INDICATORS, FACTORS, AND RULES TO LIVE BY

Excerpted from Chapter 4 of *On Track Investing* by David Hebert

Play The Strategy, Not The Stock

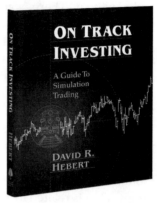

The word strategy, as I understand it, means a set of rules, or factors, that when followed produce desired results. The strategy is a process. You need to concentrate your attention on the strategy first, then go and find stocks that match the strategy criteria.

Bringing our personal likes and dislikes about a company, is a common error when deciding on a trade. It would be backwards to find a stock and then try to pigeonhole it into a particular strategy. There is also a tendency, especially when you take a loss, to make yourself determined to make money on a particular stock for reasons other than it being a good strategy candidate.

Maybe you think that Microsoft is an awesome company and that you should be able to make money buying Microsoft stock. That may or may not be true, but why not use the strategy first. If Microsoft happens to fit your strategy, by all means, go for it. If it doesn't fit, don't force it.

A common mistake is that when you lose money on a particular stock, your tendency is to want to recoup your losses on that particular stock. Why? Revenge has no impact on the stock itself. Options have no joy. Covered Calls do not get depressed. Stock Splits do not have multiple personality disorders. We, as human beings, are the ones with emotions. We need to keep this in perspective.

Also, try not to be led by your emotions when making investment decisions. Don't get me wrong. I highly value emotions and believe that they are an integral part of life. Without our emotions of happiness, sadness, loneliness, and bliss, this world would indeed be a dull place to live.

However, emotions tend to get in the way in investing. You can get really happy about a particular trade. This may sway you from getting out at your pre-arranged exit point. You may believe that the stock is going to go up another 10 or 20 points, but if you have arrived at your exit point, get out. If the trade looks that good, maybe it still is within your game plan. If so, just wait for another buy signal and get in again.

Three rules of strategies:

1. If you don't have a clear buy signal, don't enter the trade.
2. If it is not part of your game plan, don't enter the trade.

3.   If you don't know your exit points—your target profit and target loss—don't enter the trade.

Only buy when you know your selling point. If you can determine your selling point, and place a GTC, what is left for you to do? Just check the stock periodically to make sure the trend is still in your favor. Check the moving averages. Check and make sure that your targeted loss has not been reached. If everything goes as planned, your GTC order will be filled. You will have hit your target directly—a bull's-eye.

In order to hit the bull's-eye, you must be able to see it and focus your attention on it. Know by just a simple comparison of two numbers whether to invest or not. Use yes or no questions. If you target your loss at 20%, figure out exactly what that means. If you have a $10 stock, 20% would be $2. If your $10 stock becomes an $8 stock, you need to exit the trade. No ifs, ands, or buts, just exit, sell, buy, or whatever it is to close out your position.

GTCs are like sighting out a target bull's-eye and letting loose an arrow. We may have to wait to see if the arrow hits, but the concept can be the same. The point is to have set targets, to know your outcome, to know when and if you get out before you enter the trade. This is like a trading ninja tool. It seems that only the people that get to be good at these strategies understand and implement this skill.

There is the element of hunch, or intuition. I mostly use this as a gut feeling not to get into a trade. If the indicators are showing me the green light, but something tells me not to enter the trade, I don't enter the trade. The reverse, however, is not true. If the indicators are showing me a red light, and there is not a clear buy signal, don't get into the trade no matter what your emotions and intuition tell you. The best trades happen when you have a good buy signal and you feel good about the trade.

The way to overcome the emotional factor in investing is to concentrate on the logic of the strategy. Go through the process one step at a time, and then evaluate the trade with the criteria on your game plan. If the strategy process gives you the green light, enter the trade, of course, after you have already determined your exit.

Fundamental Analysis

It is a good idea to use Fundamental Analysis in evaluating your potential position. Up to this point, we have been talking about technical analysis—charting and adhering to a strategy. Fundamental analysis can tell us something about the company we are investing in.

Here are some fundamentals and a brief definition:

1.   Earnings or P/E Ratio: Earnings show us the state of the cash flow of the company that we are investing in. I've heard it said that cash flow is the lifeblood of a business. Without it, you can bleed to death.

Price tends to follow earnings. If the cash flow decreases, it logically follows that the price of the stock will most likely decrease. The company will not have cash flow to pay for things like investment for growth, excess debt reduction, paying taxes, and a host of other things. Without the cash to pay for things, most businesses have a difficult time operating smoothly, if they can operate at all.

Most of the time earnings are shown in the form of a Price to Earnings Ratio. You figure this by dividing the earnings per share into the price of the stock to get a percentage.

There is no magic number for earnings. There are, however, factors to consider when you look at the P/E Ratio. What sector is the company in? What are the standard P/E ratios for the stock's competition? Are there earnings for the last twelve months, or are they projected earnings? I would say that a good benchmark for earnings is to look at some indexes, like Standard & Poor 500. See what the average P/E Ratio is. Only invest in companies that have a P/E Ratio of 40 or less.

If you want, you can get more "fundamental" and research the earnings of a company more fully (This is also available on W.I.N.™). Look at the P/E for the "sector" or other businesses that do a similar kind of business. Research the average P/E for the stock exchange that your stock trades on. Most brokers have access to P/E Ratios and can tell you what the average ratio is for other companies doing the same kind of business. Have a peek at their financial statements. This alone can reveal oodles of information.

If you follow good earnings, you add more percentage points to the probability that your trade is going to be successful. If you will look on the Simutrade Worksheets, you will notice a place to put the P/E Ratio for the company. You may want to give a good ratio a plus (+), an okay ratio a zero (0), and a high ratio a minus (-). For me, I try and stay away from companies with high ratios. The stock is probably overvalued and I don't want to pay more than something is worth. Earnings are a solid indicator and will not let you down. Avoid investing in companies with a high P/E Ratio.

2. Return On Equity: Return on stock equity is a way of calculating the company's after-tax profits divided by the book value. What you want to see is this figure increase year by year.

3. Debt Ratio: This fundamental shows how much money the company owes compared to the equity of the shareholders. As you can guess, the less debt a company has, the better off the company is going to be if it runs into hard times. It's just like our personal finances. If your bills are almost the same as your income, what happens if something happens to your income level? Well, you simply can't pay all of your bills. If your debt ratio was low, say for every $100 dollars that you took in you only had to pay out $20 in debt, how would that be different if your

cash decreased? It would be much easier to keep current on your bills. So it is with corporations. You want to see low debt ratios. You want to target the debt ratio of companies you invest in to be under 30%. If a company's debt ratio is 50% or higher, move on to another deal. It's just not safe.

4. Cash Dividends: Companies sometimes pay out dividends in the form of cash to shareholders. There is actually a strategy called Dividend Capturing where you search out companies that pay dividends, purchase the stock just before the dividend is paid, receive the dividend, then sell the stock. You receive a Return On Investment (ROI) that is equal to the dividend. You count the time lapse for this strategy in days. Cash Dividends are not a major factor in the overall scheme of things. However, if a company pays out a good dividend, it would appear to me to be better than a company that does not. Do research on your own if this interests you.

5. Book Value: This fundamental answers the question, "What is the company really worth?" This is the dollar amount that you get when you subtract all the liabilities from the assets. You then divide this amount by the number of outstanding shares. This is the "real" value of the shares. You can imagine Book Value as what you would get as a shareholder if the company decided to close its doors and stop doing business, then liquidated its assets and dispersed this sum to the shareholders.

Margin

It is possible to have more buying power than you have money available. You can spend more than you have. Buying power is the money that you can use right now to purchase stock, money that is not being used on another trade. In a regular brokerage account, your buying power is the difference between the amount of money you have in your account minus the amount that you have spent on open trades.

Being able to buy on margin is like getting a line of credit at the bank. You can now use somebody else's money and pay them back later with some interest for the service. If you don't already have a margin account, ask your broker about margin requirements—what does it take to open a margin account?

Why would you want to have a margin account and use someone else's money? One simple little answer: higher yield. If you purchase 1,000 shares of stock at $7 per share, that would be $7,000. If you had a margin account you may be able to only put up half the money. Now your cost on the 1,000 shares would be $3,500 ($7,000 divided by half equals

$3,500). Or, you could still use $7,000, but now you could buy 2,000 shares. You have just created the potential of doubling your rate of return and your yield.

You must employ good money management principles with a margin account. The broker lending you the money will let you keep the profits of the trade. All he wants is interest. You pay him a going rate, maybe 8% annual interest, and he stays happy with you keeping the profit. However, if you take a loss, that's your responsibility. One of the worst things about a margin account is a Margin Call—you receive a telephone call from your broker telling you that you must deposit more money into your account to cover the trade. If you employ good money management techniques, like always leave 25% buying power, then you can avoid margin calls.

You can't buy options on margin. I would not want to anyway, as they pose more risk. A margin account can double your profits, but can also increase loss on the downside. It's best to use safer strategies to purchase on margin. Try using a Margin Simutrade account utilizing Covered Calls and Rolling Stocks. This way, you can experience first hand the wonders of margin, without experiencing the downside.

THE GAME PLAN

Excerpted from Chapter 2 of *On Track Investing* by David Hebert

The most crucial element to a successful, profitable stock market trading campaign is to know what you are doing before you do it. Then do it consistently.

You must know when to get in, when to get out, and why. You need to have a consistent course of action that works.

What a great value it would be if you could have someone available that could make good decisions for you. Simutrading is about making you that person.

If you had a map in front of you with your entrance and exit shown in detail and all you had to do is follow the map, could you succeed? If you have a good financial map and you have the skill to follow it, you will get where you want to go financially. The problem then becomes, where do we get our hands on a map to our financial success? For that, we need to tailor our own financial game plan.

Your game plan is like a map of your journey to financial independence through the stock market. If I were to take a trip across the country to a place that I had never been, I would purchase a map. The map would show me which roads to take and guide me to where I want to go. This concept is so simple, yet so crucial. We use maps and plans every day. Have you ever gone to a restaurant and ordered from a menu? The menu is a map of the restaurant. It lists what choices are available to you, describes the benefits of each item, and lists the price so that you know what you will be charged before you order. Have you ever gone into a restaurant and said, "Oh, just give me something to eat and charge me whatever you want?" I doubt it.

As investors, we need a map to guide us. Because we can't afford to fail or financially get off track we need a map so detailed that we can know at a moment's glance what we should do, in any situation. I call this investment map a game plan. Before you finish this chapter, you should have a game plan. You can then follow your game plan just like you would a road map until you reach your financial destination.

Once you have a game plan, you need to develop the skills to follow your game plan. This is important. Sometimes we let our emotions get in the way and we make a decision that deviates from our plan. We "hope" that our stock goes up. Do you think that hoping will increase the likelihood of the price of a stock increasing? I doubt it. A successful investor once told me, "Hope rhymes with dope." Maybe this was not very nice, but it is quite true in cases of finance. I believe strongly in intuition and hunches. I believe that there is a part of us that is aware of many, many things that we do not consciously think about. I suggest that you try to listen to these hunches, but make sure that they are in line with your game plan.

I will venture to say that the majority of investors do not have a detailed enough game plan, if they have one at all. They may target a particular strategy with a vague goal in mind, but will end up deciding when to get out after they are already in the trade. The lucky ones eventually learn to use a game plan, have enough money to lose during their learning curve, or just get out of the stock market altogether. For the rest of us who want to succeed and can't afford to fail, we need a game plan.

11

Trading on Company News

Lately, I've spent a lot of time in my seminars talking about and showing people how to increase their powers of observation and apply that to increasing their profits. For example, if you see patterns, say a connection between a company's stock dipping or rising at certain times as the stock goes through a split, can you not take advantage of this pattern? Can we not make better trades? Get in at more opportune times and get out with more cash?

The obvious is not always so obvious. I demonstrate this in classes by getting everyone to sing "Twinkle, Twinkle, Little Star" as a group while I sing "Now I Know My ABCs." These songs have the same melody, as does "Baa Baa Black Sheep." The point is that these are two of the songs most widely sung by American children, who learned them from their parents, and rarely does anyone realize they are the same melody.

We need to get better at making connections. I look for connections in the stock market all the time and then try to figure out how to capitalize on those observations. I've recently discovered something so pervasive, so recognizable, that once you know and "get it," it will literally shake up a lot of things you do. It will help you avoid mistakes. It will help you trade better—better execution and more cash profits.

What I am about to explain is a price movement phenomenon based on the market's reaction to events on the corporate calendar. Many people have observed parts of this phenomenon. Others see one angle of it but don't see the connection. Still others see the same patterns and time periods but don't understand the "why" behind the stock movements. If you don't truly understand this cause and effect, it's hard to build faith in the process—to formulate your "law" and put that law to work for you.

Your stockbroker or financial planner may claim to have known about this concept. If so, chew that person out for not telling you. Anyway, I doubt they know the entirety of this process. I've not talked to one person yet who understands all of this before I explained it—no broker, surely no news writer or journalist, and no other author.

You are about to read probably the single most important thing about trading in the stock market you have ever read or ever will read. I call it "Red Light – Green Light.™" This pearl of business wisdom was found through years of struggle, and you minimize this process at your trading peril. Watch and be wise.

Chronological Connections

In May of 1995 I took our company public. Our assets grew rapidly and we became a reporting company June 30, 1996, when the quarterly SEC reports are filed. The June 30th reports actually had to be filed within 45 days, or by August 15th. This important point will come back into play later. Read on.

For years now my accounting and legal departments have worked on our quarterly and annual reports. During this quarterly process, there are windows which open or close on what I as a CEO, Board member and insider can say. There are also specific time periods when I can and cannot sell my own company's stock.

Let's take our first time out. I can pretty much *buy* stock whenever. It's in the selling of that stock or other stock holdings where restrictions exist. If I buy stock in a company wherein I am considered an insider (a person with information that the general public does not have access to), then I have to hold onto the stock for six months. If I do sell it before six months are up, say to recover my cash, I will have to give back to the company any profits I've made. This is called disgorgement. I'm not allowed to make a profit on the stock based on "inside" information. These rules are good. They protect the investing public.

After years of complying—being careful when to buy and sell (actually as of this writing I've never sold any stock in WCFC; I want to own more of it), and being careful of what I say and when—I started observing things. Here it is plain and simple: News drives stock prices. Everyone knows this. But it is only one component, one piece of the puzzle.

Here's the question I asked myself. If I, as a CEO, am under all these restrictions—these open and closed window periods of time—then what about the 25,000 or so other CEOs, CFOs, COOs, CLOs, Boards of Directors and other insiders of all publicly traded companies in this wonderful country? Are they not under the same requirements?

Important Dates

This is where the next piece of the puzzle falls into place. When can "insiders" talk? When do they have to go silent? And what effect does this quarterly phenomenon have on the rise and fall of their stock prices? We'll explain all of these as we move along, but first some important dates.

December 31   This is the year end for most companies. SEC filings must be submitted for the whole year, and this document must be audited by an outside firm. The filing deadline is 90 days later, or March 31.

These are calendar quarter ends. Quarterly SEC filings may be unaudited. Filings are due 45 days later, on May 15, August 15 and November 15. Do you see an overlapping time period in the March 31 area? December 31 filings for the previous year need to be made as a company is just finishing up its first quarter.

Another point: Some companies may use months other than December as their year end. Most companies have a December 31 year end, but even if they don't, they usually choose a calendar quarter to be their year end. Why? The answer lies in this quick but powerful observation: Companies must file their 940s and 941s (and other Federal and State filing requirements). That's it. 940s and 941s. Now if you've been in business you've already thought, "Aha, I got it!" But some of you have never had to do quarterly employment filings. Our benevolent government makes everyone file at the same time—in this case on a calendar quarter. If you chose a different year end other than a calendar quarter, it will seem as if you have to have two sets of records—one for yourself and one for the government. Hence, for ease of paperwork most companies comply and have their year end on one of the four calendar quarters. This one fact alone will have dynamic effects as a vast majority of companies fall in line and march together, doing the same thing at the same time. You'll see the dramatic effects of this process as you learn more about "red light, green light" news periods.

So, to summarize, not all companies have the same calendar year end (December 31st), but almost all companies have the same calendar quarter ends. Some don't, like Dell. The patterns that follow quarterly reporting are somewhat predictable depending on the quality of the news. We'll get to that very soon.

News—Changing Perceptions

Okay, let's start down the path. It's about June 15th—a few weeks before the quarter ends. People start to talk. Analysts adjust and readjust their expected earnings numbers. The CEO of Big Company comes out in interviews or news releases and downplays the numbers, saying something like, "Sales have been good, but we have a charge off, so earnings will be $1.12 instead of $1.32." The stock drops $5, from $86 to $81. Now towards the end of June other news—mergers, share buy-backs, takeovers, stock splits, other sales figures, new product announcements, et cetera, et cetera—hits the streets. The stock wavers but heads back up.

Of all these newsy items, the type of announcement most followed is any announcement having to do with earnings. See *Wall Street Money Machine, Volume 2* (formerly titled, *Stock Market Miracles*). I've written about earnings, or P/E, in many other places. Many people base what they are willing to pay for a stock on the P/E, or price-to-earnings ratio. A typical NYSE company has a P/E of around 20—let's say 19.2. In short, this means that the stock will cost $19.20 for every $1.00 of earnings. The stock may be at $250 or $5 or 50¢, it matters not. Now a static or isolated P/E is not the only factor in price determination even for those who only follow P/Es. Other important considerations include these questions: Are earnings growing or contracting? How does this company's earnings compare to those of other companies? Are earnings even a viable measurement in certain sectors? Internet stocks are a scary diversion from sound rational practice in stock choices. Many have no "E" in their P/E.

Back to the point: Earnings is the most widely watched measurement of stock values. Because of this, all CEOs must be very careful what they say about earnings.

Let's move down to the first week of July. The quarter is over, but the actual filing (10Q) has not yet been done. That will happen in a few weeks—at least by August 15th, the filing deadline. Now, think this through. If the CEO, CFO or other corporate bigwigs comment about actual numbers before the proper documents are filed, it is assumed that he or she knows what the numbers should be. Do you see? Even if the accountants aren't through with the complete consolidated numbers, it would be determined that he or she should know. Because of this there is a complete news shutdown (shh! no talking, no talking!). No one will talk until the 10Qs are filed and the news release is out. Funny thing—the stock gets back to $86 and even up to $88. How does this happen? There is something happening here. Paranoia strikes deep. It is as if a whole group of people know something we don't know. In fact, we're the last to know.

Here's the pathetic, yet comical irony. Now the news is out—it's official. The interviews or press releases start up with something like this: "Earnings are ahead of expectations by about 10%. They are $1.22 per share." As the report goes on, you'll see an interesting twist. "We're pleased with the numbers and growth, but we contemplate a slowdown in sales next quarter (or year) and may not be able to maintain these high numbers."

Is this crazy or what? They good-mouth and bad-mouth their numbers in the same breath. Why? You must understand the fear these CEOs and others live under. They do not want to be seen hyping their stock. They couch the truth behind caveats. They pad everything. This is the way it is.

Now another unusual thing happens. Many times the stock goes down in spite of good news. It is a strange phenomenon. I'm still perplexed when it happens. It's part of the "buy on rumors, sell on facts (news)" syndrome. Sometimes it has to do with what has happened to the stock in the few weeks or months before the report. It has a lot to do with sentiment—expectations and the like. There are too many variables to mention in this report. It's a mystery wrapped in a conundrum engulfed by an enigma.

Based on many other news developments, so goes the stock. One event is particularly important: the Board of Directors meeting. The date of this event can be checked out, and nothing happens until they meet. This is significant. They discuss profits, available cash for dividends, mergers, share buy backs, stock splits, business plans, et cetera.

Do you see how important these topics are? Think of all the guesswork going on by people following the company. Rumor fires are easily kindled. Sometimes they get out of control. However they start, whatever they are, it all ends when the actual numbers and news hit the street.

All of this is very important, but then what? Where's the sequel? Where's the new news? It's now the end of July or first week of August. (The same could be applied to the end of the October/November or January/February or April/May periods.) The news is out. We don't have to wait as long as we did for Episode I—The Phantom Menace to come out in the Star Wars series, but wait we must. In short, in the absence of news, "this stock ain't going nowhere." The balloon isn't going up without hot air. The car isn't leaving the garage without gas. Superman isn't flying without his cape.

Here's a problem. What if we purchase stock at the height of this incredible (pre) news time? The stock has risen to $92. A big firm puts out a buy rating. Others follow. The company has even announced a stock split for August 20th, a Friday. It just looks peachy—how can you lose?

Oh, and what if you like options? Those funny little derivatives which rise and fall as the stock does—and erode as the time moves on toward the expiration date.

Options present an awesome opportunity to make money as long as the stock moves exactly like you want it to. If you buy a call option, the right to buy stock, you want the stock to go up. If it goes down or stays the same, you lose. Now ask yourself: Why am I buying this option when all the news has played out? At least ask, why did I buy the option with a near term expiration date? Maybe I should have bought the option with an expiration date at least into the next news reporting period.

Now all in all, observing this "news—no news" period should help us make wiser decisions. Decisions when to get in, decisions when to sell. Here is an important question: "What compelling reason does this stock have to go up?" More importantly, what compelling reason does this option have to go up in value? The answer is simple, but far-reaching. If there is nothing to drive it up—no news, no rumors, no nothing—then watch out.

Do you see where I now come up with "Red Light, Green Light?" A time to buy; a time *not* to buy. Now, notice I didn't say a time to sell. There are times when we should not be buying options. This goes back to a premise I've taught for years: the way to win at the stock market is to not lose! We need to avoid making mistakes. Buying a call option when a stock has nothing going on to help drive up the price is likely to be one of those mistakes.

A Look at the Calendar

By now you should have picked up on the important quarterly news periods. It helps sometimes to lay out a timeline or picture of the process. Before I do so, let's look again at a few things.

1. There are no set dates on which all companies start announcing newsy things. The dates vary. They are different because the board may meet at odd times. After the board meets the company may still make no announcement for several days or even weeks.

2. Many companies make very few pre-announcements, if any at all. Some make a lot. These announcements start about two weeks before the quarter end. Often you'll hear, "Well, we're entering the earnings season," meaning that news is about to come out. Some people "get it" on this part of the whole process. What you'll never hear from TV and newspaper reporters is this: "Well, we're leaving the earnings reporting season."

Before I go on to (3), let me tell an interesting story: We were having our speaker training two-day session in March, actually the Ides of March (March 15th) and the day after. It was in Seattle. We were discussing Microsoft. It's on everyone's mind in Seattle, as it's a Northwest company. There are news reports on it almost daily in our region.

The stock had been floundering from the middle of February through that time. I was explaining this whole new "news–no news" concept to our instructors. After awhile, the subject of Microsoft came up. It was about 9 or 10 A.M. on Monday. I pointed out that the stock was down and had been stagnant for a few weeks. I said, "Microsoft needs March 15th. Oh, it is March 15th! So the news announcements should start soon."

Shortly, news came out over the wire about the company laying a foundation to break up into five divisions in anticipation of a lawsuit settlement with the Feds. The stock went up a couple of dollars. A little while later there was more news. This time they announced that they might enter an agreement, or that they were in talks to possibly end the lawsuit. Up another dollar or so.

The next morning, March 16th, the word on the street was that they were going to blow away their numbers—meaning they were making more money than expected. All in all the stock was up something like $7 to $8 in those two days. I looked at my great instructors and said, "Seeeeeeeeeee?"

It doesn't take a genius to figure out that if there's bad news, especially about earnings, or no news, that the stock will go down. Anticipation and expectation of news reports play a big part of this game. If there's good news or rumors of good news, the stock reacts accordingly. The old expression, "No news is good news" is out the window here. It's the opposite now: "No news is bad news" is more like it.

This leads up to number (3).

3.   A lot of stock movement depends on the quality of the news. At the time of this writing our economy is mediocre. Some companies are earning a lot of money. Some are struggling. My guess is that 60 to 80% of today's news is bad and about 20 to 40% is good. This will change.

So with a lot of cautious news hitting the streets, why do some stocks go up while other stocks go down? Sometimes, on good news stocks go down. Then conversely, on bad news stocks go up. One answer is that many investors base their purchases on the anticipation of future earnings. Dell, for example, went up (had positive earnings announcements) 32 quarters in a row. One quarter—the winter of 99—they just hit their earnings estimates and the stock got tanked. They're still a great company, earning millions, but some anticipate future sluggishness and the stock reacts. The marketplace is a giant auction. A stock goes for what someone will pay for it. Built into this are many factors, and one of the most important is anticipation of future earnings growth.

Check the quality of the news. Watch for news on one company and how it affects others in the same field. Observing this will let you see many buying and selling opportunities.

4.   Not all companies follow the same exact time schedule. Many space out their announcements over a few days. Many make all of the news announcements at one time.

Often these announcements are known "on the street" way before the press conference. Ask your broker about the "whisper numbers." See what other companies have

133

done. Try to get a handle on the direction of the stock. Most importantly, be careful of buying call options on stocks going into or in the middle of a "red light" no news period. Look for compelling reasons for a stock to increase. If you find none, watch out. Back off. Consider selling your calls or stocks in the midst of the newsy "green light" period—wait through the "red light" period, and buy again on dips on the other side of the red light time when the new news starts up again.

If the news is negative or the "red light" period has started, consider buying puts or doing Bear Call Spreads (see *Wall Street Money Machine Vol. 4*). In short, time your entrance and exit points for later.

The Year—Ups and Downs

Look at the following 14-month graph. Note, this is a generality. *Any particular* stock's movement is based on many things—certainly not just a chart in a book.

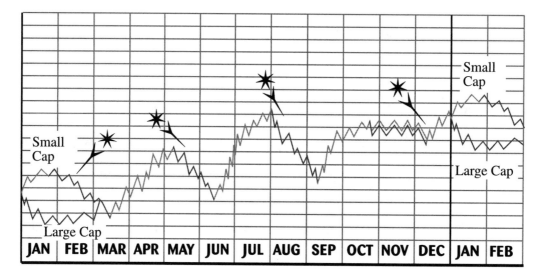

Observe:
1. The serious dips are in Feb, May, August, a neutral November and bad first two weeks of December.✳
2. October is a strange month with many erratic stocks.
3. Look at the arrows. These represent the start of the news talk, the "green light" period.

4. The months following the year end are erratic because of the quality of the news, plus share buy-backs and stock splits.

Imagine now with me the following:

1. A company's stock goes up $10 in March. In late February or early March they announced a 2:1 stock split. The stock is splitting in the middle of May, though— a "red light" or no news period. Look at the following charts.

2. A high tech stock has good news and several more rise up with it. But look at the subsequent month or so. They all move up or down based on news and no news.

Look at 4 graphs of the Dow 30 stocks. Even if the stock is on an up-trend or a down-trend, the good (news) months and bad (no news) months are pronounced. Remember irregularities are caused by the quality of the news and other factors. Be careful when you buy options which expire in Red Light months. The big gaps in the stock line usually represent a stock split.

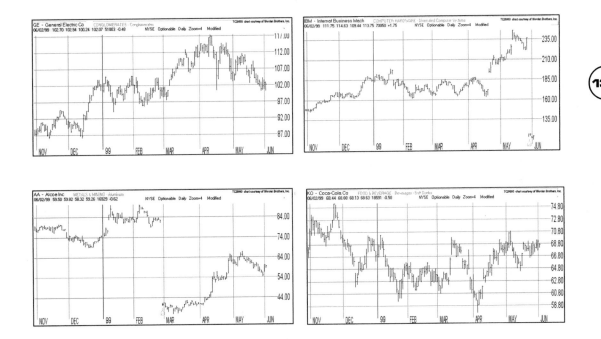

135

A Few of the Dow 30

I'm going to include four more Dow 30 stocks here so you can see how they fit the pattern. I'll comment more in the *Red Light, Green Light* book where I look at exceptions, pattern breakers and how to use my 13 cash flow strategies in light of the "Red Light, Green Light" process. Look for the book in 2002.

Also, after I shared this information with one of my stockbrokers, he sent me a 40 plus year history of market ups and downs. Now look at 40 years of S&P research on a monthly graph, superimposed with the news graph. Again, look at February, May and August. You may want to consider going on vacation. At least play bearish strategies going into these periods. The chart doesn't show a bad first two weeks of December, as the year-end rallies have bailed out the whole month and made the Decembers look good. However, look at the 9 graphs from 1991 through 1999 on the following.

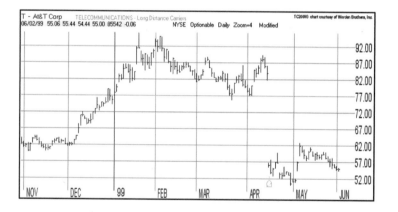

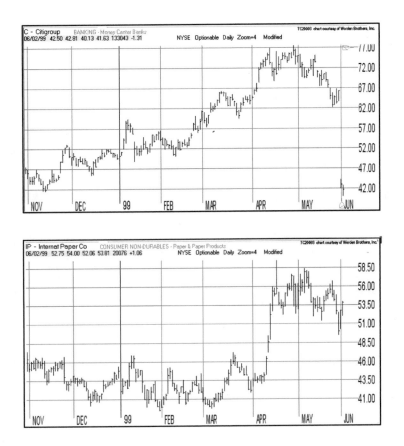

Also, after I shared this information with one of my stockbrokers, he sent me a 40 plus year history of market ups and downs. Now look at 40 years of S&P research on a monthly graph, superimposed with the news graph. Again, look at February, May and August. You may want to consider going on vacation. At least play bearish strategies going into these periods. The chart doesn't show a bad first two weeks of December, as the year-end rallies have bailed out the whole month and made the Decembers look good. However, look at the 9 graphs from 1991 through 1999 on the following page.

137

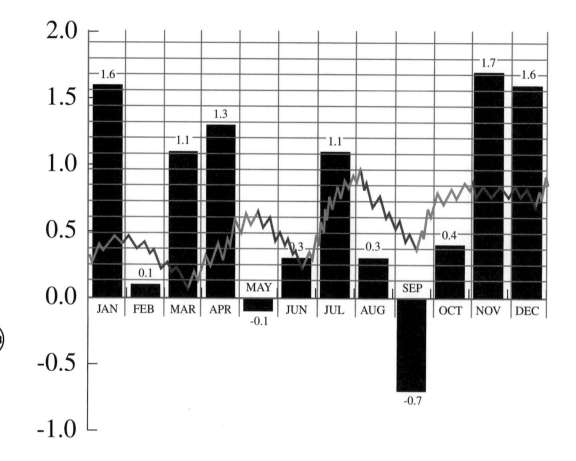

The following two pages are not only given to show the quarterly patterns, but to show the downturn in the first part of December and then the rally into the end of the year (except 1997). After looking at the graph above, you'll wonder why I've even commented on December (first part) being a cautious time. The answer is that December usually closes higher at the end of the month than where it began. However, if you play options, they expire on the 3rd Friday. If the stock (hence, the options) dip, they may not recover by the expiration date.

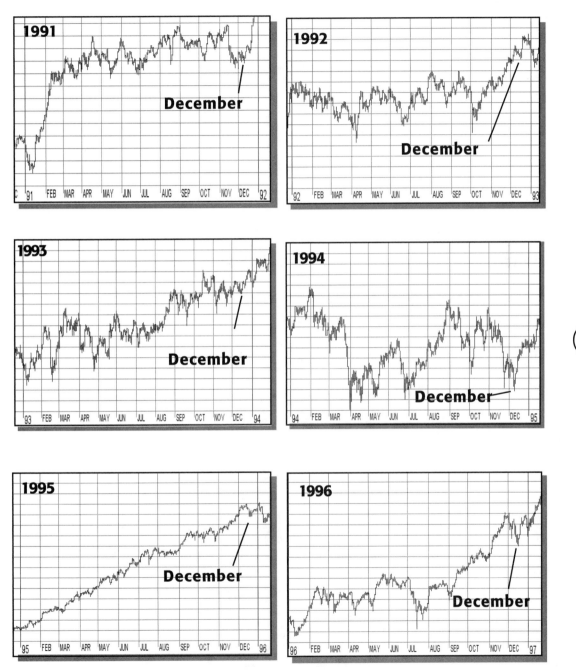

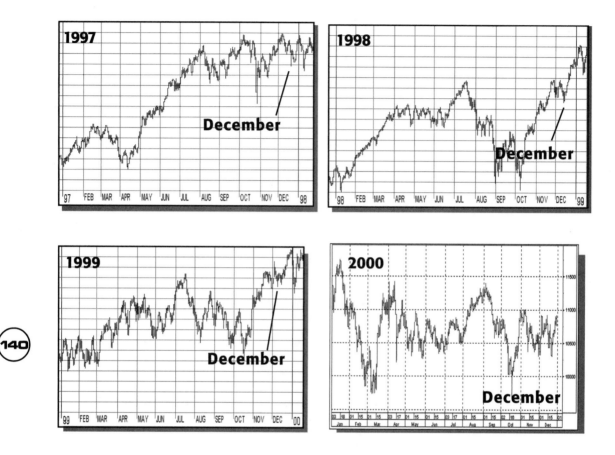

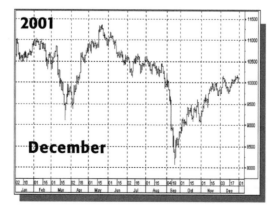

MOVING ON

Now let's look at a 40 year breakdown by the days of the month. Do you still see trends? Please don't think that because a particular day is bad historically, that it will be so this year. Yes, this year is different. Every year is different. It takes high days and low days to get an average. Averages don't tell you exactly what Sept. 14, 2004 will do. All this information is good for is to add to our knowledge base so we have many (hopefully) contrasting opinions upon which we base our decisions.

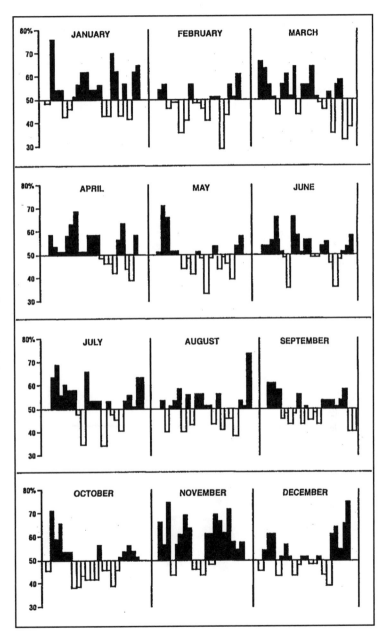

Summary

This chapter is about making better decisions, timing our entrance and exit points for more enhanced cash flow. The more dots we connect, the better for this process. The better for our bottom line. We also discussed the quantity and quality of news—how even the company's "anticipation of news" period drives a stock up or down. Option trades need movement in the right direction to be profitable. Before buying calls or puts, ask the all-important question: What compelling reason does the stock have to go up (or down for puts)? If you don't have a good answer, then refraining from trading may be the best trade.

12

Selling Puts

Many years ago I made a bold statement about selling puts. To paraphrase, I said, "Selling puts with the roll out feature is a strategy where you can't lose." Now, with thousands of trades under my belt, I'd like to revisit that statement. Was it true then? Is it true now? Does it bear up under scrutiny? Should it be amended or ended? You decide.

First of all, this sentence, written and spoken, has to be put into context. Either in books or in seminars, this and all other Wade Cook strategies are formulas with a beginning, a middle and an end. These formulas have rules. These formulas are to be used in a specific market situation—"A time to hold, a time to fold." The "How to's" are important, but the "Why to's" are oftentimes more important. Diane Ravitch said, "The man who knows how will always have a job, the man who knows why will always be his boss."

Selling puts, for example, is a bullish strategy and should only be used in bull markets or when a specific stock is moving up in a bullish manner. If used at other times, it could spell disaster.

Selling puts also has basic rules. Two basic criteria are, first: you like the company and either want to own the stock, or at least wouldn't mind owning the stock. Second, you like the stock at this particular price (strike). No one should ever sell a put on a stock they do not want to own. Backing up these two simple rules is a whole foundation of wise decision-making strategies. For example, to know whether you want to own the stock you should check company fundamentals, check earnings and earnings growth, yields, debt levels and analysts reports. It would be naïve to isolate one particular strategy and ignore all the other rules—including using common sense.

Now, one more point. No one should invest or trade without a good, effective stockbroker. This is a basic rule of all my books and seminars. Most retail stock brokers know little of effectively trading options. Simple things like getting the best price off of four different option marketplaces; or cross market trades; or even the margin or hold requirements when an uncovered put is sold. Many of them do not know how to unwind trades. NEVERTHELESS, it is paramount that an investor work out "trade suitability" with their broker. For example, we teach formulas—the ins-and-outs, the entrance and exit points, the "how's" and "why's", but that does not make the formula right for that particular person and it surely does not make that specific trade right at that time. These determinations have to be made by each person's professional stockbroker.

This is why we have our students sign an agreement that they will get proper professional help. We guarantee no results.

In fact, we encourage our students to simulation trade (simu-trade) or paper trade. They should do each type of trade at least fifteen times on paper, of which ten in a row should be profitable, before they ever use real money—and then, again, only under the direction of their stockbroker. In fact, they should paper trade with their stockbroker to get him or her up to speed. This also helps their stockbroker learn what the investor is either expecting in profits, or what they would tolerate in losses.

Next, another basic tenet of what we teach is to only use a small portion of investing capital on riskier trades. So, for example, if someone has $100,000, only $5,000 to $6,000 (maybe $10,000 if the investor has more experience) should be used. We realize some stockbrokers will allow or even encourage some people to put the whole $100,000 into riskier trades, but as we are the company that teaches "safety first" we discourage this.

In fact, some brokers will not even allow their clients to sell uncovered puts unless they have $50,000 in their accounts. They know of the risk, but do not show the downside. We do.

Last, when you sell a put you are giving someone the right to sell you stock ("put it to you") at a predetermined price. Back to rule #1: Why, oh why, would you sell to someone the right to put you the stock if you don't want to own it and don't have the money to buy it?

With all this being said, let's explore the "can't lose" statement in the real world. Selling a put option is a cash flow strategy. A put is the right to sell stock to someone at a set price, called the strike price. Many people buy puts when they think a stock is going down. Look at this chart:

Stock	Strike Price	Put Price BID ASK
$44	$40	$1.50 X $1.60
$42	$40	$2.25 X $2.35
$40	$40	$3.00 X $3.15
$38	$40	$3.50 X $3.70
$36	$40	$4.75 X $4.95

This chart does not speak to the erosion of time, but is given as a simple statement of how puts increase in value as the stock moves lower. Many people *buy* puts on a stock which has moved up in price, but may back off. This put then protects against downward movements.

Selling puts is substantially different. In selling puts, we take in money for taking on an obligation. We get paid money now for giving someone the right to sell us a stock. In selling puts, we think the stock is going up. Buying puts is bearish, selling puts is bullish.

Let's use the chart on this page. If the stock is at $42 and we think it's going down, we could buy the $40 puts for $2.35. Option contracts are in groups of 100, meaning 100 shares, so to buy one contract would cost $235. We would have the right, but not the obligation, to put this stock to someone at $40. We would do this if the stock drops below $40. However, we don't have to put this stock to someone to make money. If the stock drops $2, to $40, your put could be worth $3, or $300. Sell the put and pocket $65. Ten contracts would cost $2,350, sell for $3,000 and make $650 (minus commissions).

Now, lets sell the put. Remember, though, this time we think the stock will move up. We've checked the fundamentals (story line) and technicals (support levels, moving averages, etc.) and we're confident the stock has bottomed out and is going up. We sell the $40 put at the bid of $3. Ten contracts would generate $3,000. That's cash from selling the put and $3,000 will be in our account the next trading day.

What have we done? Yes, we've made $3,000, but we've taken on an obligation to let someone put (sell) us this stock at $40. Again, we've got to like the stock and like it at this price. However, we're not necessarily selling this put to get the stock. We're selling the put to keep the cash, the $3,000.

So, how do we keep it? If the stock stays above $40, we will not get the stock put to us and on the expiration date, the obligation expires and we keep the $3,000, again minus transaction costs.

If the stock goes up, and remember, that is what we thought would happen, we won't get it put to us. If the stock stays the same, around $42, it won't get put to us. If the stock goes down, then we have to be careful. If it goes down a little, say 50¢ or $1.50, we would still be okay. If it goes below

$40 and stays there, on expiration we would get put the stock at $40. We would have to have cash to pay for 1,000 shares at $40.

One of three things can happen when the stock drops below $40.

1.   It can go back up above $40 and expire wherein we just keep the $3,000.

2.   We get put the stock. This will only happen *before* the expiration date if there is virtually no "time value" left in the option premium. In most cases the stock is not put to anyone early. That would require someone (we don't know whom) exercising their option and the OCC (Option Clearing Corporation) randomly selecting us to get the stock. This rarely happens if there is still premium (time value) in the option. The point is, most options are exercised on the expiration date. This gives the trader ample time to clean up his position, ie., end it.

Note: Again, as the company which teaches safety first, and eliminating risk, the trader should have his "stop out" points. For example, if the stock goes down, he would be out at, say $4, or $4,000, with a $1,000 loss. (Sell for $3,000, and buy back for $4,000 = $1,000 loss.) this is much better than taking the stock at $40, if the stock is at $35.

3.   Buy back the option to stop the obligation. As noted above, as long as there is an "open" position, the position can be ended by "buying back" the option. This is a simple process and it can be done at a profit, loss or break even.

A.   Profit. We are able to buy back the position, the $40 put, but it costs us less than $3. The stock goes down to $41, but time has elapsed. On the Monday before the third Friday expiration date, the option is $1.25. We buy it back for $1.25 (A simple 30 second phone call) and we make $1,750 ($3,000 minus $1,250 = $1,750, minus costs).

B.   Loss. We have to pay $4, or $4,000 to buy back ten contracts with the same expiration date. This process ends our position. It ends our obligation. It ends our margin hold and we're free to move on.

C.   Break Even. The stock tanks, but this time it goes below the strike price, to, say, $37.50. Time has elapsed. The $40 put is now $3.00 It costs us $3,000 to end the position. We are at break even, but lose a little because of two commissions.

This is a lengthy discussion to get to the point at hand. We now need to delve into point B above. That of a loss.

When we sell a put, we're primarily selling the time value, or speculative value. Rarely do I sell in-the-money puts. An in-the-money put would be selling the $40 put when the stock is at $38. This stock price is under the strike price. This is called in-the-money. Now, to keep the cash of $3,500 ($3.50 each 1,000), the stock needs to _go up_ and stay up above $40 to capture and keep 100% of the option premium. You'd have to be excessively bullish on this position to do this. I frown on in-the-money sell put plays. Yes, the premiums are larger, but the risk is greater.

I like to sell out-of-the-money or at-the-money puts. The stock is at $42 and going up. I want that $2 pad between $42 and $40. In fact, the $38 put was going for .75¢ more. That might be the better deal. Okay, back to the $42 stock. All of the $2.25 is time value. Even the $40 stock, with a $40 strike price, makes the whole $3,000 time value. None of it is in-the-money.

If we are in a loss position, and if we don't want the stock to get put to us, which is usually the case, then we can buy back the put and end the risk. You see, when we sell a put, we create a synthetic stock position. We have all the downside risk of owning a stock, but our upside potential is limited to the put premium we sold. If we get a stock at $40 and it goes down to $25 or $5, that's bearish and a huge potential loss. We could still wait it out, write covered calls while we're waiting for the stock to recover, or sell the stock and put our money to work in a better place. We don't want this to happen, so if we didn't put our "stops" in place to get out of this position and we see that the $40 put is going for $5, we'd better close the position and end the chance that the stock will get put to us.

$5. Hmm. That would cost $5,000 and we would be underwater by $2,000. Remember, we originally took in $3,000. Now, we're not here to lose, but we're down by $2,000. If you still believe in this stock—again, check the storyline, the news, etc.—then look at the $40 puts the next month out. You are selling "time." The $40 puts for the next month out are going for $7. Sell ten contracts for $7,000. You took in $3,000 six weeks ago. You spent $5,000 and were temporarily down $2,000. Now this $7,000 puts you up $5,000. You just might have bettered your position. You had better be really bullish to do this trade. You now still need this stock to go above and stay above $40 for the whole $5,000 to remain yours.

You might want to consider two more things:

1) Sell the $35 puts for $3. You take in $3,000. You're $1,000 profitable again, but now the stock needs to stay above $35. This is a safer position.

2) Get your money away from this stock. If it's fallen in value, maybe the bad news isn't over yet. Move your money and take in $7,000, or $3,000 on a totally different stock with a better chance.

Okay, what if you sell the $40 put and the stock still goes down? Its at $32 and near the next expiration date (October). $40 puts are now $9, or $9,000. You were up $5,000, you're now down $4,000 ($9,000 minus $5,000 = $4,000 loss). The $35 puts for the next month out are $6, or $6,000. Sell and you're $2,000 ahead. The stock goes down over the next month. It cost $5,000 to buy back the $35 puts for November, but the $35 puts for December are $6, or $6,000. Again, from $3,000 behind to $3,000 ahead. You can do this month after month. Eventually, the stock should turn around. If it doesn't, get your money out of there. Buy back your obligation put and sell one to recover cash in a better trade.

Yes, this process takes careful "babysitting," but the results are worthwhile. One caution: diversify. Don't tie up too much money here. The "hold" amount in the account is about 20% plus the premium. This amount is on hold until the expiration date, or sooner if the position is ended early. You should discuss this with your stockbroker. The opposite side of a 20% coin is 80%.

147

$10,000 could mean $50,000 in stock purchase commitments, which might happen with a serious dip in the market.

To me, selling puts is still a favorite. Why? Because you have a $2\frac{1}{2}$ chance out of 3 of making money. Also, when you buy options, time is your enemy. When you sell options, time becomes your friend and ally. Also, major traders make their money selling, I think we should too.

Lastly, if we practice trade, find a really good broker, keep in mind "all" rules of trading, baby-sit our position and effectively work the buy back/roll out strategy, there is a good likelihood of success.

A Sell Put on Krispy Kreme

Real Life Example #1: Here is one of a "sell put" that went bad on us. You'll notice that we came out okay.

Trade	Description	Running	Total
1st Trade:	On August 27, 2001, before the terrorist attack, we sold 20 contracts of the Krispy Kreme Sep. $30 puts. They were $1.50 each.	Positive Income	$3,000
2nd Trade	On September 21, 2001 (expiration day) we "rolled out" to the November $27.50 puts. This roll out consists of two trades. First, we bought to close 20 contracts of the September $30 puts at $2.40 each.	Money Out	(-) $4,800
3rd Trade:	The second part of the roll out is to now sell 20 contracts of the November $27.50 puts. They were $3.00	Cash In	$6,000
4th Trade:	On October 4, 2001, after the stock had moved up a bit, we bought to close the 20 contracts of November $27.50 puts at .65¢ each.	Money Out	(-) $1,300
Expenses	Transaction Costs	Money Out	(-) $400
	Total Profit		$2,500

SUMMARY: Cash In, Trade	#1	$3,000
	#3	6,000
		$9,000
Cash Out, Trade	#2	4,800
	#4	1,300
Gross Profit		$2,900
Minus Estimated Trans. Cost		400
Net Profit		$2,500

In spite of the trade not going our way initially, we still came out on top with $2,500.

A Sell Put on Microsoft

Real Life Example #2: Another example of a "sell put" that went bad on us. You'll notice that we came out more than okay.

SUMMARY: Cash In, Trade	#1	$2,200
	#3	53,050
	#4	1,100
	#5	600
	#6	65,051
		122,001
Cash Out, Trade	#2	110,000
Gross Profit		$12,001
Minus Estimated Trans. Cost		900
Net Profit		$11,101

Trade	Description	Running Total	
1st Trade:	On August 22, 2001, before the terrorist attack, we sold 20 contracts of the Microsoft September $55 put. They were 1.10 each	Positive Income	$2,200
2nd Trade:	On the September expiration we were assigned 2,000 shares of Microsoft at $55. We spent $110,000, but about $55,000 on margin. We could have bought back the contracts, but we wanted the stock.	Money Out	(-) $110,000
3rd Trade:	On October 2, 2001, we sold 1,000 shares of Microsoft for $53.05 per share, to use the money elsewhere.	Money In	$53,050
4th Trade:	On October 4, 2001, we wrote a covered call on Microsoft stock—1,000 shares, our remaining stock for $1.10, taking in $1,100. This was the $60 strike price call.	Cash In	$1,100
Expiration:	On October 22nd, the $60 calls expired. We kept the stock and the $1,100.		
5th Trade:	On October 31st, we sold 10 contracts of the November $65 calls for .60¢, taking in another $600.	Cash In	$600
Expiration:	On November 19th the $65 calls expired; we kept the stock and the $600.		
6th Trade:	On November 26, 2001, we sold 1,000 shares of Microsoft—some at $65.01, some at $65.09 and some at $65.10, taking in $65,051	Cash In	$65,051
Expenses	Transaction Costs		(-) $900
	Total Net Profit		$11,101

We made a little over $11,000 and only originally wanted to make $2,200.

13

Bottom Fishing: A Unique Approach

This chapter is my attempt to shed light on the process of expensing assets gone sour. First of all, let me restate some of the nomenclature of the current era. One can frequently read financial reports with the words, "one-time expense," or "one-time charge." Also used are expressions like, "non-recurring charge," and even "one-time write-offs" or "write-downs." A common similar statement is "restructuring change."

This is simply a process of taking an investment and turning it into an expense. These investments are usually in the form of business purchases, as in Boeing buying McDonnell Douglas. Sometimes these investments are stock or partnership unit purchases in other companies. Once in awhile these investments are in divisions or subsidiaries a company has started, still holds, or has spun off. Also of note is the term "blue sky," or someone's guess as to the value of an existing business or part of it. This term "blue sky" is often associated with the value of employees—say, the business they create. News reports of 28,000 people being laid off may contain additional facts that the company is "taking a $200,000,000 charge for blue sky." One last charge or write-down could be from the discontinuance of a product line or the loss of a copyright or lawsuit.

All of the above "investments" are carried on the company's books as some type of investment. It is listed in the financial section under assets. It could be "non-marketable securities," in the case of stock ownership in another company. It could be "real estate" or "business owned" in other cases.

One interesting side note with extensive dynamics is just how the asset is carried in relation to its real value. According to Generally Accepted Accounting Principles (GAAP), an asset is carried on the books at the cost (basis) or market value, whichever is less. This offends the sensibilities of most non-accounting types. "You mean the $1,000,000 apartment building, which has been depreciated to $800,000 but is worth $2,000,000 or more, can only be listed on the books at $800,000?" The answer: YES.

Adjustment to these asset values should be adjusted to each Securities Exchange Commission ("SEC") for public companies filing—with each financial statement, so long as there is a substantial or noticeable change since the last filing. Let's explore this. Company A is a 20% investor in Company B. Company A has purchased 5,000,000 shares of stock at $1 per share. It's been two years. The B company is doing great, but needs more money. The next offering (PPM) is for $20,000,000, but this time the shares go for $2 each. Yes, Company A's shares in Company B might now be worth $2 each, but they still have to be carried on the books at $1 each, or $5,000,000.

Now, let's go the other way. Company B is not doing too well. It needs more money. This time, shares (the same type) are offered at 50¢ each. Now, sadly, Company A's investment is reduced to this amount. It's $5,000,000 investment is now valued at $2,500,000. We'll get to the other $2,500,000 in awhile.

All of this is done, regardless of the fact that this Company B goes public in one year and the stock goes out at $14 per share.

Let's return now and see how an investment, carried on the books under assets, becomes an expense. Then we'll explore the stock valuation and tax implications. There are two basic financial documents in every SEC filing. Yes, there could be hundreds of back-up documentation forms and pages, but these have a genesis in either the Income Statement (some might still call it the Profit and Loss statement) and the Financial Statement or Balance Sheet. This Financial Statement, once again, lists assets, liabilities, then the net worth at the bottom.

Once an asset has shrunk in value, or if either inside accounting or outside auditors feel that the asset is no longer viable, a decision is made to write it off. Quite simply, it disappears from the asset column (all or part of it) and finds its way to the expense side of the income statement. Its treated, pretty much, like any other expense.

Now, two things have happened. One, the company's net worth is less. The other is that the company is now making less money. Let's explore this aspect first.

A $100,000,000 write-off could seriously reduce the current profit, or earnings of the company. Many people follow earnings. They base their stock valuations on earnings. It takes a savvy investor—ever a student of the market—to read behind the headlines. For example, recently JDS Uniphase (JDSU) had headlines reporting a "$7.9 Billion" loss. The stock tanked. If you were to read the report, you would have read that it had operating income of 2¢ a share. "How," you ask, "can a company which is making money report a $7.9 billion loss?" Simple. They just wrote off $7.9 billion dollars worth of investments, purchases and "blue sky."

Boeing was set to announce fairly good earnings one quarter last year. The stock had risen nicely over the previous nine months, but especially so in the two to three weeks before their earnings announcement. Then, suddenly, they announced a $280,000,000 charge-off—a non-recurring item—for their previous purchase of McDonnell Douglas.

Recently, Microsoft announced quarterly earnings of only $1,200,000,000—a noble feat by any measuring stick. If you read on, however, you would have found a $1.3 billion charge for "poor investments." I guess some of their dot.com escapades didn't pan out—like who hasn't had bad dot.com investments? Are you getting these numbers? That's $2,500,000,000 in net earnings without the charge off. And this $2.5 billion is after taxes.

TAXES AND WRITE-OFFS

Let's stick with the Microsoft example. $1,300,000,000 as an expense creates a $455,000,000 tax savings at a 35% tax bracket. That's money the company can use to expand and grow and further build shareholder value.

Oh, and if an expense is large enough, it could wipe out all the net income this year, create an NOL (Net Operating Loss), which can be used to offset net profits from previous years or in future years. That's right! A loss could generate a return check from the IRS.

To recap: earnings are bad, the stock might go down; earnings are bad, there might be substantial tax savings. Do you see why it's so important to read further on in these reports and try to ascertain the true health of the company?

STRING OUT OR TAKE IT NOW

Obviously, not all investments a company makes are accomplished all at once. Likewise, all of a company's investments do not all go south simultaneously. Many companies write these bad assets off over a period of time, but there has been a dot.com fiasco of late of epic proportions.

The high-tech downturn, even if not directly invested in by a company, has been felt by everyone. Imagine now, that you're on the Board of Directors. You have the auditors report and some of your investments don't look too hot. In fact, some are worthless. You know it's going to look bad so what do you do? First choice: string out the bad news. Take some now, some next quarter and if possible, some at the end of the year, or next year. Second choice: pile on the bad. Get the bad news out of the way. Take the hit now and get on with life.

As of late, many companies have taken huge write-downs. And while for some companies, these investment write-offs are complete, others are still holding some bad assets, while others have assets which haven't completely soured yet. These "one-time expenses" occur all the time. They have just been more pronounced lately.

Also note another phenomena waiting in the wings. Just because a company has written off an investment doesn't mean that it no longer owns the investments. It's carried on the books, at a new zero-basis—maybe just a footnote in a supporting document, page 79. What if, just what if, there is a Phoenix? What if the asset can be sold, or the start-up eventually makes it? I know it's rare, but life has many mysteries. In this case the company re-books it as an asset (especially in the case of publicly traded stock) or claims the profits as income.

STOCK VALUATION

Any type of negative news, even the anticipation of news, can impact a stock. Rarely will a good investment a company makes be treated with equal time as its mistakes. In fact, there's no real place to report this type of good news. You won't see: "Company A's investment of $5,000,000 in Company B is now worth $60,000,000 after Company B's IPO." You'd have to be an expert financial report reader to find it out.

Bad news gets a lot of press. But remember, press reports are fleeting. They are on to tomorrow's story. You still own the stock in this company, with all the bad news. Do you hold, sell, or generate income, say by writing covered calls? Well, first, check the real story. Is it making money, or not? Are earnings growing or contracting? Again, was it truly a one-time charge, or is there more bad news around the corner? Listen carefully to what the company's leaders are saying. Are they bullish or not?

This next part is most difficult for us armchair investors. We need to kick the tires. We need to find out what the company is made of. Okay, it's had some bad investments, but has it had any good ones? How are they carrying assets on the books?

You see, assets are carried on the books as of the last Quarter's SEC filing. Some of these assets could be worth a substantial value more than how they are listed. However, it would be rare to see assets carried at less than their value. Remember, (GAAP)—"cost or market—whichever is lower."

Picture American Airlines with its land, gates, airplanes, etc. It could have billions of dollars carried as millions. WeyerHauser has millions of acres of land—with trees and other resources. Some of this land was purchased around the turn of the century—NO, the last one. Companies have invested in other companies with the hype of it going public. They're still waiting.

Book Value is a determination of a company's value based on the break-up and sale of the components. The Book Value is easy to find out—just call your broker, or most good computer programs (stock search) will list this value. It is not uncommon for a company's stock to be trading at two to three times Book. Many are at eight and ten times Book Value.

Let's look at this a little more closely. I can't stress enough, though, that the listed Book Value is how the assets are being carried, according to GAAP, and according to those values as of their last Quarterly Filing. Take a look at how many banks have been buying up regional banks. Granted, banks have odd reporting requirements. They carry loans on their books a certain way. These loans, plus assets, make up their Book Value. Their stock is at $20, but the Book Value is at $24. Their stock is at a discount to Book Value. They are a target for a takeover. Conversely, another bank's stock is at $14 and the Book Value is $10—AND it's still a target. Maybe even more so. Why? Because the true value of its assets are larger in real life than how they're being characterized on their books.

Now, away from banks, but let's still explore a takeover, or merger. Often, these transactions are done with stock, with little or no new cash. Sometimes, the assumption of debt is involved. It doesn't matter. There still is a valuation placed on the deal. It is carried on the books at that price. Do you see how the valuation of the stock in one company can be almost instantaneously affected by the rise or fall of a sister stock?

RESTRICTED TRADING TO FREE TRADING

Many companies have invested in private companies with the hope that this new company would go public. This private stock, once the company nears the going public process, is often called Rule 144 stock, or restricted stock. There are other names, but these will suffice. If the new company goes public, the investing company is under serious restrictions as to when and how fast it can sell the new stock.

The holding time is now just one year. So, Company B goes public. Either the stock Company A owns is registered in the IPO (unlikely and it still has selling restrictions) or Company A submits Form 144 and registers an appropriate amount of stock for sale. This registration is good for 90 days. If selling volume increases, a new registration can be done, even before the previous 90 days have expired. However, even though the company has registered this stock, it doesn't necessarily mean it has to sell this stock. Maybe the price drops, or news comes out that something good is about to happen with the thought that the stock might go up. They wait to sell. For this discussion on valuations, the important point is this: this registered, now free-trading stock, can be listed on the books at the current stock market price. For years, all of this stock still had to be carried on the asset portion of the ledger at the original cost. Do you see how our $1 stock, now worth $14 or $114 could be carried at the original lower value?

This is important. Once again, it is possible that a million dollar investment, now worth billions, is carried at the original cost until it goes public and is registered.

INCUBATORS

This discussion will take on added meaning when we explore a few incubator-type companies. Incubators in this regard are companies which have as their business plan that of investing in or helping companies to go public. There are simply not many publicly traded companies that do this. Here are a few: Safeguard Scientific (SFE); CMGI (Ticker the same); and Internet Capital Group (ICGE). You might recognize one or two of these. They had stocks in the $100 to $200 range. What happened? Many of their holdings, and most of their work, was in the high-tech companies—some primarily in Internet companies. The bottom fell out on this arena and, while hundreds of companies were set to do IPO's and go public, the last few years have seen this IPO business, once a fire hydrant of activity, come to a trickle.

Okay, the "take public company" is almost dead, but as Billy Crystal said as Max in *The Princess Bride*, "He's only *mostly* dead." These companies still have huge investments in companies which have gone public (SFE was 20% of Telelabs: TLAB), or are still private, but waiting to go public.

So, before I go on, I want to pose a question. Please ponder this and come up with an answer. One of these companies owns stock in say 30 different companies. Some of this stock has been owned for four to six years. Some of the little companies have totally gone out of business. This original list was 52, now 30. Some are making good money and most are just waiting for the IPO market to turn around, then they will go public.

Here's the question: how are these assets carried on their books? Cost or Market? More or less? Could the asset be worth less than their original investment? Yes, in the real world. But...but...even though the company is making money; and even though it's ready to go public at $30 a share, their $1 purchase priced stock is still on the books at $1. My point: Kick the tires. I'm not recommending these stocks, always look at their share price compared to their Book Value.

As of 10/29/01

Company	Stock Price	Book
SFE	2.49	4.70
CMGI	1.65	5.92
ICGE*	0.79	0.87

* Note the closeness of the stock price and Book Value. Remember, this is *Internet Capital Group, Inc*. All of its holdings are Internet related. Could this be the reason its Book Value is so low?

These value comparisons are from incubator-type companies, but lest you think these are the only companies trading at less than Book Value, look at the following. I've thrown in the Price/Earnings ratios for fun.

Company	Stock Price	Book	P/E
ITWO	5.13	16.67	—
CNET	5.15	14.50	—
LENS	4.28	5.63	—
MIND	4.95	6.04	—
ITX	4.87	11.64	10
COLT	7.71	10.91	—
CREAF	5.89	6.14	2
SKS	7.03	15.96	12
OPTV	7.90	29.23	—
MTZ	4.61	10.48	3

I want to reemphasize that these Book Values are out of each company's latest SEC Filings. It is possible, but highly unlikely, that the Book Values shown here could be less than what's listed. However, it is highly likely that any one of these companies' book values could have assets, valued in the real world, at substantially greater values than what is listed. We're told in life to accentuate the positive. The SEC tells us to accentuate the negative.

SUMMARY

This discussion has two punchlines, or two endings, if you will. Both of these insights are valuable. I come at this as a president of a publicly traded company (Wade Cook Financial Corporation: WADE) I live this discussion every day. Simple things affect our stock. For example, when we register stock (Rule 144) which we own in a company which has gone public, it becomes a marketable security. Not only does its value increase to the street value, but it now shows up as a short-term asset. The ratio of short-term assets to short-term liabilities is important to some analysts, so we like restricted stock to become free trading stock. I could go on for hours, as we have investments in several companies which have gone public or we hope will soon go public.*

Okay, the two endings:

#1) One-time expenses seems to be a current epidemic. Hopefully the waterfall will be over soon, and we'll return to a more peaceful cascade of water. To me, this means opportunity. Stocks are low. P/E's are low, even from the historical 15% P/E averages. Stock prices today are as low as option prices a few years ago. Add the shedding of bad investments, with a tax cut, lower interest rates and an economy beaten down, but trying to recover, and I feel good.

Please note: these charge-offs, one-time expenses and the immature way the media reports them are not over, but much of the bad news is past tense.

#2) With Book Values written down—GAAP-wise—it's time to find real bargains. Once the economy revives, two things will happen: (A) Companies will start doing IPO's (going public) and hence their stocks will reflect a truer value, and (B) companies will start aggressively taking over other companies. They'll look for a relationship strategy first, then they'll look for value. And as far as I can tell, there is value everywhere.

So, for me, the glass is half full. I'm looking for value and opportunity. I want to get my money in the way of movement. A small part of that money will be in companies which own stock in a diversified slice of the American Pie.

14

My Favorite Value is Companies with Recurring Cash Flow: Excerpts from W.I.N.™

The following is excerpted from Wade's comments on W.I.N. (Wealth Information Network) on Thursday, January 31, 2002.

Good morning everyone! This is Wade.

I would like to do a quick commentary on some of my purchases recently in regards to some Bargain Hunting and Bottom Fishing I have been doing. I am specifically talking about Arkona Inc. (ARKN). I want you to know up front that I am not an insider to this company. I do not have any special information, nor do I want to be an insider. I can go to their website and check out some of the news items and read their prior notices that come over the wire just like anyone else.

I do, however, want to note that I am an investor in this company purchasing restricted stock. This is Rule 144 stock, and I have to meet all of the requirements under the SEC regulations for holding that particular stock. For example, holding the stock for one year—and then being able to only sell so much at one time when the hold period is up. However, at the current time, I am also buying stock on the open market.

In Bargain Hunting and Bottom Fishing, I go looking for companies that have a really good product for sale, in conjunction with a dynamic management team. I have often said to "bet on the jockey, not on the horse." I made a trip to Sandy, UT to check out this company and to meet with the management team, and I was very impressed. There obviously are no guarantees that a business plan (as presented in a company's literature) is going to succeed, but when there is a really great product – indeed a superior product – then it could create a situation where the "world beats a path to your door."

Before I say any more about this product, let me tell you one of the things I look for. For any of you that have attended my seminars or read my books, you will know that I am big into monthly cash flow. Let me state that another way: I am big into perpetual monthly income, or ongoing revenue streams. What that means is that actions today, or work performed now, should produce income in the future.

Let me give you an example: Those of you that are in business know that the cost of purchasing a copy machine is significant. But sometimes not as significant as the ongoing expense of keeping the copy machine working. You have maintenance contracts, labor and parts, and continuous problems with copy machines. I sometimes wonder if the sellers of the copy machines make more money off of the actual sale of the machine or off of the ongoing service and maintenance?

A similar situation would be an automobile dealership. I know that, in spite of their advertising to the contrary, they make money off the sale of a car. But again, I wonder if they make just as much money over the long term off of the service and the maintenance of the car. When you think about the parts that are sold, the excess accessories, and the back room maintenance of a car dealership, I think that is where the steady income can be generated. In fact, even if a car dealership has a bad month from time to time, the labor charges and the sale of parts can, I think, substantially sustain a dealership. I could list hundreds of other businesses that operate the same way.

Mentally, to my students, I have encouraged them to try and build up a positive monthly income. For example, Writing Covered Calls or Selling Puts on a monthly basis, and to in fact use the stock market as a cash flow machine—a business enterprise that can potentially support not only the ongoing enterprise, but also provide money to pay the bills and support their families. I have often quipped that a PMA, or a positive mental attitude, is so much better when you have PMI, or positive monthly income.

I go looking for companies that have ongoing revenues, especially revenues that can be derived from work done today. I will give you a fictitious example: If I had a chance of buying into a company that supplied clothes hangers for dry cleaning businesses, and had an ongoing business relationship with numerous dry cleaning businesses, that to me would be a very exciting business. I realize that it is not high-tech, I realize it doesn't have glitz, and I realize it doesn't have the jazz and pizzazz that a lot of other businesses seem to have.

However, I also realize in a business like this, there would likely be low volatility, therefore option prices would not be very high for selling purposes like in selling puts or writing covered calls. This type of business excites me because they have monthly income to sustain their current operations and hopefully monthly income that will continue to grow. This should speak to the growth of earnings, which could also speak to the current price of the stock and the future value of the stock or its growth potential.

Even in the company where I am the CEO, Wade Cook Financial Corporation (WADE), we are looking for different enterprises that have ongoing income streams. If someone purchases a seminar from me, unless they purchase another one, the income from that customer stops. So we are developing Daily I.Q.™ and several other business enterprises that will not only provide quality continuing education for our students, but also produce a steady cash flow.

Let me now speak to one of the things that I would like to do. I see that a big part of my future may be in an "incubator" type operation. By that I mean, in finding undervalued companies; finding and discovering assets that are way below value; and finding and helping other companies go public.

I think that the valuation of a private company going into the public arena is quite a substantial leap, and I want to be involved in that process with many companies. The last few years have been most difficult in the IPO marketplace. The going public process has been hampered with the downturn in the stock market. It just seems that people in general have been mentally in a rut, and have been in the doldrums to the point that they don't have high expectations for the future.

For many of my stock market strategies, this type of attitude is okay. But for those that are hoping to take a company public and raise money from potential investors, this has put a real damper on prospects. In all of this, I see the opportunity for Bargain Hunting and Bottom Fishing. In fact, I have come across several companies that fit these two strategies. There is obviously no guarantee that any of them will go public, and it is quite possible to "make it in ours, lose it in theirs."

Now I have mentioned several of these companies in a new question and answer formatted message to our shareholders which we are putting in the Investor Relations section of www.wadecook.com about Wade Cook Financial Corporation. Please go there and read it and also make sure that you read the disclaimer, which is the "Forward Looking Statement" disclaimer.

One of the companies I invested in as a private investor was a company originally called Sundog Technologies. They did a name change to Arkona, Inc. I have made numerous references to this company in the past. I started buying some of the free trading stock at .18 cents and .22 cents a share, which by the way was substantially less than some of the restricted stock that I had purchased. I even had an agreement to buy more restricted stock, again, which must meet securities guidelines on hold requirements. I also believe in this company's product.

In fact, I am very excited about this company's product, because it has all the characteristics I mentioned before, including that of creating ongoing revenues. Here is a company that over the last five years has developed a software program for running and managing car dealerships. Once again, it sounds like a "coat hanger special", but I love this type of business. You can go check out exactly what they do at www.arkona.com. They have a really high quality, state of the art software program that manages all aspects of car dealerships, both new and used.

The program would help dealerships manage not only accounting, payroll and commissions, but also inventory, parts, the backroom and all other aspects of their businesses which could include all kinds of peripheral items like advertising and marketing, sales promotions and things like that.

This company seems to have been very successful as of late. They have approached Mitsubishi of North America and are rapidly installing the software program in many dealerships. They have also approached Ford Motor Company and General Motors and have been approved to put their software program into those dealerships. I hear they are so busy right now that they can hardly keep up with their demand. Once again, the reason I like them is not only because their product is good, but because the service and maintenance of their product once it is installed in a dealership, should produce ongoing revenues. This bodes well for the future if it continues to be successful. This company could be a buyout candidate and could also be a candidate for other investments – but it is definitely a candidate for ongoing revenue streams.

Yes, "Excessive profits breed ruinous competition", but right now, this company has a foothold in attracting new customers because it has what I believe is such an awesome product. So until other companies catch up with this product, or in fact buy this company out, and then shelve or use this product, this company has a bit of a head start. I hear that the ongoing revenues for the service and maintenance of software dealerships is just over a billion dollars a year. Even if this company gets a small slice of that pie, it could potentially mean a company that not only has earnings in the near future, but increasing earnings for the long term.

Having said all this, I want you to know that last fall I made an agreement to fund into the company $100,000 and gain the right to buy the stock, again restricted stock, at .25 cents a share. When I did this agreement, I think that the stock was around .28 cents a share on the open market. So why am I able to get it at .03 cents less? Simply because I have to hold onto this stock for a year. At that point in time, it wasn't that good of a deal. Now the stock is trading at over .75 cents per share, and the right to buy a little bit more stock at .25 cents a share, I think is a very good deal. But I still have to hang onto the stock. The stock could go up to $2.00 or $10.00 a share or back down to .20 cents a share before that one year is out. That is the risk you take when you buy restricted stock. The only reason I agreed to do so, is because I have every hope that this stock will do well in the future.

I am hearing all kinds of rumors of impending events. I have made comments about Arkona in the past, so I ask you to go back and review some of the things I have said about this company over the past few months. However, all I am hearing now are rumors and there is no substantiation. Because I own restricted stock in the company, I am sure that the corporate executives of the company would tell me different things that are going on, but I have specifically avoided making any phone calls to the company because I do not want to be considered an insider. I have not talked to the CEO, CFO or anyone in the company except in regards to completing the purchase of their stock.

The point is that I am not an insider, and I do not have insider information. But I, like everyone else, hear rumors and I am specifically waiting for certain company announcements to tell of the direction of the company and some of these arrangements that they are making. Check out BottomFISHing.com.

I have made money on some of these companies and I have lost on a couple of them too, so there are obviously no guarantees—and there would be no guarantee of anyone else investing in the company, even at the current level. However, I have even purchased stock in the .70 cent range as of late because I truly believe that this company fits my strategy. Learn to study companies like these, and to at least paper-trade and you should look hard for companies which have good potential revenue.

This commentary is not intended as investment advice or an endorsement of any company's stock. Do your homework and consult your personal financial professional before taking any action that affects you.

Now that I've mentioned our ownership and hope for the future, let me include a "Forward Looking Statement" as a disclaimer.

This material contains statements that may constitute "forward looking statements" within the meaning of the Securities Act of 1933 and the Securities Exchange Act of 1934, as amended by the Private Securities Litigation Reform Act of 1995. Such statements include but are not limited to future company products and services, proposed businesses, models, or other company expenditures. Additionally, this commentary is intended for educational purposes and should not be construed as investment advice, or the endorsement of any particular stock(s). For factors that may cause actual results to differ materially from those contemplated by such forwardlooking statements, please see the "Risk Factors" described in Exhibit 99.2 to the company's Quarterly Report on Form 10Q, filed in November 2001, and in other filings on file with the SEC, which Risk Factors are incorporated herein as though fully set forth. The company undertakes no obligation to update or revise forward looking statements to reflect changed assumptions, the occurrence of unanticipated events or changes to future operating results.

163

15

Attitude is Everything

Publisher's Note: Wade Cook has written 33 Special Reports. The series is entitled Soar with Eagles, *taken from Issaiah 40:31. See the end of Appendix 4 for more information. This report is #714.*

I have attended some of the best motivational events one could possibly attend. The theme banners say a lot: "Think High and Fly;" "Your Attitude Determines Your Altitude;" "As a Man Thinketh…;" and so on. The speakers were even better as they gave specific ways to succeed. I've read some of the best books encompassing some of these same themes and much, much more. Motivation is big business in America.

This report will be different. You see, I have a problem with these promoters of success. It's not really with them but with what they teach, which boils down to this: "Buy my tapes or books, learn this new system and you will be successful." Or, "Here's a catchphrase that will turn you from a loser to a winner." Managers and corporate bosses think that if they can only get their employees, salespeople or whomever to a meeting and get them fired up with the latest motivational gadgetry, then their company will move ahead. My problem with all of this attempted motivation is that the "mystical, magical" something is always external. Nothing has to change in the character or the internal processes of the person. "Rah, Rah" is only good for one game. But, by doing business this way, no one, not even the boss, has to take responsibility for real change.

Real change only comes from something internal. Said another way, and for me personally, there is no one on this earth who I want to go to, to change my personality. That should come from a higher source: from God.

Oh, I know some of these books and seminars might help briefly, but the ways of the world are just fads. Unless the system, the method, the process is grounded in God's word, its chances for success are limited. I want the chance at unlimited success. That is why in my books, Business Buy the Bible, A+ and Don't Set Goals, plus all of these Soar With Eagles Special Reports, I use the Bible for my source. Most graffiti is useless, but I saw one that read, "God Rules." I agree and it's because His Rules are best. Let's return to God's word often.

I remember as a teenager I really started getting into quotations, maxims, and thoughts. Now that I'm older, I look at those thoughts and realize many of them, which I learned and loved 30 years ago, have their basis in the Bible. I actually thought James Allen wrote, "As A Man Thinketh." Not so: "For as he thinketh in his heart, so is he…" Proverbs 23:7. All good things have their genesis in God. I've collected some of the greatest quotes ever (in my Power Quotes book), but none of them have the majesty, the power, or even the precise advice, offered in the Bible.

What does this mean? You won't find meaningless cliches and overworked motivational methods in the Bible. People with great attitudes don't need them and they're only a temporary fix for people with poor attitudes. The Bible deals with changing the heart and aligning people's character and will with God's mind and will. Actions will then follow belief and real conversion.

In another report I've written that options (not stock options) and optimism have the same root prefix. It is difficult to find a person with a lot of opportunities—a lot of "people to see and places to go"—who is down in the dumps.

Education, study, connecting-the-dots and good associations present opportunities. You can have the best attitude in the world and then, by your lack of a specific modus operandi, remove yourself from the success path. Keep your optimism high by having and cultivating opportunities.

How to Get and Keep A Great Attitude

Are there methods that will keep your attitudes high? There are, but first a choice needs to be made. From the way I see it, you have two ways to get and keep a positive attitude. One is from external sources and the other from somewhere internal. Let's explore each. Don't fudge here on which one you need.

<u>External</u>. Is it always something outside yourself which gets you pumped up? Do you need pep rallies and pep talks? Do you need friends to pat you on the back and to constantly encourage you? Do you need motivational books and tapes to keep you going? Now, don't get me wrong, all of these things have their place. But you've got to

decide what it is that makes you tick. Contrast all of this external feedback to the following:

Internal. Are you naturally positive? Do you find the best even in bad situations? Does external feedback just add to your good attitude? Do you get back up when you get knocked down? Do you feel that you could write a book on having a good attitude and inspiring others? Are you sought out by others for help, encouragement and a pat on the back?

The choice between external and internal is easy but loaded with consequences. If you're in need of external stimuli, admit it, and then seek the best help you can. Most people fall into this category. I submit that you'll be happier if you are an internal person. Your radiance will shine, your attitude will exude out of you. You will be peaceful with yourself—with who you are. God's words have an incredible effect on you. We all have a spark of the divine within us. Your light shines because you're excited about something.

As I said, the choice is simple: external or internal, but then the work needed to achieve desired results will be different. I'll assume that you want to move in the direction of being internally motivated. It's rare, but so much less expensive than paying for all the external "stuff."

Here are four ways to help the process:

1. **What is your viewpoint?** Where does your view originate? From being down? From other people's opinions? From wealth or poverty? Does your past control how you look at your future? Does this way of looking at your life serve you or hurt you? How has negative baggage (ie: anger, sarcasm, etc.) served you?

2. **What is your focus?** On what do you train your thoughts? Are your actions helping or hindering your movement? On what set of principles do you base your decisions? Is God's word really important to you, or just semi-important? What and who influences you? What can cause you to get sidetracked, and why? How long can you stay focused and "put blinders on" to reach your target?

3. **What is your love or passion?** You simply cannot get and maintain a good attitude if you do not have a passion for what you're doing.

You will probably never sell to others a bigger life insurance policy than the one you own on your own life. Do you believe in it, really?

You cannot get excited about your team if these people do not have good skills. Yet, one team member with a great attitude can turn an unpleasant situation around. One negative person can undermine a whole project—even a whole company.

You will be ineffective working at your company if you do not believe in and "walk the walk" with your product. Is it "my company" or "the company?" Do you drive a Chrysler and sell Fords?

Do you get the point? Internal motivation is crucial to maintaining a great attitude without the next sales meeting, without the weekly pep talk.

Our Associations

I think it is detrimental if we minimize the importance of carefully selecting those with whom we associate. Hardly anyone, even someone with a great attitude, can withstand negative associations. I realize "birds of a feather, flock together," but if you're a sparrow with a huge attitude you may want to hang out with the beautiful swans.

I used to travel extensively and speak at real estate investment clubs. I would get to the hotel early and listen in on the conversations. One group (6 to 10 people) in the back corner of the room was very negative. "There are no good deals." "I don't have any money." "This is a bad time for real estate." They spouted a thousand other excuses why it wouldn't work.

On the other side of the room was a lively bunch. "I made three offers this week and got a really good deal." "I just bought a pre-foreclosure worth $200,000 for $120,000, with zero down." And on and on. These people stood a few inches taller. They were into solving problems, being creative and making deals.

Choose which group you want to be a part of. The choice is crucial.

Lately I've been addressing audiences with my "Passion, Precision, Profits" lecture. How dare anyone think they can get profits without the precise _____ (you fill in the blank: details, procedures, equipment, etc.)? And then, why would anyone think they will have the persistence and drive to learn and use the precise detailed (whatever) if they do not have a passion for the product or service?

We who lived in concentration camps can remember the men who walked through the huts comforting others, giving away their last piece of bread. They may have been few in number, but they offer sufficient proof that everything can be taken from a man but one thing: the last of human freedoms - to choose one's attitude in any given set of circumstances- to choose one's own way.
~Victor Frankl

If you do not think God is precise, then go to Ezekiel 40-42 and spot read even a few verses and you'll see the minute detail God expounded upon for the building of His temple. Example: "And the little chambers thereof, and the posts thereof, and the arches thereof, according to these measures: and there were windows in it and in the arches

> *thereof round about: it was fifty cubits long, and five and twenty cubits broad. And the arches round about were five and twenty cubits long, and five cubits broad. And the arches thereof were toward the utter court; and palm trees were upon the posts thereof: and the going up to it had eight steps.*
> —Ezekiel 40:29-31

So, what do you love to do? It seems to me that integrity is a conjunction of the following four verbs: it occurs when what we <u>think</u>, <u>say</u>, <u>do</u> and <u>are</u> — are the same. Disappointment, unhappiness and despair are the results of any other attempt at attitude building if our integrity is not intact. If what we think about is not what we talk about or do, then we'll be mediocre at best. Make sure that these four things are in alignment—only then will we build and maintain a good attitude and achieve the results we want.

4. **What is your methodology?** Do you have a plan? Refer back to the question: internal or external? Do you need external assistance? Then fine, get the best help you can.

However, make sure you believe in what you're doing. Enthusiasm is crucial to success. Again, where's your heart? Look at these scriptures and look at the attitude needed:

> *Be of good courage, and he shall strengthen your heart, all ye that hope in the Lord.*
> —Psalm 31:24

> *Create in me a clean heart, O God; and renew a right spirit within me.*
> —Psalm 51:10

> *All the days of the afflicted are evil: but he that is of a merry heart hath a continual feast.*
> —Proverbs 15:15

Now explore these "tudes" with me:

An Attitude of Gratitude. Live with a thankful heart. Express your thanks often and in many situations. You will garner to you like minded people.

Our Attitude Does Determine Our Altitude. Have an attitude of working a plan, getting educated and associating with good people. If you're mired down in the pits, you need to check your attitude. Let's not expect a high altitude without a high attitude.

An Attitude of Rectitude. The dictionary says of rectitude, "moral integrity," and "the quality or state of being correct in intellectual judgement." Take time out to think, ponder and determine a wise course of action. Plan for success in the battle before you find yourself in the battle.

An Attitude of Magnitude. Think big—but in a whole bunch of bite-size pieces. Think lofty and noble ways. Involve God in every step of the process. You're not alone.

This attitude of "bigness" is not what I call the "multi-level" mentality. You know the type. A friend does that little "If I get two people and they get two people and they get…" thing. These are classic external people. There is always something outside of themselves that will get them rich. They want the prize without paying the price.

Don't misread this. I know of a few (maybe two) of these people who are truly internally motivated. Their passion is in helping people and building organizations. In fact, these two are so good that they are highly sought after to lecture and motivate others. Note, though, they are internally motivated but are invited to encourage people who need external motivation.

Being "big" is being magnanimous. It is searching for and achieving all that God wants us to be.

Attitude in Solitude. Having a great attitude doesn't necessarily mean you have to be a cheerleader. An explosive demeanor has little to do with fortitude, drive, kindness or any other worthwhile attribute. Great leaders are reflective, graceful and gracious. Here's a scripture we can set our course by. It's from the Apostle Paul:

"Finally, brethren, whatsoever things are true, whatsoever things are honest, whatsoever things are just, whatsoever things are pure, whatsoever things are lovely, whatsoever things are of good report; if there be any virtue, and if there be any praise, think on these things." Philippians 4:8

An Attitude of Plenitude. Abundance is God's free lunch for us. We can fill up our lives and live full. There is no credible law or theory of scarcity. A life of plenty awaits anyone who wants it. Reach out and grab it.

Apply Amplitude to Our Attitude. Do this and we'll live a fuller, more abundant life. To amplify God's goodness, to exercise godly wisdom, to walk uprightly in His ways will benefit us in immeasurable ways.

What we all need is more vitality, more exuberance and enthusiasm. We don't need to be obstreperous, pushy or manipulative—and attitude makes all the difference in the world. Our attitude determines who our friends will be. Our attitude determines what grades we'll get.

Our attitude determines what kind of a relationship we'll have with our spouse, our children, our friends. Our altitude determines how we'll react to God's Word.

Attitude determines our course of action, our resolve and therefore our destination.

The attitude you take towards problems and difficulties is far and away the most important factor in controlling and mastering them.
~Norman Vincent Peale

I cannot finish this without sharing my witness; my testimony. I think I have a pretty good attitude. But then, so does everybody. Not one person I've ever met thinks they're negative. Throughout my life I have not had to work too hard at developing an attitude of success. One reason is that since my youth I've known that God exists. My parents raised me well: with respect and reverence for God's ways. I saw that truly great people, people who lived large, were humble and quietly observed God's Laws and walked in His ways. They unknowingly reflected a spiritual exuberance. I learned early that our destiny is not of this world.

In times of trouble and times of success I've been led back to the Bible. Jesus is my hero. I want to be successful with Him. I love so very much what He taught, what He did and who He is. There is but one course only if I want the proper attitude for my daily walk through life. It is to follow Him. This desire is echoed by me when reading Paul's words to the people at Corinth:

For who hath known the mind of the Lord, that we may instruct him? But we have the mind of Christ.
—1 Corinthians 2:16

When I look at life from this perspective and focus on Him; when I check frequently my motivation and what I have a passion for; and when I make sure my methodology is based on godly principles, then all goes well.

All my problems have their solutions in Christ.

Summary

The long and the short of having and maintaining a good attitude is easy to talk and write about. But, unless the outcome of sharing the information involves meaningful conclusions or actual achievements, then there really is no reason to speak of the necessity of having a good attitude. It seems that whether you have a good attitude and a quiet disposition, or a good attitude and a zealous spirit, if you do not finish projects the attitude has no meaning. It is easy to think about having a good attitude, but unless that attitude is used to serve others and carry action to the point of accomplishment, what use is it?

Having a good attitude needs to be translated into meaningful activity and actual conclusions. I wrote a paragraph in my book A+ about finishing things, and I'll quote from

171

there, even Jesus' last words on the cross when he said, "It is finished." John 19: 30. Another example is the apostle Paul in his scripture where he said, "I have fought the good fight, I have finished the race, I have kept the faith." 2 Timothy 4:7

You know when you have a good attitude, even when it's a temporary good attitude. A temporary good attitude is usually in relationship to your enthusiasm or excitement about a particular project or cause. We could have a good attitude one day, and not a good attitude the next day, literally depending on how we feel. We could have a good attitude for a certain school project, or subject in school, and a bad attitude toward another project or subject. Whatever our attitude is, will determine the outcome of whatever we are attempting to finish.

If accomplishing things and finishing tasks is important, then all I've written here about getting and maintaining a good attitude will come into play. You'll realize in your own life, as you've seen in the lives of other people, that those who have the best attitude are also the very people who accomplish the most.

Appendix 1

Knowledge is Cash
Flow Potential

To say that this appendix is unique would be an understatement...way under. I'm going to throw everything at you but the kitchen sink. I'm going to show you really cool stock market angles. I'm going to reason with you. I'll try to uplift, inspire, elucidate and do all I can to help you make the only logical conclusion that these words are meant to accomplish: to get you to financially commit to coming to my Wall Street Workshop.

Oh, you'll have to do your part. You know the old adage…"you get out of something what you put into it." Nothing you've ever read will be like this. Nothing I've ever written has been like this. It's a brief journey through words, sentences and paragraphs—all designed to help you on the greatest journey of your life.

TIME OUT! Yes, even before the game gets going, we have a DELAY OF GAME. But oh, so worth it! I offer here a few powerful insights that will hopefully make this report more meaningful, so dear reader, spend a few pages with me before the actual appendix begins.

Okay, right up front, let me give you the punch line: if you want to kick some major fanny in the stock market, you need to attend the Wall Street Workshop, learn (by doing) my strategies, and build more income. Now that I've cleared the air by telling you the results I want this Special Report/Marketing Piece to achieve, let me share a dilemma with you.

> *Somewhere, something incredible is waiting to be known.*
> –Carl Sagan

You bring with you into every situation the culmination of your experiences (good or bad), your opinions (whether they're on target or off target); your dreams (both active and dormant); your attempts (both successes and failures) and your prejudices (both helpful and hurtful). For me to convince you to do anything is a major accomplishment. To say the least, it's an uphill struggle.

However, I have hundreds of thousands of people who have benefited greatly because I refuse to give up on them. I am who I am and I want to be the very best, the #1 financial educator in the country. To many, I've made it, but probably not to you....

So, let me tell you straight away, I know I can help you achieve a success beyond your wildest dreams if you'll just give me a chance. I positively know I can make a *small, great, HUGE* difference in your life. You choose. I've helped people who are in no way as smart as you. I've made a difference in people's lives who have much less money than you have. I've definitely helped people with less luck than you have. In this uphill battle to sell you something and do good in your life, I have a three-way challenge. I must convince you of three things:

1   *You Can Do It.* You can. I know you can. You can get rich—whatever that means to you. You can quit your job shortly. You can pay off your bills. You can pay a large tithe to your church, etc., etc. But how? I'm glad you asked. The stock market can make a perfect part-time business. All you need is a phone. No computers, no gadgets. You don't need all the usual expenses of a regular business. *Trading* (not *investing*) has entrance and exit points (usually three to five weeks). Buy wholesale to sell retail. There are learnable, workable formulas that are really cool—because the extra cash flow lets you accomplish so much.

> *These systems are not easy, but by knowledge, by practice and by a clear understanding of the components, you can work with your money and it can (YES, it will) replace your day job. Again, I'm confident you can qualify yourself for admittance back into the American Dream. I won't give up on you. If you become one of our students, you deserve the best fighting chance to kick your life into high gear.*

2.   *You Can Do It Here.* (where you are) In your back bedroom, in your car, on a coffee break, you are minutes a day from stirring up more cash flow than you can spend.

Yes, it may be tough at first as you go through the learning curve, but believe me the results are worth it. Just imagine having hundreds of thousands of dollars waiting for your retirement. Look at the words of just a few of my students.

My first option trade four days after Microsoft announced a stock split. $11^{1}/_{2}$ months after my first option trade, I've made $1,338,081.43 net profit. I originally started with $36,000 so that makes it a 3,716.89% actual increase on my investment. WOW!!

–Myke L., WA

Knowledge is Cash Flow Potential

I started trading on 10-19-95 with $2,900... I recently took an account from $16,000 to $330,000 in two weeks, and $35,000 to $2,484,000 in six weeks. I made $1.25 million in one day.

–Glenn M., IL

I had $36,000 and turned it into $460,000 in less than 3¹/₂ months. In another account, I took $100,000 and turned it into $400,000 in four weeks, and then, in another, I made $30,000 in one week for a total (account balance) of $960,000.

–John T., OK

They did it, you can too. Just imagine, a free and clear house, no debts, a new car, great vacations, helping others. Where would these people be if they had listened to the average stockbroker? If you keep doing what you've been doing, why would you ever expect different results? Isn't that the definition of insanity? If you want this great life, it's yours for the taking. And...just imagine doing all of this in your pajamas.

3.   *You Can Do It Now.* Yes, now—in this crazy volatile market. Actually, most successful stock market traders love volatility and learn to use it to their advantage. You play the market at hand. Don't be fooled—the energy flows are real. There are fortunes being made all around you. You don't need luck, you need expertise. There is no such thing as negative energy, but you can sure do things to block positive energy. Stop it.

Get in the flow. You can't get rich on a mental desert island. Surround yourself with achievers. Lose the losers. May I humbly ask that you consider, as an alternative to the old rut you're in, a new place to go and a new group to hang out with—yes, me and my "Team Wall Street™." We're not perfect, but we're students first, educators second. We are doing what we teach and teaching what we do. We are always improving and all this is to your benefit.

I've always enjoyed a good sales presentation. I appreciate honesty and integrity. My personal style of selling has been to get people excited with knowledge. That is a constant theme of our marketing efforts. I'll share, you learn and try my strategies. You decide. "Don't trust me, test me," is a quote in many of my books and seminars. I'll not back off this style here in this appendix, but I will apply it with a slight twist. I won't try to sell you on me and my seminars, but I'll try to sell you on you: that you can make a big financial difference in your life with the application of small methods for cash flow—my infamous "meter drop™."

> *It's amazing what ordinary people can do if they set out without preconceived notions.*
> ~Charles F. Kettering

The attempt and achievement are worth the effort. One of my students, a successful but bored Real Estate broker, said, "When the pain (of staying the same) is worse than the pain of change, people will change." He, like thousands of others, has found that the decision to change may have been slightly painful, but our educational process to effectively and quickly get you through the learning curve can be quite enjoyable.

I am excited about my future. I am 72 years old and have a new burst of energy. I have made over $250,000 in just three months selling covered calls and have definite plans to realize all my life's unfulfilled goals. What a rush!!

—Dwight H., CA

I am a retired attorney, real estate broker, and financial planner who was looking for a new direction; something lucrative, but fun. I came (to the Wall Street Workshop™) with great interest and am leaving a ball of fire. Is this fun or what!

—George R., ID

Three words: Vision, Scope and Perspective. I thought I had had all three before. I realize now I've been trading in the dark—(the instructor) turned on the lights! I'll be back.

—Rod M., UT

Now, as I said before, you bring a lot of baggage on this trip. To get off the ground, we need to discard much of it. Misplaced skepticism never accomplished anything. Again, test, don't trust. I'm coming up on a major (earth/mental moving) challenge, but first this quote by Patrick James, one of the Stock Market Institute of Learning's instructors. "The person with a theory is always at the mercy of a person with an experience."

> If you'll do for a few years what most people won't do, you'll be able to do for the rest of your life what most people can't do.
>
> ~WADE B. COOK

I want you excited again! Oh, not so much excited by what we teach as by what you'll be able to <u>DO</u>. The American Dream is alive and well. We're here to help you live that dream to its fullest.

And while I have this brief time out I'd like to interject these comments by Carol Floco who writes for *Lifestyles* Magazine. She came to our Wall Street Workshop™, like many, to find fault. She was as impressed as you will be:

"Again, great care was taken to caution the class that buying and selling options can be risky business. While the idea of a substantially smaller investment turning potentially sizable returns is extremely appealing, the novice trader can get himself or herself into a negative cash position quite quickly. We were tutored in the common mistakes that are made due to a lack of experience and urged to begin with paper trades and continue the practice until eight out of ten of those trades turned a profit.

"Cook has assembled and trained a top-notch team of facilitators and support technicians to teach, uplift, and encourage all who participate in his programs.

"RISK was the first order of business. I was deeply impressed by the fact that Cook wants his students to fully understand—before getting caught up in the excitement of the learning curve—the risk of loss associated with investing in the stock market.

"No rookie to the motivation and self-improvement workshop circuit, I have had the opportunity to make the rounds and acquaintance of a number of engaging public speakers and idea entrepreneurs. From Zig to Tony, I have listened, laughed, learned, and, on occasion, come away disenchanted.

"Wade Cook is the first person to step up and say that he doesn't have all the answers, nor is he promising a miracle. He has made his share of mistakes, and even gone broke. Critics have accused him of motivating followers to make rash, ill-informed investments. I disagree, feeling rather that I now have the incentive and confidence to take control of my own financial future. I left the Wall Street Workshop™ feeling that I had been given the gift of a new skill—one that could potentially change my life. It is now up to me to hone that skill and put it to practical use."

I have no investments for sale. I share useful knowledge. I get nothing out of what my students do. They learn and earn.

Right now, I must convince you to put aside all of the mental games you play that serve you not. Read on in this appendix. You'll learn a little about the stock market, BUT you'll learn a lot about you. I don't really need to convince you about the stock market, but I do need to convince you that "you're the one."

I feel that you need to find again that "better you." I humbly ask that you consider me: my Zero to Zillions™ home study course, my tutorial service on the Internet (WIN™—Wealth Information Network™), and my powerful two-day Wall Street Workshop and one day B.E.S.T.™ (Business Entity Skills Training) seminars.

Respectfully: you can do so much more with me on your team. I pledge you my support, my continued quest for "cash flow" knowledge, my ongoing desire to keep improving and my faith in God and his desires of Abundance for us. Our lives can and will be so much better when we put Him first.

Do you see how tough my task is? So I pose this question: if you do not believe in your own ability to succeed, will you test me to the point that you'll believe in the systems I've developed? I say trust no one (but God), test everyone. Later you'll read our actual results; you'll read heartfelt testimonials; you'll be asked to think, consider and decide.

Herein lie the tools to help you decide. This is an important decision. The consequences of your choice will affect your life and your family's life for generations to come, or your decision will leave you alone—where you are. If where you are is where you want to be, that's great, but if where you want to be is a small or great distance from where you are and you need a sturdy vehicle to help you get there—all of us at the Stock Market Institute of Learning, Inc.™ invite you on the journey. We're glad we can be a part. Bon Journee.

> *Inherently each one of us has the substance within to achieve whatever our goals and dreams define. What is missing from each of us is the training, education, knowledge and insight to utilize what we already have.*
> ~ Mark Twain

> *Knowledge is of two kinds. We know a subject ourselves, or we know where we can find information upon it.*
> ~ SAMUEL JOHNSON

I honestly think the last thing you need is more useless information. I also feel that the last thing you need in relation to the stock market is old worn out methods and ignorant strategies, which get even the best traders in trouble...

In addition to this, I have seen people follow stockbroker's advice into risky and even boring investments with disastrous results—setting their wealth process (nest egg) back years.

I have learned by sad experience that people who use "asset allocation" as their primary strategy suffer immensely. They need "formula allocation," which only the Stock Market Institute of Learning, Inc. shares. All of us need to be careful of the "get-the-commission-at-any-cost" financial professional.

This seminar and Wade's books have filled in the gaps in my stockbroker education. As a stockbroker, I learned how the markets work but not how to personally make money. The firms I have worked for focus on selling (creating commission) and on customer service... not on learning strategies beyond buy and hold. Thanks for showing me what I was missing.

—David S., TX

As a former stockbroker and current commodity broker, everything I ever wanted to do to help people make money in the markets was here at the Wall Street Workshop™. This is a dream come true for me and I can never truly explain how much of an impact was made on me today.

—Richard M., FL

Knowledge is Cash Flow Potential

I have 25 years experience as a broker with three major firms, and I was convinced I had nothing to learn from Wade Cook. How wrong I was! It was the most professional, dynamic and thoroughly enjoyable series of meetings I have ever attended. I plan to write my clients and advise them to seriously consider attending the next Wall Street Workshop the next time one is scheduled. Once again, it was a profoundly educational seminar.

—Carl G., CO

I am a financial planner who works primarily in mutual funds and life insurance. Any financial professional who criticizes Wade's strategies is simply speaking out of ignorance. My practice with my clients will undoubtedly change in the future because of the results I <u>personally</u> have experienced.

—Christopher M., OH

> It is important that students bring a certain ragamuffin, barefoot, irreverence to their studies; they are not here to worship what is known, but to question it.
> –Jacob Chanowski

You just read four comments made about us. I use tried and tested safe cash flow strategies. Indeed I think that the stock market makes a wonderful full or part-time business—<u>if</u> you treat it like a business. Many people wonder what that means. First of all, I am absolutely against day trading—defined as level two, or S.O.E.S. (Small Order Execution System). Investor carcasses now dot.com the landscape. I am into posi-trading, or position trading. Yes, call this home trading, or call it phone trading if you will, but it is built on cash flow/business principles.

I use certain formulas for generating cash flow—actual cash money each month to pay the bills, get out of debt, retire and live a valuable lifestyle. I show how to know your exit before going in the entrance—and don't go in if you are unsure of the exit (profits). I use simple to understand fundamental, technical, or OMFs (Other Motivating Factors) like stock splits (five times to get in and out), earnings, share buy backs, mergers, acquisitions, etc., to sharply increase our skills at entrance and exit points. Just two to five trades a month can generate $5,000 to $15,000 per month of cash flow.

… my portfolio has increased $50,000 - $60,000 per month…

—Alden F., CA

I have left my full-time job, and continue to make large amounts of money each month. Thank you for helping me fulfill my dreams!!

—J.S., CO

"Mr. Binky, I quit!" ...Will go to Europe in March & May and play in a golf tourney in April. Single parent (of) 22 years, daughter just graduated from college and got engaged. I'll be able to pay for her wedding and college all on my own and I'm happy about that!

—Nancy H., TX

I also know you are really cheating your bottom line (and brokerage/bank account) by not having this knowledge. These trading skills are easy to master with the right facilitators. Quit expecting your commission/fee based financial pro to teach you. That is not what they do. They educate only to sell you things. We educate to protect you.

Wrote Covered Calls and made an average 17% per month return. Gave control to my broker and now I'm broker. As soon as I violate Wade's rules and strategies, I start losing in the market. Now we are back on track! Thank you.

—Don G., CA

So, what is the difference between someone making $50,000 a year, and someone making $250,000 per year? And $2,500,000 per year? The answer is the effective use of specialized knowledge.

That's where I come in. The stock market isn't for everyone, but for those who look to the market to find answers to their financial needs I am here to truly help them see and work the alternatives. Working formulas for cash flow—actual income on a monthly basis—is what I do, and what we help our students gain. Here are several testimonials that speak to our effectiveness. This is monthly cash flow that these people *would be living without* had they not learned and applied our unique, powerful, yet very safe "income formulas." Please read the paragraphs following these people's personal experiences to get a good comparison of Stock Market Institute of Learning, Inc., vs. the other financial professionals.

Since I attended the Wall Street Workshop in October 1998, I have done Covered Calls and I am averaging between 25% to 35% monthly returns.

—John B., NY

We're making our living by trading now. Each event fine-tunes our trades and helps us see more clearly where we need to improve and where we're succeeding.

—Renita S., WY

In 1999, (I'm) averaging about $5,000 per day.

—Neal L., MA

Knowledge is Cash Flow Potential

Quit my job and am making twice as much as I was there in the stock market. Will end the year with 5X the income I otherwise would have had. The best part is being more available to my family.

—Janet S., ID

Virtually every financial advisor in this country is trained in a certain way. The focus or methods from one to the other are different, but all of them sell people things for the future—their future retirement, estate, etc. This is a noble endeavor, and while we disagree with some of their methods and most often with their fad products, that is not the point here.

I have been a (Wealth U™*) person since September 1999. I am averaging $30,000/ month...

—Edward A., HI

We show, tell, educate, facilitate for the *here and now*. People need more income. They need to get out of debt. They have dreams and plans—like putting kids through college, buying a bigger house and traveling to visit the grandkids. We believe that if a person learns how to get their money to work harder—yes, even to the point of generating "pay the bills" income, they can live better now and the future will take care of itself. In fact, here's a shift: we want to help you get more money now so you can fix your lifestyle, and then spend all your extra profits buying these other people's investments.

So look at the following two lists, and realize for yourself how we are widely and wildly different from others, and then we'll help you figure out what this means to you.

The opposite chart shows the major difference between Stock Market Institute of Learning, Inc.™ and the other financial professionals.

Notice the first one on our list. We like great stocks also and we know we have the greater methods to elucidate this arena—indeed, to keep you out of trouble and away from risky investments promoted by people who usually don't even buy these same investments.

Also, notice if you didn't catch it that we have 13 formulas that are street-tested ways to put your money to work. Check this out: even in our own accounts, the one strategy that causes us the most concern is the buy and hold—be out of control—formula. The other twelve are methods to help you quit your job. *We want to help you quit your job.*

I do many radio and TV talk shows. Many hosts ask me the difference between me and everyone else. The obvious answer is that they sell investments, I educate. They have stodgy old methods, which more often than not produce bad bottom lines. I share formulas for cash flow. I put the emphasis on selling, on meter-drop income (consistent predictable cash profits), on rational, logical ways to use the stock market as a business—a business that will support people and their families so they can get on with their lives.

Even within this educational process, everyone needs to realize that each of my thirteen strategies is different.

1. They have their own beginning, middle and end—entrance points and exit points.
2. Each has its own set of rules or factors which make it work.
3. Each has a specific time to be used and only works or works best at that time—or market occurrence.

Again, we share—you learn and earn.

I've pretty much offended every stockbroker and financial professional in the country. Most of these people, who you think would be up on these cash flow methods, know little about them. When this cab driver took on Wall Street, I had no idea what a commotion I'd cause. I'll apologize to them in advance, and invite them to attend the Wall Street Workshop. We should charge them double to pay for all the anguish they've caused people. Profits are waiting. All you have to do is grasp the knowledge, gain an understanding, and apply it for profits.

Consider what everyone gets out of this. Brokers get commissions. I get book royalties. You get profits today and more profits tomorrow. You actually take control of your financial destiny. You. You and only you. No one will learn and understand your financial situation like you.

You have choices. One is to keep trading your time for money; the other is to put your knowledge to work and get your money to work as hard as you do—even harder. Expect more from your money, learn what it takes and then get more from your money.

On the next page is a matrix. Find yourself—your risk/reward tolerance, cash flow needs, safety requirements and future growth needs; then look at market conditions and movement and see what it takes to gain an expertise so you get the results you want.

So Just Who Is Attracted To Us?

Our strategies are not for everyone. People who like a lot of risk (yes, the returns <u>could</u> be higher) don't like our safe "calm-down" multiple small profits methods. People who like someone else spending their money probably should put their investments with money managers. People who are contented with 8% to 12% annual returns (even the worst money managers can do this) should put their money in mutual funds. Time out: if this is you, at least find a *good* index and put your money in that fund. I, Wade Cook, with some of my "hold" money, park it in Spiders (SPDRs—Standard and Poors Depository

Knowledge is Cash Flow Potential

Strategies/Courses	Zero to Zillions CD/Video Course	Blue Chip Trading	Rolling Stock	Options (Calls & Puts)	Stock Splits	Writing Covered Calls	Selling Puts	Bull Put Spreads	Bull Call Spreads	Bargain Hunting/Turnarounds	Wall Street Workshop	IPOs	Spin Offs	Rolling Options	Range Riders	W.I.N.—Internet Tutorial Service
Market Conditions																
Whole Market Bullish	○	●	●	●	●	●	●	●	●	●	○	●	●	●	●	○
Whole Market Bearish	○	●	●	●							○		●	●		○
Sector Moves	○	●		●	●	●	●	●	●		○		●	●	●	○
Hi-Tech Trades	○	●		●	●	●	●	●			○	●		●	●	○
Low-Tech Trades	○	●	●	●			●	●	●	●	○	●		●	●	○
Stock — going up	○	●		●	●		●	●	●		○				●	○
Stock — going down	○			●		●		●		●	○			●		○
Stock — going sideways	○		●	●		●		●	●		○			●		○
Your Condition																
I need cash	○		●	●	●	●	●	●	●		○	●		●	●	○
I need steady income	○		●			●		●	●		○			●	●	○
I need growth	○	●				●	●			●	○	●	●			○
More safety	○	●	●			●					○	●				○
More risk—more profits	○			●			●			●	○	●		●	●	○
Little time to trade	○	●	●			●		●			○					○
Quick Turn Profits	○		●	●	●			●	●		○	●	●	●		○
Retirement Income	○	●	●	●		●		●	●		○			●		○

183

The following shows the major difference between Stock Market Institute of Learning and <u>all</u> the other financial professionals.

STOCKBROKERS FINANCIAL PLANNERS FUND MANAGERS	STOCK MARKET INSTITUTE OF LEARNING
1. They receive commissions for selling investments, regardless of returns to client.	1. We sell no investments. We get nothing out of what our students do.
2. They advise clients on specific investments.	2. We explain formulas, methods, and techniques to work the market. Stocks are mentioned as working examples. No specific advice is given.
3. Many financial professionals get paid a percentage of asset base they manage, whether assets increase or decrease.	3. We teach. The students learn and earn. They work the formulas, after paper or simutrading, and keep all the profits.
4. They sometimes get investors involved in risky investments.	4. We show students how to avoid and minimize risk with a dedication to knowledge and specific tools like low-cost options, spreads and writing covered calls.
5. They preach "asset allocation" placing portions of investor's money in harm's way.	5. We teach "formula allocation" for cash flow, tax write-offs, and growth. We help students learn to find certain stocks/options that fit the formulas.
6. They constantly sell investors the new "investment du jour."	6. We teach and show investors how to work the formulas, spread out risk, avoid losses and not get caught up in erratic and fad investments.
7. Most do not show their trading results, they surely do not publicize their personal trades.	7. We tell all, show all. All trades are listed on our award winning Internet site at wadecook.com.

Receipts). Have your money person check out SPY, MDY, DIA and QQQ. You can create your own so-called mutual fund.

To continue. If you don't need more income, or you don't have anyone in your life (kids, friends, parents) who needs more income, then you probably don't need us. Now, we still think you do for even more safety in your out-of-control buy and hold trades. We could go on—literally forever—and give you testimonials, reasons, strategies for why you need to align yourself with us, but first, what is it that you need?

We're about results. Do you need better results from your financial activities?

We're about effective training. Do you need to learn skills that could possibly make you millions?

I turned $200,000 approximately into $1.2 million in six months.

—Larry G., CA

(This class) sharpened my knowledge and confidence to avoid making past mistakes. Using Wade's strategies has made me a millionaire.

—Frank A., CA

Building Your Team

Once in a seminar I asked who they thought was the hottest basketball player in the country. Michael Jordan was the overwhelming response. I then asked, who the worst team at that time was. The Dallas Mavericks (though they are so much better now) was the answer.

Then I asked, "Who would win in a game between the Dallas Mavericks and Michael Jordan?" Though it was debatable at that time, the audience finally agreed the team would beat the one, single player. Now, I've seen Michael play. He seems to defy gravity. He has an incredible work ethic—he is willing to pay the price. His attitude is a powerful force. Michael once said, "I've always tried to lead by example. I never really tried to motivate by talking, because I don't think words ever mean as much as action." But still, five on one would be too much, even for him.

The team. The players. Who can you pass the ball to? Who is your go-to guy? Who protects you? Who helps you be better and get better? Our whole company exists to be a team player for our students. Yes, sometimes we're the coach, oftentimes we're on the floor, playing defense, offense, and making plays.

Back to basketball. Bill Walton summarized it this way, *"In basketball, you can be the greatest individual player in the world and still lose every game, because a team will always beat an individual."*

Choose your team wisely.

- We have a passion for helping people. Do you need someone on your team who is in-the-trenches every day working wonders and has a mission to help you better your precision that results in profits?

Note: Passion, Precision, Profits, the three Ps, cornerstones to successful achievement. They go together—you hardly can have one without the others. Point. So many people focus on the prize, not on the price. They want to win without learning and working the process. *And there is a process.* We'll show it to you in our awesome "TELL-SHOW-DO" format.

- We show our results. We lead the way. Do you need someone to talk the talk or to *WALK the WALK*? Who else do you know who puts their trades (win, lose or draw) on an Internet site as a tutorial service for the whole world to see?

You can see these trades on WIN at www.smil-inc.com. Keep asking yourself: so what? What does this mean to me?

Remember: Cash Flow (Being Rich) Success comes from the effective application of specific knowledge. Many trades on WIN are put forth in a unique way. It's a process—once again, totally to help our students make more money in less time with less risk.

> *It is impossible to estimate how many good ideas are abandoned every day as a result of difficult-to-manage relationships.*
> ~John P. Kotter

I just wanted to let you know, that I was able to play one (rolling) stock over a three week period, seven times, and was able to realize a $7,000 profit from a $500 investment.

—Thom A., TX

When Thom came to our Wall Street Workshop we didn't promise him this kind of profit, but he did it anyway. Do you need promises or results? We help <u>you</u> get results, and you don't need much to get started.

I've made $100,000+ in five months starting with $5,000.

—Ricky I., VA

> *I can give away enough money to feed a man for a day or I can teach him how to earn enough to feed himself for the rest of his life.*
> ~Unknown

$5,000 turned into $100,000. Wow. What could you do with $100,000? If you would then switch to a safer 10-15% monthly cash flow formula, this will generate $10,000 to $15,000 (or $20,000 to $30,000 if you trade on margin) by using our "Writing Covered Call" formula. Is your IRA (or pension money) making 5% to 10% monthly cash flow returns? Could you quit your job in six months to a year—even starting with less than $10,000? These students did:

Retired within one month of first Wall Street Workshop September 1998. Made more in 1999 than ever working for a living.

—David B., WA

At age 50, my wife and I have now been retired for six months. Trading is making it possible to take time for ourselves, our children, and our community. (Our trading strategy is) conservative, but it makes us about three times our money each year.

—John S., WA

I have been able to retire and live wonderfully off of selling covered calls on large cap stocks.

—Lee H., TX

You need WIN today and forever. It's just $3,600 per year. That's peanuts for the quality and value you get. Just one medium trade gets you this back and more. To some, this $3,600 is a chunk. We hope within a few months you'll realize what the value of this is. Oh, we realize we're probably the most expensive Internet site in the world. But this cliché definitely holds true here: you get what you pay for. You don't need mediocrity. You don't need a half-done job. You need results. We get results!

I am an RN...for a labor and delivery unit. I mentioned to a friend (he sells life insurance for New York Life) that I was learning so that I could start investing in the stock market. His comment was, "Leave the stock market to the big boys." This rather incensed me and became the catalyst to learn all I could so I could be successful and prove this friend wrong.

—Suzanne E., CA

What would you do with more money?

Had to retire and then discovered I had prostate cancer and needed surgery. Insurance ran out and I was cancelled. Now 'high risk' insurance is $850/month. Trading pays for it and a lot more. I have peace of mind.

—David E., CA

I am a single mom. Sold my business within one year of taking my first Wall Street Workshop. I'm now trading full time at home, and spending more time with my 13 year old son, and doing things together that we love to do. I just bought an SUV Benz and a Rolex watch to go with it! Wade's seminars have changed my life.

—Susan R., HI

Are there people in your life who need help?

I trade full time, (bought a) six bedroom home with swimming pool and tennis court, helped others who needed work (they work on my house now and I pay them with what I make in the market). I know if I lost everything, I could start with enough to buy one contract and make it from there.

—Garland H., FL

Can your church or favorite charity use more money?

My life has changed by spending less time running my computer business and more time with my family. This has also allowed my wife and I to sponsor many new programs through our church. My minister wanted to put 100 teenagers through a program about waiting until marriage for sex. We (anonymously to all other members) offered to match ALL donations received to this program for two weeks. The other members donated enough to send 75 teens through the program. With our matching funds, our minister was able to do 150 teens or 150% of his goal.

—Dwayne G., OK

Donations: $25,000 to son's school building fund, $25,000 to church building fund, both this year on stock account gains.

—Raymond B., FL

Are you living a great, noble life of compassion and passion? How would more time and more money help?

Helping others, gave over $30,000 in last four months to charity from earnings!
—Larry K., MI

These success stories are real. We want to help you become your own success story. That's how we measure our effectiveness. But frankly, we cannot help you if you do not attend our Wall Street Workshop. We can hook you up with dynamic and far-reaching methods of wealth enhancement, but we can't do this if you don't come.

You see, you have a choice. (1) Learn these strategies on your own! (2) don't learn them (in fact, if you do not attend the Wall Street Workshop™, you will not even know they exist; or (3) learn these strategies from people with experience, passion, and achievement.

> *Some drink at the fountain of knowledge... others just gargle.*
> ~ Anonymous

The best choice is to walk with people who are walking the walk. To quote from a special report I wrote called Wise Choices:

In the Bible is a series of wonderful lessons on gaining wisdom. A simple lesson stands out: 'walk with wise men.' [Proverbs 13:20] It stands true of listening to and following God's word in spiritual matters, as it does in other matters.

> *Through the commendations and the condemnations, I will stay the course. I will help others honestly so as to win their recommendation of our services to their friends.*
> ~Wade B. Cook

You should not settle for second best. Your family is too important, your retirement is too close; your life too worthy to surround yourself with mediocrity. Oh, to be sure, Wade Cook's Wall Street Workshop is one of the most expensive courses, but again, what are your alternatives?

Why, you ask, is this course so good? And why should I give you two days (three with the B.E.S.T. Seminar) of my life? What can I possibly learn in that time that would let me retire in a year or so? We'll answer these questions with a question—If you keep doing what you've been doing to build up your wealth, increase your net income and retire at 32, 42 or 52, will you make it? Do you have a good answer?

Well, we do. However, our answer will not be what you think. Please don't judge your future potential by your past. You'll miss a major point, and missing this point will be detrimental to your financial health.

> *Experience is the best teacher, but it's so darn expensive.*
> ~Anonymous

> *Experience is a hard teacher, because she gives the test first, the lesson after.*
> ~Vernon Law

So what is the point? The information is awesome, but that's not it. The methods are results oriented. No, the methods aren't the difference. Maybe the insights and exit strategies are it. Nope, they're wonderful, but it's much more than this.

Simply put, it is our unique and fantastic method of delivery. It's not what we teach, but *how* we teach—indeed, it is how you learn that makes all the difference in the world.

We use an efficacious "Tell, Show and Do" experiential learning process. You learn, see and then do (on paper or for real) the actual strategies. It's undisputed we are the best at teaching you our methods. No one can show and explain these processes like we do, BUT, if that were all, we'd be like dozens of others. The "Do"—getting you to do the deal, or into the trade, and as much as possible, we "watch over" you and help you truly "get it." If there was a better educational delivery method we'd adopt it. THIS IS THE BEST. You learn, you see the trades done, then the whole class goes on break, or is excused to go (on the phone or online) and make the trade. Most students do these on paper until they become proficient. You've heard that "practice makes perfect." That's a half-truth that breeds many failures. You can practice something for years and if you are practicing wrong or ineffectively, you've still got it wrong.

> *To teach a man how he may learn to grow independently, and for himself, is perhaps the greatest service that one man can do another.*
> ~ Benjamin Jowett

"Perfect practice makes perfect." This works. We put on our wonderful Wall Street Workshop on a regional basis to help people learn how to practice perfectly.

> *Practice yourself in the little things, and thence proceed to greater.*
> ~ Epictetus

Do not delay coming to this class. Even a one or two month delay could cost you tens of thousands of dollars ($$$). That's the kind of money most people only dream about. We'll help you make your dreams gone blue become dreams come true. We do it all the time.

Thank you Wade!! We made money enough to travel throughout Western Europe because of your strategies. We fulfilled a lifetime dream. Thank you, Thank you, THANK YOU!
—Patricia J., CA

For five years, my husband has worked 300 miles away Monday through Friday. We commute on weekends to be together. Our small town has no good paying jobs, but is an excellent place to raise our three children. Pete is quitting now and returning home! I have been trading options for just over one year, and have been quite successful. We plan to travel extensively during summer vacations. We've already been to the Bahamas twice for a month each time, but without Pete. Now he'll be joining us! I should add that Pete has been in a very stressful job that has been wearing on his health and our marriage. We both look forward to our future now. I have also been able to give heavily to my church – something I've always wanted to be able to do. Thanks Wade!
—Suzanne G., CA

I began attending Wade's seminars my junior year in college. I graduated in 1999, and I did not get a job. I will never have a job in Corporate America. Just in the Fall of 1999 I

190

have already nearly made the average starting salary of a college grad. Thanks to all of you. I am living every man's dream, I am 24 years old!

—Dan D., TX

Another knowledge point. We want you to not only learn the "how," but the "why."

> *The man who knows how will always have a job. The man who knows why will always be the boss.*
>
> ~Diane Ravitch

To come to this kind of understanding where else could you go? We contend—"There Is No Place Like Our Home." Please come visit.

There is a critical aspect to this educational process that will bear you much fruit once you employ it. We'll get to it after you look at the topical agenda for Wade Cook's two day "experiential learning" Wall Street Workshop:

Day One

Getting Started

- What you expect and what you will get.
- Strategies of Engagement: Take notes, hang around positive people, working lunches, papertrading.
- Three-step training process: Tell, Show, and Do.
- Learn the basics and practice, practice, practice!
- Creativity: If there is a way, take it; if not, make it.
- To whom are you listening? Sources for information and advice.

Building A Great Portfolio

- Trading basics: Buying stock safely, how we make money, making effective decisions, yield calculation.
- Choosing a brokerage firm and a good personal broker.
- Market Makers: who they are and how they work.

Rolling Stocks

- Benefits, definitions and rules.
- Tools for finding (WIN, TC2000®, etc.).
- Assignments: research, real trades or Simutrades™.
- Review.

Options

- Benefits, definitions and rules.
- Risks of doing options and how to avoid losses.
- News: Other Motivating Factors (OMFs).
- LEAPS®.
- Examples and review.

Stock Splits

- Benefits, definitions and rules.
- Why companies split and how to find them (WIN, IQ Pager).
- Options on stock splits, five times to get involved.
- Examples, assignments, review.

Writing Covered Calls

- Benefits, definitions and rules.
- Wade Cook formula for writing covered calls.
- Finding the good ones.
- Examples, assignments and choices.
- Covered call power strategies: buy/write, clean house, in the money, buy back and roll out.
- Examples, questions and concerns, review.

Day Two

Early Bird Session

- Research, call brokers, do the deals (real or simutrades).

Selling Puts

- Benefits, definitions and rules.
- Examples: a strategy where you can't lose money.
- Three things to do if the stock is put to you.
- Cost basis and margin requirements.
- Tandem plays: stacking the deck in your favor.
- Bull put spreads (if time permits).

Peaks And Slams
- Benefits, definitions and rules.
- Dead cat vs. dead dog bounce.
- Can the price be sustained? Has the news played out?

Bargain Hunting
- IPOs: How to find them, when to buy and the 25 day rule.
- Turnarounds: Why are they down? Why should they go up?
- Spin-offs: Examples (Pepsi etc.), advantages.
- Penny Stocks: advantages and disadvantages.
- Range Riders: up, down or sideways; news, moving averages, money flow, events.

Pulling It All Together
- Tracking sheets—start using the words "open and close."
- Combining balancing strategies.
- My four step plan:
  Is my trading personality safe or aggressive?
  Choosing a favorite strategy.
  Research for that strategy.
  Practice. Monitor, monitor, monitor.

Day Three: B.E.S.T.™

Busines Entity Skills Training

Overview
- The goal of wealth enhancement.
- Trader's update—advantages and disadvantages.
- Key areas for success—divide and conquer.
- Three solutions for protecting assets.
- The power of entities.
- Protections, growth and tax reduction.
- The basic structure of the legal entities.

(193)

Corporations

- The basics of corporations.
- Corporate benefits — estate tools.
- Corporate structure for family dynastics.
- Who runs the store? Shareholders, directors and officers.
- Tax brackets, benefits and movement.
- The pre-tax difference.
- Corporations and the IRS.
- Splitting income.
- Why Nevada?.
- B.O.S.S. (Business Office Suite Service)

The Limited Partnership

- Tax benefits.
- Income and tax distribution.
- Ownership vs. control: general and limited partners.
- Asset protection and estate tools.
- Unearned income: getting out of the social security system.

The Living Trust

- Trusts, wills and probate.
- The courts and your estate: the problems of probate.
- How to avoid probate: Die as a pauper.
- What about control? Trustees and beneficiaries.
- Tax benefits and family ramifications.
- Will vs. Living Trust: examples.

Tax Minimization And Deferral Techinques

- Making Tax-Free investments.
- Pensions: creating a tax-free entity.
- Charitable Remainder Trusts (CRT).

It is so much fun to show this. When you really think about these topics—seven of the major ones in the Three Step Process of "TELL, SHOW and DO"—you'll realize how comprehensive this immersion learning course is. I think it's comical, yet pathetic, when all these brokerage firms spend millions on their radio and TV ads to convince you that they enable or empower the individual investor. I beg to differ. I've gone to their websites; I've seen their brochures and the only thing they do is educate you on the next thing they want to sell. It's sad.

It's like the Wizard of Oz. You learn that the big Wall Street guys are hiding behind the curtain, peddling a contraption to generate enough noise and sound to be convincing enough to keep you afraid and away from the truth.

—Tim W., VA

Along comes Wade Cook, and says, "Hey Americans, you're not stupid. You can learn and master these splendid methods of cash flow. I'll learn them from the Billion Dollar Traders and share them with the Average Guy." Is it any wonder why a typical retail stockbroker, who hasn't the foggiest idea of how the stock market really works, shoots down these ideas? If they're not up on it, they're down on it.

An interesting thing happened at the Wall Street Workshop™. I am a licensed general securities broker, licensed insurance agent, and a CFP (certified financial planner). And compared to (the instructor), I don't know jack! It just proves that institutionalized knowledge and street knowledge is about a $1,000,000+ per year difference in money making capability. Thanks for presenting difficult to understand material in an incredibly absorbable and fun way. Bravo Wade Cook strategies!

—Christopher K., FL

195

I took $4,000 to $80,000. My wife and I pulled it out and built apartments. I have $10,000 now to do it again.

—Ken M., CA

Our December (99) statement showed that we had taken a $17,000 account to $120,000. In January (00), we'd made (my husband's) <u>annual</u> salary plus a portion of mine!

—Virginia M., NJ

A Case Made For Zero To Zillions™: Home Study Mega-Course

It is such a rush for us to put these events on, almost all with real audiences, so our students are part of the action and feel the passion. We see people listen, review, retain, share with their family these time-honored, in-the-trenches ways to build up their income.

I took $4,000 with the tapes only and in $2\frac{1}{2}$ months, doubled my money.

—Marilyn M., TX

I was very unhappy with a holding of RXSD which was going nowhere. I was just going to sell it around $11 or so, when I listened to (the) Zero to Zillions tape(s). I sold a $12 call for $1^{3}/_{8}$. I was called out of seven contracts. Just listening to the tapes garnered me an additional $1,300—paid for much of the course so far.

—Stanley G., FL

Approximately $9,000 by just listening to Zero to Zillions and doing: 1) $800 Rolling Stock. 2) $6,600 Writing Covered Calls in two months. 3) $2,400 Dividend Capturing. All done in two months of active trading...

—Simisola O., MI

To add to the excitement, take a look at this extensive list of topics in a most remarkable home/car study course that explains, expounds on, elucidates, fills in the gaps and is all-in-all the most powerful and effective "college on wheels" ever assembled.

Volume 1

CD #1: Treat The Stock Market Like A Business: Introduction to Wade "Cash Flow" Cook, and what makes him tick. The need for more cash flow and how to turn the stock market into a profitable business. (Income machine.)

CD #2: Building A Great Portfolio, Part 1: Making wise decisions. Company P/Es and how to effectively measure stock valuations. Understand a "Fun-damental" approach to better portfolio building.

CD #3: Building A Great Portfolio, Part 2: More great information put forth in a "down-in-the-trenches" format. Understanding what moves stocks, why some prices contract while other prices explode.

CD #4: Building A Great Portfolio, Part 3: A technical approach to making better entrance points (open positions) and exit points (close positions). Then on to OMFs—Other Motivating Factors—the "why now" behind stock option movements.

Volume 2

CD #5: Stop And Go—More Cash Flow: The ultimate presentation on the quarterly "newsy-go-round." Don't do anything until this information enters your brain. Earnings Seasons are only a limited part of the story.

CD #6: Rolling Stocks—Repeated Waves: This is a lively presentation to bring more life to your trades. The Three Rules explained. Examples given. Charting, tips, hints, methods that work: understand three types of roll patterns.

CD #7: Stock Splits: Capitalizing On Big Moves: Stock Splits. You'll soon be able to harness the power of this workhorse. You'll thoroughly go through the five times to get involved and then uninvolved. You'll learn to watch out for Split Strategy #2. This powerful event has become a cornerstone of many other events.

Volume 3

CD #8: Options (Introduction): Safer Than Stocks? Part 1: Low-cost, limited-risk options are safer than stocks in some ways. Get the jargon down. Use leverage for magnified profits. Control without ownership and protective profit-making techniques.

CD #9: Option Optimism, Part 2: Understanding more on option/stock relationships. See price swings and gain an understanding of problems and pitfalls to avoid. See how basic options can be used in a variety of strategies.

CD #10: Option Pricing And Volatility, Part 3: Options: a unique demonstration of how option prices move. Stock movement is just part of the story. Learn the three components of Option Market Makers and computer pricing models.

CD #11: Making Options Work Hard, Part 4: Moving on up. Option knowledge and expertise most of the pros don't have. This intermediate level comes as a must for serious investors.

CD #12: Stockbrokers: Choosing (Training) A Good One: An effective team is essential. A good stockbroker, one who truly knows how to get in the spread prices, does cross-market trades, and knows the components of the cash flow formulas is invaluable.

Volume 4

CD #13: Writing Covered Calls, Part 1: This powerful cash-flow formula is a must in every trader's tool chest—even if most trades are made with more aggressive methods— this "calm-down, get the monthly check" will grow anyone's portfolio and cash flow.

CD #14: Selling Calls, Part 2: Way too much for one CD (#13) this seminar continues with more precise techniques for strengthened profits. Problems to avoid and overcome. How to better choose strike prices and expiration dates.

CD #15: Writing Calls: Cleaning House, Part 3: Only someone with hundreds (even thousands) of trades could share this information. These powerful insights for extra (get more cash now) income are creative, yet simple to implement. Buy backs, roll outs (up and down) are explained with pertinent examples.

Volume 5

CD #16: LOCC—Large Option Covered Calls, Part 1: Part of Wade's Lifestyle Investing Series. Certain stocks produce huge four to six month out option premiums—sell these, generate big time income—this seminar shows you how to get your stocks for FREE—yes, get the stock market to pay for your stocks.

CD #17: LOCC It Up, Part 2: Pick off (pre-capture) large option premiums now. Offset stock purchase prices. Switch to plan B for more cash flow. Retire within one year (if you have $25,000 to start) or two and a half years (if you have $5,000 to start). Also, explained is the stock repair kit for down stocks—this is awesome!

CD #18: Puts For Income And Protection: Puts have a definite place in every trade arsenal. Protect large upside moves in your stocks by buying puts. If stocks dip, puts go up in value—sell for cool profits. Also, learn about puts for bear market trading.

Volume 6

CD #19: Spreads For Safer Cash Flow: The amazing bull put spread is Wade's favorite cash generating strategy. Build on basic selling puts—buy insurance with this credit spread. (Credit means you get paid cash to put it in place—yes, you get paid.) This is a wonderful way to go for the safety conscious, and it's oh-so-simple.

CD #20: Bargain Hunting, Part 1: Don't delay listening to and studying this information. These deals, turnarounds, spin-offs, slams and peaks are available on a daily basis. Wade's creative insights are powerful, not to mention necessary for finding and playing these detailed formulas.

CD #21: Bargain Hunting, Part 2: Huge discounted, undervalued stocks are out there if you know what to look for. Wade moves on with street wisdom in regards to IPOs (Initial Public Offerings). The problems with trying to get in, but then the 25 day (quiet) rule is explained.

CD #22: Make More, Keep More, Part 1: Asset protection and wealth enhancement the entity structuring way. You learn about Nevada Corporations, Living Trusts, Pension Structures, the (Family) Limited Partnership, and the effective CRT (Charitable Remainder Trust). This is an extremely informative event.

CD #23: Make More, Keep More, Part 2: Grow your wealth and protect your assets as you pay less taxes, lower your exposure to lawsuits and other problems, and prepare for a great retirement. The best of all worlds: cash flow, tax write-offs, and growth. These entities are blended together for unequaled efficiency.

Plus, Two Bonus CDs

<u>Hidden Wealth</u>™: A passionate presentation on structuring your financial affairs—for beginners and everyone else. Also, an introduction to the Wealth U.

<u>Building A Quality Life</u>™: Wade's heartfelt seminar for enhancing the nobleness of our life is wonderful. Based on the Bible with use of powerful quotations, stories and experiences. This is great for teenagers and anyone else wanting help in achieving great results.

This course also has four videos. Again, you can sit and watch me at work, in a professionally set studio—most with live audiences—and professionally taped and executed. You get the best information quickly, using sight and sound, but given at a pace for you to emotionally awaken to the extent that your emotions, your history, your own skills and your desires step up and go to work for you. Look at a brief description of the videos:

On-Growing Stock Market Profits™

This video alone is worth thousands, seriously. I come at stock market trading in a whole different way: I explore how people learn and use some of these different mechanisms, coupled with real life examples to bring these systems alive—to hit home with you in a way that will affect you and cause you to gain the attributes of trading success. Seriously, these formulas can be used repetitiously for on-growing (not just continuing, but increasing) cash flow.

Position Trading™

Do not go near the stock market until you watch and absorb the knowledge (wisdom) in this video. I explain the "news/no news" cycle. As CEO of a publicly traded company, with SEC reporting requirements, I've discovered the anticipation of news inside the company versus outside news, and when it starts and ENDS. You'll learn how to get your money out of harm's way to stop losses, and also how to get your money in the way of progress.

It's what I call "position-trading," or "posi-trading." It makes so much sense. This video could help you make an extra $200,000 to $400,000 a year.

Enhancing Your Wealth™

As a former financial planner, I thought I knew a lot about securities and the market. As a current attorney, I thought I knew a lot about companies and securities. Now I know I knew nothing about companies, securities, and the market.

—Michael R., WA

Back in the studio I went, to put out the most concise strategies for asset protection, tax reduction, risk avoidance, and estate structuring. This video presentation will help you gain a working understanding of:

<u>Nevada Corporations</u>: secrecy, privacy, tax reduction and estate planning capabilities.

<u>Living Trusts</u>: extensive probate avoidance, tax savings, good for the family, yet estate-sharing limitations.

<u>The (Family) Limited Partnership</u>: asset protection, distribution of assets, awesome tax ramification and bequeathment attributes.

<u>The Pension Plan</u>: tax deductibility, control, tax free growth of all types of income, acceptability.

<u>CRT or Charitable Remainder Trust</u>: deductions, cash flow and asset control, growth and income and possibly an awesome "tithe" on your build-up of wealth. This last one, the CRT, is my favorite. It's awesome (in every cliché of this word "awesome.")

I'm into entity structuring and design. Truly you'll hear a symphony when you see and know how to use these different "instruments" to produce notes, then chords, then beautiful music.

"After a decade of being in practice as a surgeon, I found myself in the classic American mode: a holder of assets that demanded always more cash, forcing me to work longer and harder so I could continue to add to the legacy of government taxation—now more than $1,000,000 since I had begun my practice...

Enter Wade Cook.

...I learned that my malpractice is only another sandwich spread on the buffet table for the ravening wolf known as a trial lawyer. After the malpractice insurance has been collected in a suit, a doctor's home, practice, stock accounts, or any other assets are fair game to take. The best way around that was to incorporate, and distribute one's assets in a number of legal entities so nothing was owned, but all the powers of decision were retained. Where was this stuff ten years ago?! Why didn't my friends and legal advisors tell me about these things?! I had to learn it from a taxi-cab driver! Not only would I be shielded from lawsuits, but from taxes. "No, you didn't have to pay the government that million dollars," I heard. (I had to ask that twice.) So immediately that day I paid the $6,000 to start the creation of my legal entities. It was a bargain, even if $60,000. Thanks Wade!!"

—Dr. Steven N., OR

Precision Trading™:
Presentations Of Our SUPPORT Speakers

We want to be the company that will stick with you until you make it. We won't abandon you. Our Team Wall Street™ instructors, originally chosen and trained by Wade, branched out into their own designs and profitable methods. They built on his foundation, but now have fine-tuned various aspects of trading. They're wonderful, and so passionate. When you see the precise discoveries they've made, and their effective ways to enter and exit trades, you'll simply wonder what you've been missing—so will your stockbroker.

Topics include:

Stock Splits: More insights, trading methods and tips. Note: Darlene Nelson.

Sector Trades: Get in the way of movement as money moves from one arena to the next. Note: Doug Sutton.

Charting: Use trends, support lines, money flows, gaps and much, much more.

Spreads and Safety for Income: See and earn maximum profits with leg-ins and outs, emotionless trades.

News Trades: Develop expertise to use tools (Daily IQ™ and WIN) for daily profits.

Tax Saving, Asset Structuring: Even more effective ways to make more and keep more money.

You would never think of hiring on a new employee without training. Could you imagine a farmer expecting a tractor to plow straight rows without someone behind the wheel guiding it? Trading is no different. You earn from a formula just in proportion to how much you learn from it. There is no substitute for knowledge, understanding and application on a never-ending cycle of quality improvement. We live in a society and economy with so much available information. But how do you learn to profit from it? How do you capitalize on you? Where our company rises and shines is in bridging the gap between knowledge and understanding. In this never-ending cycle, we facilitate the application process to increase your understanding and the cycle goes on and on and on.

Why Home Study Courses?

You get seminars personally tailored to fit your time and schedule. With videos, you can literally design your own workshop, picking and choosing what strategies to focus on. Review as much or as little as you choose, whenever you can!

You get the visual dimension. See the charts being explained, follow along with the examples, and get the facilitator's full instruction. Using sight and hearing at the same time increases attention and comprehension, and that leads to more successful trades! Most of our courses have blank manuals for your notes plus a filled-in version.

You get instant replay! If you miss something, run the tape back and watch the example again. Stop the tape, try it out, come back and review immediately to see the right result. You can go over a concept or strategy as many times as it takes to really be comfortable with it.

Share the education with your friends and loved ones, for no additional charge. You can take just one volume or the whole course anywhere you want to watch it. Only video provides every chart, strategy, tip and technique as you learned them (except for the live experience). If you can't get folks to the Workshops, take the Workshops to them!

Video copies of Wade Cook's seminars and workshops are like getting free college courses forever when you pay for just one semester! Every time you review a strategy you learn something new. Our most successful students attend courses every month. Having your own video copy essentially allows you to attend as often as you want at your own convenience.

You can review on demand. Did you ever have a trade go wrong and wonder what happened? Would you like to have a mentor on hand any time of the day or night to go over the strategy with you? That's what video makes available—the opportunity for immediate course correction any time you get off track, for years to come.

The handsome multi-volume reference libraries keep you in action toward your goals. Just by sitting on the shelf, our video sets remind you of what you could be doing with your time and money to achieve your dreams. And you'll be able to act on them, whether you want early retirement, freedom from debt or simply a better lifestyle for your family.

Zero To Zillions Is A Must

Here, in one extensive, detailed course, exists 23 full-blown audio CDs, plus two wonderful bonus CDs, and filled-in manuals with charts, diagrams, explanations, analysis and seminar notes—after all, these are seminars, workshops, demonstrations and presentations. You'll be there, to some degree, learning, reviewing, pondering these formulas, methods, systems, concerns, techniques—and then, yep, you figured it out—you'll use these new-found strategies when you place your orders; when you eliminate bad trades, and as you make more money.

> *It is the glorious prerogative of the empire of knowledge that what it gains it never loses. On the contrary, it increases by the multiple, of its own power all its ends become means; all its attainments lead to new conquests.*
> –Daniel Webster

A Comprehensive System

You are just a quart or two of knowledge away from having and keeping the cash flow necessary for a great lifetime of giving. Ask yourself: if I don't get this knowledge what will I do? I don't like any answer or scenario you'll experience without knowing and using these powerful tools.

Zero to Zillions is worth way more than the low cost of $1,695. You'll make that back in a trade or two. You'll make more, keep more, and have more growing for you to produce income now and more income later—when you really need your money to work for you.

Our promise is to give you "fox-hole soldier" information, not ivory-tower, useless mumbo-jumbo. You deserve the best, most effective knowledge and a delivery system to match.

At the time this special report was written, Zero to Zillions was given for FREE with paid attendance at the Wall Street Workshop. It's worth the whole $1,695 and much, much more, but we were trying to prove a point: "We always give more than we promise." Call 1-877-WADECOOK for details.

The teacher's task is not to implant facts but to place the subject to be learned in front of the learner and, through sympathy, emotion, imagination and patience, to awaken in the learner the restless drive for answers and insights which enlarge the personal life and give it meaning.
–Nathan M. Pusey, President, Harvard

Your Emotions And The Stock Market

Here are a couple of major dilemmas I have in trying to convince you to "take the bull by the horns," get trained and learn by experiencing my trading methods.

People don't ask for facts in making up their minds. They would rather have one good, soul-satisfying emotion than a dozen facts.
~Robert Keith Leavitt

<u>Dilemma number one</u> – one of the easiest ways to sell an item, especially if that item is not well-known by the customer, is to compare it to something that the customer can relate to. It's sort of an "it tastes like chicken" scenario. The Wall Street Workshop has no equal—it literally stands alone.

There is no other seminar in America that is done in this workshop format, wherein we use real-live stock market experiences, actual examples from what is going on that day, and even that minute, in the marketplace. We could use hypothetical situations, but it is so much more interesting and educational to use real live stocks. So if we're buying a call option or selling a call option on a stock, it is best to use a real stock, even though that stock price is just a snapshot in time.

But the students get to see a real deal being done. Then, as they're excused in the TELL, SHOW, DO format, whether they're doing paper trades or real trades, they can go out and get a stockbroker on the phone and get real live quotes, and start to get a feel for how the deals are really put together.

We have Direct TV at my home. It is hooked up to our TV, which is hooked up with a VHS, DVD, stereo (et cetera) system. My wife and son point, click, relax and enjoy the show. Not me. I can sit there for 30 minutes moving the buttons, pushing, clicking, and then step 5—go get my wife or my 13-year-old son to help me get my show on.

I ask them for help! They grab the remote gadget and in six to ten seconds the show is on. I say, "No, let me hold it." At first, they still reached over my shoulder and pushed the buttons. I was frustrated. I said, "No—stand over there and tell me how to do it. Let me push the buttons. *Let me learn how to do it myself.*"

It was hard for them, I know, to let me do it myself. I needed to see it done, then do it. TELL, SHOW and DO. That's how we teach. You study, practice, understand and do.

One comparison that might shed a little light on this would be reading a cookbook, as compared to attending a cooking class, where you actually make a soufflé, or a cake, or meatloaf. Again, I think everyone knows that you can just learn so much more by doing. It's wonderful to read, it's good sometimes to watch a video, but to use another comparison, if you're going to learn how to snow ski, there is just no substitute for buckling the skis on and hitting the slopes. All the books in the world, all the videos in the world, will not help somebody become a master at snow skiing. So while there is no other course like our course, there are a few comparisons that help people see what we do to try to bring the stock market to life in the lives of our students.

The second dilemma is this: every sale is an emotional sale. The purchase of a car or stereo was done to satisfy some emotional need.

I've tried to get you to think about getting rich. I've attempted to show and teach you in this brief format, strategies for cash flow. I've used testimonials of big bucks being made, others of steady income, others to show you don't need much money to start. I used others from stockbrokers and financial planners to give credibility and credence to my methods. Have they worked? Did they produce an emotion in you to grab the phone, take your financial destiny into your own hands and get to a class?

I've tried to get you to not judge your future by your past—to come with us as we train you in our simple, easy-to-follow formulas.

> *Things may come to those who wait, but only the things left by those who hustle.*
> ~Abraham Lincoln

> *No steam or gas ever drives anything until it is confined. No Niagara is ever turned into light and power until it is tunneled. No life ever grows great until it is focused, dedi-cated, disci-plined.*
> ~Harry Emerson Fosdick

Does it help when I show you how WIN works and that some months of WIN are available FREE with your tuition? You get this tutorial, do-the-deals site for your profit convenience. Can you see the wisdom and power of having Zero to Zillions so you can master these processes—and turn all that wasted time in your car into instructive, constructive time? Time that will now help you make more money. We get really emotional about this for our students. Are you focused on the hard work necessary to gain these skills, or on the thrill and fun of achieving results?

I need help here. I can't do this alone. I need you to get emotional. You need to do your part. So sit back and ponder with me.

Imagine a big 'ol huge check—a few times a month—in your mailbox. You didn't have to go to work and punch a time clock. Your money produced this extra money. Does this feel good, or just okay?

Imagine quitting your job. Again, how does this feel? The fear—don't worry, you'll have extra, extra, extra cash flow for medical/dental insurance. Remember—your financial future is controlled by you, not your boss, not a union, not a fading industry.

Are you still with me? Now imagine sitting in church this Sunday and paying a tithe of $10,000 (and it's not even much of a sacrifice), because there's more on Monday. Imagine donating $25,000 to the American Heart Association.

Picture yourself in your car. A Mercedes passes on your left. Now sit in a new Mercedes dealership and write out a check—$86,000 and it's yours. No credit approval, no filling out credit apps. No debt. All cash. Turn the radio up, roll your window down—let the wind blow through your hair.

Now let's keep thinking. Look around your house. Now close your eyes and imagine a beautiful home with a huge yard for your kids. Mentally sit on your new beautiful furniture. Kick your feet up and relax.

Imagine paying cash for your kids to go to college; or helping your mom and dad retire more comfortably.

Can you feel it? Can you see yourself in better circumstances? We can—that's what we help people do.

Thanks Wade, I now work the market as a business daily from my home. I was a former stockbroker working for a bank brokerage. I now have financial independence and freedom to be with my family and travel.

—Richard P., AZ

A year ago today, we were living on 20 plus credit cards and had a second loan out on our home. Today, we're down to two or three cards and that second loan has been paid off. And we don't owe much on the cards. Up till August 1st, we did not have a computer. A personal message for Wade Cook with regard to each and every one of his critics: MAY ALL OF HIS CRITICS GET A TERRIBLE CRAMP IN THEIR TONGUE!!! That's a very old Yiddish curse. But his critics deserve no less. Much thanks for helping to turn our lives around!

—Joel and Jennifer D., CA

My husband has worked two full time jobs since our son was born three years ago. He put his aspirations for a career and education [on hold] so I could be home with our son. Since I started trading with real money in 12/99, he has been able to quit a job and will be starting school to be a computer network engineer. Quite a big deal for a farmer from El Salvador who came here look-

ing for asylum. Without stock trading, we would have to live on low income or dump our child in daycare.

—Gayle G., CA

You pick out and *use the emotion you need*. Don't delay! Riches and cash flow await you. Our place in this is simple. We'll teach you. We'll inspire you. We'll cheerlead you. We're in your corner. We're behind you and we want the job of helping you make it big time.

If you don't choose us to help you, then who? If not now, when? If not this current stock market and our workable cash flow ways, then what? When will it be your turn? Yes, most people are not rich because they don't deserve it. What experiences have they had, what knowledge have they gained which qualifies them to be rich? It's time to give up the heavy baggage that doesn't work. It's time to ditch old stale formulas and it's definitely time to give up the excuses.

So, lets move some earth. Please read this carefully. This should shake up your thinking a bit—maybe a lot.

> *You can make money or you can make excuses, but you can't make both.*
>
> ~Don Berman

I have been criticized by some of the most influential financial "gurus" in the country. Their attacks are relentless, because they represent the status quo for the firms in the industry, and I must apologetically say about them, they do not want to help or serve the little guy. They have their job, I have mine.

> *Keep away from people who try to belittle your ambitions. Small people always do that, but the really great make you feel that you, too, can become great.*
>
> ~Mark Twain

> *I expect to pass through life but once. If, therefore, there be any kindness I can show, or any good thing I can do to any fellow-being, let me do it now, and not defer or neglect it, as I shall not pass this way again.*
>
> ~William Penn

It's time to jump up and get going.

> *Getting an idea should be like sitting on a pin. It should make you jump up and do something.*
>
> ~Kemmons Wilson

One last thing. I have been very, very successful in my life, and I hope I can make a difference in your life. I want to be the very best, but I want to be here to serve people. I don't want to charge a price that is so inexpensive the class won't be valued.

Every time I attend a Wade Cook Seminar I realize how little I know. Thank you Wade for giving of yourself to help us students achieve this wonderful course in stock market strategies. I attended my first Wall Street Workshop in Boston in 1998. I made $8,000 on PFE. It paid for my course plus. Thank you!

—Victoria K., CT

So let me give you all the incentive you need to take action on your future and get yourself into this incredible event! The Wall Street Workshop retails for $6,295. Keep reading—you're about to be blown away....

> *Knowing is not enough; we must apply. Willing is not enough; we must do.*
> ~ Johann Von Goethe

I know travel involves extra expense, and I want to help in every way I can, so I'm offering a $1,000 (one thousand dollars!) Travel Discount. Since my staff can't possibly book everyone's travel, I decided to keep things simple and offer you this $1,000 discount. The Wall Street Workshop is such a dynamic event, if it isn't in your town, get on a plane and get there—your trip has just been covered!

If you think I've already done enough, think again—I want to do more! I know how hard you work. I know everyone expects to pay for their education. I know some people even pay more for their education than it's worth. Well *you* are going to get more education than you pay for! I am offering right now, for a very short period of time, one additional Scholarship Discount. Anybody who calls right now, I will knock another $1,000 off the price! That puts the Wall Street Workshop within the realm of virtually everyone! I don't want you to say no. These two discounts cannot be used in conjunction with other specials.

I feel like I've been in college for one year but I've only been in class (Wall Street Workshop) just two days!

—Barbara D., TX

At $6,295, we knocked off $1,000 for a discount for travel, and now we've knocked off an additional $1,000 for this Scholarship Discount! Now, you don't have to take this discount. You can say, "I want to ignore Wade's Scholarship Discount, and I'll pay the extra $1,000." But, I'm offering it to you, and I would love for you to take advantage of this. I want you to say YES!

> *By wisdom a house is built, and through understanding it is established; through knowledge its rooms are filled with rare and beautiful treasures.*
> —Proverbs 24:3-4 (NIV)

Knowledge is Cash Flow Potential

I don't have any secrets—I could make a lot more money trading in the stock market for myself, but I have such a love, a passion for sharing this information! I was going to say "teaching," which I used to believe in, but I don't believe in it anymore. There's an old proverb that says "When the student is ready, the teacher appears." I believe in learning. I believe in education, but all you will learn something when you need it, and you'll learn at your pace. I want to be a facilitator in your life, helping you along that path to wealth, those stepping stones to success.

The American Dream is alive and well! I want to be one person in your life that will lead the way and help you get it; help you get the understanding, the knowledge and the application skills that will help you re-enter the American Dream. You deserve it! What are you waiting for??

Okay, if you still need a kick in the pants, there's one last thing I want to do for you. The spouse, or companion rate (and I really recommend that you come as a family) right now is $3,695. Usually the spouse rate is about half, but I'm going to do even better than that. I just knocked off $2,000 from your price for the Travel Discount and for the Scholarship, and I'm going to knock off *another* $2,000 from the spouse rate! So, it's only $1,695 for your spouse or your Mom or Dad, or your business partner. And, what's more, I'll honor that price for *two more people*! So if you want to bring a spouse *and* your Mom and Dad, their price will only be $1,695 each!

You will get the $1,695 Zero to Zillions, and when you get that, you will say that this one item is worth every penny of the entire package price. You're also going to receive three months of WIN, our incredible Internet tutorial service (a $900 value). What I'm trying to say here, is anything that my company can do to help move you through this educational process, we will do it. It's all part of our desire to stick with you until you make it. At the time of printing, we were offering more than three months of W.I.N. Call to see if "more" are still available.

That's right. All this for a price that one good trade will pay for. I know it's hard to believe, but I realize we as Americans want value and quality. Come learn with us, and you'll have value, quality and abundance fill your life to overflowing.

People say "Is this guy real? Is he just using the Bible because it's convenient?" I'm serious, I get that question every now and then. People come to my seminar and say "OK, you talk about the Bible; do you live it?" I say "Well, talk to my employees. Talk to my family. Talk to my students."

I am so grateful for people like Wade and his terrific (staff)…this is the stuff that will make it possible for anyone who wants it, to have a better life. Thanks so much to all of you. After my first Wall Street Workshop… my account went from $2,500 to $60,000 in about nine or ten months.

—Trish K., AZ

So, if you like my style, and if you like me, I invite you to this experiential learning workshop. Put us to the test. We want to get you through this learning curve, and again, help you to make all the cash flow you need so you can truly live a great lifestyle. A lifestyle of nobility. A lifestyle of quality. A lifestyle of caring and sharing for those people in your life. And if there's anything that my staff or I can do to help you in this endeavor, then please join with us. If you're going to buy stocks and bonds, take stock in knowledge and bond with us!

I am very encouraged by the Wade Cook Seminar System. Most people I talk to want to go out and make some things happen so they can afford the seminar and that is backwards because it will cost them money [not to go] and they may get discouraged and they won't get the education. I'm endorsing [the] Wade Cook seminars because every time I go to one, my income goes up. If my income is going up, why shouldn't I be excited? I'm writing covered calls, buying a few options and doing rolling stocks, just the basics. I am finding a 20-30% per month income. I am simply implementing the tools provided and the teachings by the staff [at the Stock Market Institute of Learning™]. Everyone thinks that there is an easy way out. I will tell you that I've never seen anything easier than following within the guidelines of the Wade Cook seminar system. Wade, in his wisdom and tenacity of going after knowledge and never letting down, has created something that will live a long time. We can provide for our family—generations and generations deep. This is SINCERE, REAL, DOABLE, can be done, and should be done. Why waste another minute in your lives without seeing the potential and the fruit on the tree?

—David E. FL

Note: At the time of printing, we were marketing our MAP Program. MAP—Mentor Apprenticeship Progam. It's even a better deal. Call 1-877-WADECOOK.

Appendix 2

A Conversation With Wade

And Other Officers
Of The Company

About our Company:

Wade Cook Financial Corporation is a publicly traded company (OTCBB:WADE). The following are excerpts taken from a recent Shareholders update. To read the Shareholders update in its entirety, please go to our website at www.wadecook.com or call Investor Relations at 1-206-901-3000.

A Message to Shareholders of
Wade Cook Financial Corporation, Inc.

The following is an interview conducted with Wade **Cook** and several other officers of Wade **Cook** Financial Corporation that transpired over a one-month period of time, from about mid-December 2001 through January 15, 2002. Questions answered by Wade **Cook** will be prefaced with **Cook**, and the other officers of the company will be noted as follows: Robert Hondel, COO, WCFC—**Hondel**; Cynthia Britten, CFO, WCFC—**Britten**; Robin Anderson, CEO, SMILe—**Anderson**.

Many of these questions have come in the form of letters and emails from shareholders and students to Wade **Cook** Financial Corporation Headquarters.

Many statements below fall under the "Forward Looking Statement" category as defined by the Securities & Exchange Commission. Please see full disclaimer on page 218

#1 Q: If you were to give a State of the Company Address, what shape would you say the company is in?

A: Cook—As everyone knows, we have gone through a really difficult time for the last two years. One of our major subsidiaries, the Stock Market Institute of Learning, Inc.™ (SMILe) has primarily been sponsoring and teaching Stock Market seminars. For many years, we taught Real Estate seminars and Asset Protection seminars and, while we are still teaching many Asset Protection seminars, our primary flagship seminar is the Wall Street Workshop™.

We have let shareholders know for a number of years that our sales, basically our fortune, is tied up in how the Stock Market is doing. We could in fact lay our sales reports on top of one of the indices, like the Dow Jones Industrial Average, and you will see an amazing correspondence. The point is, as the Stock Market was going up during that rampaging bull market, our sales increased dramatically. We had incredible referrals coming into our seminars, meaning our existing customers were sending their family and friends, and that bolstered our sales immensely. Our books, through one of our subsidiaries, Light-house Publishing, were selling like crazy in the bookstores. We had at one time three books on the New York Times Business Best-selling list, on Business Week Best-selling list, on Entrepreneur Magazine Money Best-selling list and in the USA Today Business Book Best-selling list. This all brought so much attention to the company. With the two down years, it has been tough to get people really excited about the Stock Market, and yet we now see that changing.

We have also seriously reduced our costs during this time. We have put many control measures in place to better monitor each advertising dollar. We feel very hopeful that as the market turns around, and as we add a new product mix to our seminar base, our sales will continue to increase. We are hoping to help this momentum by keeping our costs low, therefore bringing a better profit to the bottom line.

Anderson—The Stock Market Institute of Learning,™ Inc. (SMILe) is continuing to add dynamic new speakers with exceptional products in an effort to diversify. These new names and faces are becoming household names in the industry.

Hondel—We have our costs under control. Example: 1ˢᵗ Quarter 2000, our costs were $4,000,000 per month. Today, our costs are at $2,000,000. We watch every dime. We monitor everything.

Britten—The state of the company is a continual dedication to improve, and increase the profitability amongst all obstacles. The feeling at the company is of pride. As I walk down the halls I pass employees who love their jobs and continue to support the company at all costs.

The past year has had a positive impact on the company by the demand to take a closer look at expenses, employees and our dedication to our consumers. The reduction in revenues have only made the company stronger.

#2   **Q:** Fill us in, if you will on the 1:10 reverse stock split.

A: Cook—The Board of Directors and the Officers of the Corporation feel that it is really important to get our company listed on the NASDAQ or one of the major exchanges. We are willing to take some drastic measures to get the company listed.

We want to get back to our core business, and get the company extremely profitable. This involves keeping those entities that have the highest likelihood of making a profit, and disposing of the others—basically to concentrate all of our efforts on the core business and get our sales back up while bringing better earnings to the bottom line.

Wade Cook   **Robert Hondel**

Cynthia Britten   **Robin Anderson**

Another drastic measure would be this 1:10 reverse stock split. As many of our students from my seminars would know, I have not been a proponent of reverse stock splits. I have been very leery of them. As you can see from reports elsewhere, reverse stock splits usually are not a very healthy move. However, the ones that have been successful are companies that are profitable or soon to be profitable, as we hope to be after this downturn.

We see really good signs that our company will show profitability. Other companies have done reverse stock splits to STAY listed. That is not the case with us. We want to GET listed and therefore one of the requirements for NASDAQ is to maintain a share price, in the Microcap division, of $4.00 per share for 90 consecutive days. We meet all other requirements to have our stock listed.

Let's say for example, that our stock is at .20 cents, which it was about the time this answer was given. In a 1:10 stock split, that would put the stock at $2.00. If it would just double or more from here, we would be up to the $4.00 range.

Hondel—Our motive is simply to get listed. For that to happen, we need our share price above $4.00. A reverse split is a method that reduces the number of a company's outstanding shares, and that, at the same time, increases the price of the individual shares. The total value of your shares, however, remains the same. Your investment is worth the same dollar amount as it was the day before the split.

There is little direct benefit of a stock split, but when you get a good profit to the bottom line, your stock price should reflect this better.

For example, take a company with a $2 stock, 6,000,000 shares outstanding, and a profit of $6,000,000. This reflects a healthy earning of $1 a share before taxes. This is what I mean when I say that in the end, the only thing a company can really do to guarantee a major league listing is to run its business successfully.

When the company is steering to get listed on NASDAQ (or one of the other major exchanges), you will see the stocks move up on good earnings reports. This attracts institutional investors who only deal with stocks over $4.00. They don't want to deal with companies with penny-stock status.

#3 **Q:** What about the public float?

A: Cook—We have tried for many years to get our stock up off the nickel range. It has been my personal opinion based on a 'percentage times sales,' that our company could easily trade at $100 to $200 million dollars, even though it did not have the net earnings for the last few years to accomplish this. We have been highly profitable in the past and, after experiencing the downturn and retrenching and regrouping, and getting back to our core business, we see really good signs that a turnaround is forthcoming.

One of the problems has been the large float for a company of our size. We have over 63 million shares outstanding. The founders of the company and their personal family corporations and limited partnerships, have owned about 65% of the company. About 35%, or about 20 million shares, have been on the public float. The company has been in a share buyback program, and has purchased back hundreds of thousands of shares. But still, the float is so large that, according to the law of supply and demand, we just haven't been able to get the stock to rise with so much supply in the marketplace.

A 1:10 reverse split, would take that 20 million shares of stock, and reduce it to 2 million. There would then be a total of 6.3 million shares outstanding. As the Company moves towards getting a NASDAQ listing in our attempt to increase shareholder liquidity, and as we have the investing public in general looking at us and scrutinizing us, (which we welcome because of our value and our sales) we feel that all this should bode well for our stock in the future.

The Board of Directors is really determined to build shareholder value. We realize that a one for ten reverse stock split is a drastic move, but again, we are doing it opposite of what most companies have done, to GET listed on a major exchange, not to STAY listed. We are very proud of the results of our cost cutting efforts, our current level of sales compared to the expenses we have, and the direction we are taking with the uptrending market, while also adding more seminars.

If the demand is there, and there are only 2 million shares available, we feel that our company may be more fairly valued. We would therefore be in a position to fulfill the primary mission of the 1:10 reverse stock split, which is to get listed on a major exchange.

#4 **Q:** What about your earnings announcement?

A: Cook—For many years, we have felt that if we just build a great company, by increasing earnings and investing in other great companies, our asset base would eventually increase to reflect a really good shareholder value. For example, the price of the stock as compared to the Book Value or breakup value of the company.

We have not gone out and promoted the company stock, as many companies do. We have had opportunities to do so, but the presentations just seemed like a lot of hype. For example, we have had many PR-type firms come into the picture who have told us that they wanted "X" number of shares of stock to PR our stock, which also means finding new market makers who would push our stock to the investing public. The problem is, these types of companies end up with a lot of stock in the company, and as soon as they get the share price up, they dump their stock. The contract period is over and the stock goes back down. We have not wanted to play that kind of game. We want to build a great company with a strong foundation.

In December of 2001, when the Board of Directors met, they decided to change the company policy of not making earnings projections. Obviously, we are a Bulletin Board stock (OTCBB) and therefore we do not have analysts following us from the major firms. If we get listed on NASDAQ, and any of these analysts want to start following us, we would obviously at that point in time have to give them certain types of information that would help them evaluate the company, the stock price and the future direction as they make recommendations or non-recommendations to their customer base.

In advance of that, we decided as a company to very honestly and forthrightly go to the investing public and tell them what we think we are going to make. For example, we feel rather conservatively that the company, with the addition of the homebuilding profits, the profits from SMILe, a turn around in Ideal Travel (another one of our subsidiary corporations), and the huge investments we have in several companies that should go public in the future, we should in the year 2002 see net earnings of $6 million.

Again, we have never made this type of projection before and it could be more or less than $6 million. We present these types of earnings projections under the "Forward-looking Statement" guidelines by the SEC. Realize also that these guidelines are in place not only for our company, but also for all other companies which make earnings projections.

Britten—We as a company are ready to step out and let the public know the value and potential that we feel is inherent in our company. Management's sole focus is to put forth the effort required to assist in the building of each individual subsidiary to its full potential to reach the estimated net profit.

Hondel—We have a family of great companies with huge potential. We have to concentrate on each subsidiary. We have to put energy and passion into the travel division, the luxury homebuilding division, the publishing division and the investment division. Each division has had greatness in and of themselves.

#5 **Q:** What do you think $6,000,000 of earnings would do to your stock?

A: Cook—That is really hard to say. We can sit and hope all day that our stock will go up, but it just might not do so. We cannot control exactly what goes on in the minds of the investing public. We cannot control what happens, for example, when the great news we have coming out is picked up by certain news agencies, and they then seem to put a negative spin on it. I honestly don't know how this poor cab driver from Tacoma Washington can generate so much animosity in the press. I think it speaks to the fact that we are out showing the small guy in America how to trade in the market and do what the billion-dollar traders do. This has generated, obviously, a lot of heated statements about our company. I'm not saying now that the negativity has gone away, but in the last few months we have seen an abatement in those kinds of attacks on our company.

One of the things we're trying to do is clarify for people that Wade **Cook** Financial Corporation is NOT a company that teaches Stock Market Seminars. Those are taught by one of our subsidiaries, The Stock Market Institute of Learning, Inc. Wade **Cook** Financial Corporation is a holding corporation, with several great, wholly owned subsidiaries, which are diverse and yet very synergistic as a whole.

More specifically, if we do make $6,000,000 in net earnings, that would represent about $1 a share. In theory, the stock could rise to 20, 30 or 40 times earnings, and that would be nice, but there is no guarantee that this will be the case. Also, it's not really a concern at the current moment that the stock goes to $20 a share, because all we're trying to do is get listed on NASDAQ and we need the stock above $4 a share. In the open-air marketplace that we call the Stock Market, the investing public puts a value on our stock according to the dictates of their own thought processes. All we can do, and intend to do, is get them good information, accurately and in a timely manner, so they can make the decision.

Anderson—We have very capable employees, who are dedicated to building this division of WCFC. They also have a vested interest in getting our stock price up, as most are also shareholders. Our employees also understand the value of the education we teach and are actively involved in building revenue.

Britten—Earnings of $6 million or any positive movement in earnings will only relate the progress of the company to the public. The hope, of course, is to increase the price of the stock and to achieve the honor of being listed on a major exchange.

#9 **Q:** We hear good things about the homebuilding business. Can you fill us in on a few of the details?

A: Cook—Brookhaven Homes is the name of our luxury homebuilding division. We are building upper-end homes in the state of Washington. Brookhaven Homes is a major award winning company. We had one home out of six in the 2001 Seattle Street of Dreams, and of the 12 major awards, we took 8 of them.

"The Calloway" in the Seattle 2001 Street of Dreams—Brookhaven Homes

We are hoping to have between 2 and 4 luxury homes either built, and/or closed by the end of 2002.

Hondel—We are finding our niche in the homebuilding business. We build luxury homes. We put innovations into our homes that you won't find in most others—we are on the cutting edge of home technology. We are the trendsetter, that's why we took 8 out of 12 awards. We have the creativity and boldness to be the best. That's what people who have money want. They want a home that nobody else has, they want it to be top of the line and they want it now.

#10 **Q:** What is the status of the publishing enterprise?

A: Cook—The publishing business is a very difficult one to make money in. The force in the book selling industry has changed to the retail front. Old publishers like Simon-Schuster, McGraw-Hill and others used to control the day, but virtually every major publishing company we know of is struggling. Huge bookstore chains now dominate the industry.

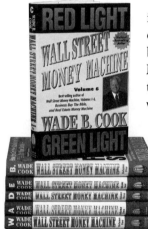

We have been very successful, however, because our books in the bookstores have brought a lot of attention our way. For example, in many of our books we have had CD's, our 800 number and our website listed. People can then get a hold of us. Many current students have come through the random selection of our books in bookstores. Darlene and Miles Nelson have written, *Stock Split Secrets*. It's a great book. Oh, and Doug Sutton's book, *The Beginning Investors Bible*, is a must read. Every trader and investor in the market should get this book before they do their next trade. It's just that good.

We also center a lot of our advertising on our books. For example, we will, in February or March of this year put out the new release of Wade Cook's *Wall Street Money Machine Series*, Volume 6, which will be entitled "Red Light, Green Light." This has been one of our most successful home study course seminar products, and we have taken the best of that seminar and have put it in hardbound book format. We are planning to do a major campaign at SMILe, as Lighthouse Publishing releases this book to the trade.

Hondel—SMILe sends out two to three million pieces of mail each year to their customers. It costs pennies to include a flyer about our best-selling book, which in turn drives people to the bookstores to buy books. SMILe spends $2,000,000 a year on radio advertising to drive people into their seminars. It costs us nothing to mention our best-selling books at the same time. In essence, Lighthouse Publishing gets the benefit of millions of dollars of advertising at zero cost.

   Anderson—SMILe has taken the model developed by Wade **Cook** in creating best-selling books and has applied this to our stable of professional speakers. This again proves our commitment to diversify and promote new talent.

#15 **Q:** You mentioned your investment in some private companies that might go public, and/or companies that have already gone public. Can you enlighten us on that?

   A: Cook—We have investments in four to five other companies which look very promising.

   As many of you know, the last few years have not been that good for the going public process. IPO's have been scarce. It has been tough for many companies to raise money in this downtrending marketplace and therefore a lot of the companies we were hoping would have gone public three and four years ago have not done so. It looks like many of them now are poised to do so, however it is two and three years past the time we thought they would go public. Our cash has been tied up until this point in time. Let me now give a brief listing of these companies. I will include their Internet site so you can get more information. You may even want to use their products and services if you need them.

   #1 One of the companies we invested in a number of years ago is Ceristar™. They can be found at www.ceristar.com. Originally, it was going to be a high-speed phone company, but with the incredible technology they have, they have become an Intranet phone company. For example, they might become the whole phone system for a complete mall. They can wire an entire office complex and it is more sophisticated and easier to use than a T-1. They are very successful. One of the reasons I like this company is because they generate continuous cash flow. Efforts today produce income tomorrow and I like that format.

   #2 About five and a half years ago we invested a half a million dollars in a company called Know Wonder. They have kept the name Know Wonder™ and it is now one of their three divisions, but the parent company has now changed their name to Amaze Entertainment™. You can find them at www.amazentertainment.com. When we first invested in Amaze they had three employees. This is a company that focuses on computer games.

   Awhile ago, they were able to negotiate a deal with Electronic Arts™ (EA on the TV screen, but ERTS is the ticker symbol), and developed a game to market at the release of the first Harry Potter® movie. This video game, *Harry Potter and the Sorcerer's Stone*, has the imprint Know Wonder on the back of the one for the PC and the one for Gameboy Color and Gameboy Advanced has the imprint of Griptonite on the back of the game.

They are selling very well. Again, this is still a private company, but they are doing very well and we hope they will either get bought out or go public.

They have just signed an agreement with Lord of the Rings® for two games. They are also negotiating for two more games for Harry Potter and a lot of other great things are happening.

Our publicly traded company at one time owned a little over 6.5% of the company, but they have done another private placement offering and raised more money, so I'm sure our shares have been diluted. However, we bought the stock at $2 a share and the last round of private placement money was raised at $6 a share. As you'll read in my Special Report called *Asset Expensing*, we still have to carry that asset on our books at $2, because it's "cost basis or market value, whichever is less." Again, we hope this company goes public, and then the stock can go to the price that the public deems it to be worth. The company has a great future.

#3 A few years ago we invested in a company called Arkona. This company has already gone public and is trading under ticker symbol ARKN. You'll find their website at www.arkona.com.

This company has a very unique, hugely popular software program for running car dealerships. Mitsubishi was getting out of the software development process after spending two million dollars to develop their own software programs for their dealers. They started using the Arkona developed system and Mitsubishi has approved this system for dealerships in North America. Arkona became the software dealer of choice for Mitsubishi. They also, soon after that, which was in the fall of the year 2001, were approved by Ford Motor Company and also by General Motors.

The future looks so incredible for this company, because they not only receive fees for installing the software, but they receive ongoing percentages of sales and/ or fees for maintaining the software.

#4 The next company is called Aradyme. I am very, very excited about this company. They have a website at www.aradyme.com. This company has a great software product for any business over ten people. It has an incredible drag-and-drop type software that makes it very easy for the IS or IT department in companies to install, maintain and run. There are up to 50 different functions that can be installed on a modular basis, so you can do one without the other. The other ERP-type software for running larger companies is so all-inclusive that everything has to be done at the same time, and a change in one area can create such drastic problems in another area.

I see this company could grow into hundreds of millions of dollars in sales, and be such a new, unique and viable product in virtually every industry. It has such a rosy outlook.

#16 **Q:** What should we, as a stockholder of your company, do now?

A: Cook—Neither I, nor any of the other management staff, would ever make a recommendation to buy our stock. People would have to decide if ownership of our stock fits into their own risk/reward tolerance level. All I can do is tell you that I know a lot of the management staff here are buyers of our stock. You'll notice I did not say, "net buyers," in that I do not know of anyone that is selling the stock.

I guess my last message to our great shareholders, who continue to remain loyal to us, is to "Hang in there." We really feel that a NASDAQ or other major exchange listing is just one answer, but a very important answer. If people ask me what I'm doing and want to follow my example, it is simply that I want to own *more* stock in this company, not less. I encourage everyone to give us a good, hard look and hope they will make a decision to own stock in our future.

One of our slogans in our seminars has been, "Before you invest in stocks and bonds, take stock in knowledge and bond with us." We realize our shareholders have bonded with us and we thank them for that. We want them to know of our heartfelt gratitude for supporting us and for being a part of our progress.

Abundantly Yours,

Wade B. Cook

Note from the Marketing Department at SMILe:

Wade Cook is just finishing up a brand new home study course called I.P.O.-P.O.P. The P.O.P. stands for Pre, Open, Post. It's very informative. It will retail for $695, but for a limited time we have a shareholder special that is so low, we don't even want to disclose the price here. Call 1-877-WADECOOK.

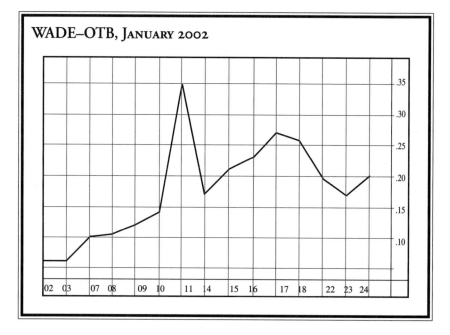

This shareholder Q&A contains statements that may constitute "forward-looking statements" within the meaning of the Securities Act of 1933 and the Securities Exchange Act of 1934, as amended by the Private Securities Litigation Reform Act of 1995. Such statements include comments regarding the Company's anticipated net earning in 2002, the expected initial public offerings of companies whose stock is held by the Company, the profitability of the Company's subsidiaries and investments and the ability of the Company to achieve a listing on Nasdaq or another major stock exchange. Prospective investors are cautioned that any such forward-looking statements are not guarantees of future performance and involve risks and uncertainties, and actual results may differ materially from those contemplated by such forward-looking statements. Important factors currently known to management that could cause actual results to differ materially from those in forward-looking statements include, without limitation, the Company's working capital deficiency and liquidity constraints; the effect that volatility in the stock market may have on the interest of customers in the Company's seminars, products and services, on the Company's own investments and the ability of the companies in which the Company has invested to complete an initial public offering at a price level anticipated by the Company, or at all; the level of resources that may be required by the Company's consumer redress program; the Company's continuing compliance with state and federal agreements; fluctuations in the commercial real estate market, the housing market and in the travel industry; the possibility of adverse outcomes in pending or threatened litigation and actions involving the Company; and damage and disruption to operations caused by the February 28, 2001 earthquake and flooding. For additional factors that may cause actual results to differ materially from those contemplated by such forward-looking statements, please see the "Risk Factors" described in Exhibit 99.2 to the company's Quarterly Report on Form 10-Q, filed in November 2001, and in other filings on file with the SEC, which Risk Factors are incorporated herein as though fully set forth. The company undertakes no obligation to update or revise forward-looking statements to reflect changed assumptions, the occurrence of unanticipated events or changes to future operating results.

Appendix 3

Resource Material

Books

Wall Street Money Machine Series, Volume 1
Written by Wade Cook

Wall Street Money Machine Series, Volume 2
Written by Wade Cook

Wall Street Money Machine Series, Volume 3
Written by Wade Cook

Wall Street Money Machine Series, Volume 4
Written by Wade Cook

Wall Street Money Machine Series, Volume 5
Written by Wade Cook

Business Buy the Bible, A+, and *Don't Set Goals (The Old Way)*
Written by Wade Cook

Beginning Investor's Bible
Written by Doug Sutton

Stock Split Secrets
Written by Darlene and Miles Nelson

On Track Investing
Written by Dave Hebert

Audio Compact Discs

Top Ten Ways To Trade Right Seminar on CD

The Stock Market is ever changing and we need to be ready, to not only change with it, but find a way to come out on top. This seminar on CD is designed to give you the edge you need to trade no matter what the market is doing, especially if the country is in a recession. (value $19.95) Now just $10, plus $3 S&H.

Outrageous Returns Seminar on CD

This seminar CD is jam-packed with education on how to capitalize on the phenomena called Stock Splits. Companies do stock splits to reduce the price of their stock to more investors. There are five times to play stock splits and this CD will cover it all for you. (value $26.95) Now just $10, plus $3 S&H.

Behind Closed Doors Seminar on CD

On this intimate CD, Wade Cook shares some of his secrets to success. Learn concepts such as, cash to asset to cash, meter drop, Wade's teaching process, and much more. His stories and wisdom will help you enjoy learning from one of the masters of cash flow and education for success. (value $26.95) Now just $10, plus $3 S&H.

Events

Wade Cook's Financial Clinic

We travel to various cities across the United States, teaching time-tested principles of wealth enhancement to information-hungry students of all demographic levels. Team Wall Street is a group of handpicked instructors who will share cash flow strategies like, Rolling Stocks, Writing Covered Calls, Options and Options on Stock Splits. You only need call to find the class nearest you – 1-877-WADECOOK. (value $295)

Semper Financial Investors' Convention

Imagine with me, an event where 12-15 of speakers take their best strategies that have helped them trade for cash flow from the stock market and share with you how to use these strategies in the current market. Now, imagine hundreds of other fellow students of stock market strategy education all mingling for three days with each other, sharing successes and pitfalls to help each other grow and learn. This convention is for everyone; from beginner to advanced, there is something for each level. You can't afford to miss this incredible three days of learning and fun. (value $999)

Home Study Courses

Zero to Zillions

Zero to Zillions is an easy-to-follow, easy-to-understand, and teaches easy-to-implement methods and techniques designed for consistent cash flow from the stock market. This mega course on stock market income formulas is taught in a lively format of real examples, great expectations, functional demonstrations and presentations to take you to the next level of trading in the stock market. Zero to Zillions has beautiful filled-in manuals (notes taken as if you were in the live events) with documentation, examples and add-on materials. (value $1695) See Appendix 1 for information.

Red Light/Green Light

This is the ultimate in making timely trades. As CEO of a publicly traded company, Wade Cook discovered a quarterly pattern of stock price behavior that corresponds with corporate news reports. Since most companies file their reports about the same time, many stocks would move accordingly. The Red Light/Green Light course shows you how to recognize and use this information to make more money and avoid losing trades. (value $995)

Miscellaneous

Travel Agency Package

The only sensible solution for the frequent traveler. This package includes all the information and training you need to be an outside travel agent for a stable company. There are no hassles, no requirements, no forms or restrictions, just all the benefits of traveling for substantially less every time. (value $29.95)

Explanations™ Newsletter

In the wild and crazy stock market game, Explanations Newsletter will keep you on your toes! Every month you'll receive coaching, instruction, and encouragement with engaging articles designed to bring your trading skills to a higher level. Learn new twists on Wade's basic strategies, find out about beneficial research tools, read reviews on the latest investment products and services, and get detailed answers to your trading questions. (value $149)

Wealth Information Network (W.I.N.)

One of the most comprehensive sources for stock market information is the Wealth Information Network (WIN). WIN is a web-based platform containing solid stock market information and strategies in an easy-to-use format. Using WIN, you can look over the shoulder, so to speak, of some of the finest stock market strategists in the country! Not only are you seeing trades that have been placed by Wade Cook and Team Wall Street, WIN also provides a centralized spot on the Web where you can access the online trading resources you need, quickly and conveniently. We are not stockbrokers and we don't get anything from your trades. We are however, an excellent tutorial service and information source for our students. (value $3,600 per year)

Special Reports

10 Indisputable and Often Gut Wrenching Rules Of Financial Success

Stop listening to people making less than what you want to make and don't miss out on a timely special report from a millionaire. Learn all about the incredible Wall Street Workshop and what makes Wade Cook and his strategies different from everyone else in the stock market arena. (value $59.95) Currently sent FREE as part of a 2002 marketing push. 1-877-WADECOOK

Videos

Dynamic Dollars

In this exciting video event, Wade gets "<u>real</u>" and tells it all. He explains cash flow strategies that <u>really</u> work. He will show you <u>*what*</u> he learned, and how he has been able to apply it to his stock market investing and "tear up" the market with some phenomenal and dynamic results. The presentation is truly astounding. (value $59.95)

Appendix 4

Soar With Eagles

The nighttime gym scene in the movie *Remember The Titans* had a part where the football players started quoting scripture. I loved it, because it was one of my favorite verses. Isaiah 40:31 *"But they that wait upon the LORD shall renew their strength; they shall mount up with wings as eagles; they shall run, and not be weary; and they shall walk, and not faint."* Years ago I started collecting small statues of Eagles.

I love eagles, but I love God's words more. The promise in this verse is awesome. Inspired by this and a passion for Biblical study, including research into the original Hebrew, Aramaic and Greek words, and a desire to see these Biblical truths brought back into our general discourse and our personal lives, I set about to write these *Soar With Eagles* Special Reports. I hope you enjoy them.

Wade & Laura Cook

#700 **Preface:** A study in itself of ancient knowledge and God's will for us.

#701 **Total Harmony:** A discussion of false myths about God. Abraham, the first Hebrew, set a new standard.

#702 **Gaining Wisdom:** Knowledge to understanding everyday uses: desire first. Learn how to make better decisions.

#703   **7 Ways to Gain Wisdom:** Functional ways to really put knowledge/wisdom to work. See tangible results.

#704   **Discerning Wisdom:** More easy-to-implement formulas for applying knowledge gained. Fun stuff.

#705   **Wisdom and Riddles:** Samson and a great riddle. Hebrew knowledge. Learn how to *project* outcomes, not predict outcomes. New Perspective.

#706   **Noble Living:** A wonderful, uplifting report on nine ways to build a quality life. Excellent.

#707   **Noble Actions:** Living, working for a quality existence. Actions which reflect Godly Values.

#708   **Seeking Peace – Making Peace:** Study Hebrew: Hebrew and its varied meanings. Peace, comfort and more happiness.

#709   **A Pure Heart:** "Incline thine ear..." A Godly heart translated into worthwhile action. Splendid.

#710   **Heart and Soul:** The nexus with God. The lamp unto the body. David's plea! A touching collection of scripture.

#711   **Trusting God:** Building a team. Faith is trust, trust is everything in our relationship with God.

#712   **Dealing With Injustice:** Fight, Flight or Forego to God. Maybe Wade's battles can help you think more clearly.

#713   **A Thankful Heart:** A key to success. Blessings acknowledgment. Keeping things in proper perspective.

#714   **Attitude is Everything:** Think High and Fly. Control your thoughts—it's the start of all good things.

The following five reports are part of our High-Teens Series (715-719).

#715   **Guard Your Heart:** Only you control your thoughts. A message of Great Importance to all—especially the youth.

#716   **Determination:** Wade's daughter Leslie shares her secret passion—drive, persistence—goal getting.

#717   **The Strength of Youth:** Wade's teen stories. "Double it" and the Second Mile thinking process. Uplifting.

#718 **Ten Laws of Success For Teenagers:** A wonderful exposé that will help uplift, motivate, drive teenagers to greater heights.

#719 **The Whole Armour of God:** Don't leave home without it. A report on Ephesians 6. This will give teenagers real things to do to better their lives. Encouraging.

#720 **Influence:** A powerful report on the influence of one. Cautions. Friends, parents, leaders—Please read this.

#721 **A Prayer for All of Us: Jabez:** A detailed study of the four components of Jabez' prayer.

#722 **Wealth: A Generous Viewpoint:** A Biblical and historical look at money and generosity. Really fun.

#723 **A Celebration of Light:** God is the Father of lights. Explore the Light of Christ. Mornings. Sunshine. Health.

#724 **Music To My Ears:** A beautiful collection of thoughts through the ages on music.

#725 **Woman—God's Supreme Creation:** Men will love this report. Finally, a great report which helps women rise above the "wisdom" of the world. Truly inspiring.

#726 **A Virtuous Wife:** A great study of Proverbs 31. Perspective. Beauty. Direct and Godly virtues.

#727 **Motherhood:** You'll want every mother you know to have these beautiful words. Mothers are such a blessing!

#728 **A Time For Everything:** Ecclesiastes 3 comes alive. Build a better, more meaningful life with these insights.

#729 **Friendship Values:** Choosing, helping, building great friendships. Friends as a gift from God.

#730 **Nine Virtues 1-3:** A study of the famous verses in Galatians Chapter 5. What are the Fruits of the Spirit?

#731 **Nine Virtues 4-6:** A continuation of Galatians Chapter 5. A discussion of longsuffering, gentleness and goodness.

#732 **Nine Virtues 7-9:** More on Galatians 5. Knowledge on faith, meekness and temperance. Insightful.

#733 **The Lord is My Shepherd:** Wade's personal testimony and insights into one of the most famous passages of all times: Psalm 23.

Eagles in a Storm: Did you know that an eagle knows when a storm is approaching long before it breaks? The eagle will fly to some high spot and wait for the winds to come. When the storm hits, it sets its wings so that the wind will pick it up and lift it above the storm. While the storm rages below, the eagle is soaring above it. The eagle does not escape the storm. It simply uses the storm to lift it higher. It rises on the winds that bring the storm.

When the storms of life come up on us—and all of us will experience them—we can rise above them by setting our minds and our belief toward God. The storms do not have to overcome us. We can allow God's power to lift us above them. God enables us to ride the winds of the storm that bring sickness, tragedy, failure and disappointment in our lives. We can soar above the storm.

Soar With Eagles Special Reports

Order Form
14675 Interurban Ave. South, Seattle, WA 98168-4664
phone: 1-800-872-7411 fax: 206-901-3006

STOCK MARKET
INSTITUTE of LEARNING
Incorporated

QTY:			QTY:			QTY:			QTY:		
___	700	$6.95	___	711	$5.95	___	720	$5.95	___	728	$5.95
___	701	$6.95	___	712	$5.95	___	721	$5.95	___	729	$5.95
___	702	$5.95	___	713	$5.95	___	722	$5.95	___	730	$5.95
___	703	$5.95	___	714	$5.95	___	723	$5.95	___	731	$5.95
___	704	$5.95	**High Teen series**			___	724	$6.95	___	732	$5.95
___	705	$5.95	___	715	$6.95	**Womanhood series**			___	733	$5.95
___	706	$6.95	___	716	$6.95	___	725	$5.95	___	All 33	$99.00
___	707	$5.95	___	717	$5.95	___	726	$6.95	___	Binder	$12.00 Free with complete set!
___	708	$5.95	___	718	$6.95	___	727	$5.95			
___	709	$5.95	___	719	$5.95	___	this set $10.00					
___	710	$5.95	___	this set $13.00							

Share the Spiritual Wealth. If you have family and friends you would like to share these reports with, you can keep yours and send them their own set. Fill out and send in your order form, and enrich the lives of those you love.
Call 1-800-872-7411 or fax it back to 206-901-3006.

But they that wait upon the Lord shall renew their strength; they shall mount up with wings as eagles; they shall run and not be weary; and they shall walk, and not faint.
Isaiah: 40:31

QTY:

Soar With Eagles Reports	___ X	$ 5.95 =$_____
Soar With Eagles Reports	___ X	$ 6.95 =$_____
High Teen series	___ X	$ 13.00 =$_____
Womanhood series	___ X	$ 10.00 =$_____
All 33 (plus bonus #700)	___ X	$ 99.00 =$_____
3-ring binder (**Free** with all 33)	___ X	$ 9.00 =$_____
	SUB TOTAL	$_____
WA residents add 8.8% tax		$_____
Add $1.00 each for S&H (max. $6.00)		$_____
	GRAND TOTAL	$_____

(231)

Customer Name: _____

Address: _____

City: _____ State: _____ Zip: _____

Phone: _____ Email: _____

check # _____ credit card: VISA M/C AMEX

credit card # _____ exp: _____

signature: _____

printed signature name: _____

print shipping address if different from billing:

Name: _____

Address: _____

City: _____ State: _____ Zip: _____